Understanding and Using
dBASE® III PLUS

Steven C. Ross

Marquette University

This book is available with or without the
Student Version of dBASE® III PLUS.

West Publishing Company
St. Paul   New York   Los Angeles   San Francisco

Copyeditor: Cheryl Drivdahl
Cover Design: Bob Anderson, Computer Arts, Inc.

Library of Congress Cataloging-in-Publication Data

Ross, Steven C.
  Understanding and using dBASE III Plus.

  (The Microcomputing series)
  Includes index.
  1. dBASE III PLUS (Computer program)   I. Title.
  II. Series.
  QA76.9.D3R73   1987   005.36'9   87-8127
  ISBN 0-314-34744-5
  ISBN 0-314-39289-0 (Student Version)

CONTENTS

PUBLISHER'S NOTE

This book is part of THE MICROCOMPUTING SERIES. We are proud to announce that this unique series is now entering its fourth year, and currently includes four different types of books:

1. A core concepts book, now in its second edition, teaches basic hardware and software applications concepts. This text is titled UNDERSTANDING AND USING MICRO-COMPUTERS.

2. A series on introductory level, hands-on workbooks for a wide variety of specific software packages. These provide both self-paced tutorials and complete reference guides. Each book's title begins with UNDERSTANDING AND USING . . . .

3. Several larger volumes combine DOS with three popular software packages. Two of these volumes are called UNDERSTANDING AND USING APPLICATION SOFT-WARE, while the third is titled UNDERSTANDING AND USING SHAREWARE APPLICATION SOFTWARE. These versions condense components of the individual workbooks while increasing the coverage of DOS and the integration of different application packages.

4. An advanced level of hands-on workbooks with a strong project/systems orientation. These titles all begin with DEVELOPING AND USING . . . .

Our goal has always been to provide you with maximum flexibility in meeting the changing neds of your courses through this "mix and match" approach. We remain committed to offering the widest variety of current software packages.

We now offer these books in THE MICROCOMPUTING SERIES:

Understanding and Using Microcomputers, 2nd Edition   by Steven M. Zimmerman and Leo M. Conrad

OPERATING SYSTEMS

Understanding and Using MS-DOS/PC DOS: The First Steps, 2nd Edition
    by Laura B. Ruff and Mary K. Weitzer
	Understanding and Using MS-DOS/PC DOS: A Complete Guide
	    by Cody T. Copeland and Jonathan P. Bacon

	Understanding and Using OS/2 by Jonathan P. Bacon

PROGRAMMING LANGUAGES

Understanding and Using Microsoft BASIC/IBM-PC BASIC
    by Mary L. Howard

WORD PROCESSORS

Understanding and Using DisplayWrite 4
    by Patsy H. Lund and Barbara A. Hayden

Understanding and Using Microsoft Word
    by Jonathan P. Bacon

Understanding and Using MultiMate
    by Mary K. Weitzer and Laura B. Ruff

Understanding and Using PC-Write
    by Victor P. Maiorana

Understanding and Using pfs: WRITE
    by Mary K. Weitzer and Laura B. Ruff

Understanding and Using WordPerfect
    by Patsy H. Lund and Barbara A. Hayden

Understanding and Using WordPerfect 5.0
    by Patsy H. Lund

Understanding and Using WordStar
    by Steven C. Ross

Understanding and Using WordStar 4.0
    by Patsy H. Lund and Barbara A. Hayden

SPREADSHEET PACKAGES

Understanding and Using Lotus 1-2-3
    by Steven C. Ross

Understanding and Using Lotus 1-2-3 Release 2
    by Steven C. Ross

Understanding and Using Lotus 1-2-3 Release 3
    by Steven C. Ross

Understanding and Using SuperCalc 3
    by Steven C. Ross and Judy A. Reinders

Understanding and Using SuperCalc 4
    by Judy A. Reinders and Steven C. Ross

Understanding and Using VP-Planner Plus
    by Steven C. Ross

DATABASE PACKAGES

Understanding and Using dBASE III (Including dBASE II)
    by Steven C. Ross

Understanding and Using dBASE III PLUS
    by Steven C. Ross

Understanding and Using dBASE IV
    by Steven C. Ross

Understanding and Using pfs: FILE/REPORT
    by Laura B. Ruff and Mary K. Weitzer

Understanding and Using R:BASE 5000
(Including R:BASE System V)
    by Karen L. Watterson

INTEGRATED SOFTWARE

Understanding and Using Appleworks (Including Appleworks 2.0)
    by Frank Short

Understanding and Using Educate-Ability
    by Victor P. Maiorana and Arthur A. Strunk

Understanding and Using FRAMEWORK
    by Karen L. Watterson

Developing and Using Office Applications with AppleWorks
    by M. S. Varnon

Understanding and Using pfs: First Choice
    by Seth A. Hock

Understanding and Using Symphony
    by Enzo V. Allegretti

COMBINATION VOLUMES

Understanding and Using Application Software, Volume 1:
DOS, WordStar 4.0, Lotus 1-2-3 Release 2, and dBASE III Plus
    by Steven C. Ross, Patsy H. Lund and Barbara A. Hayden

Understanding and Using Application Software, Volume 2:
DOS, WordPerfect 4.2, Lotus 1-2-3 Release 2, and dBASE III Plus
    by Steven C. Ross, Patsy H. Lund and Barbara A. Hayden

Understanding and Using SHAREWARE Application Software:
DOS, PC-Write, ExpressCalc, and PC-FILE
    by Victor P. Maiorana

Understanding and Using Application Software, Volume 3:
DOS, WordPerfect 4.2, VP-Planner Plus, and dBASE III Plus
    by Steven C. Ross and Patsy H. Lund

ADVANCED BOOKS

Developing and Using Decision Support Applications
    by Steven C. Ross, Richard J. Penlesky and
    Lloyd D. Doney

Developing and Using Microcomputer Business Systems
    by Kathryn W. Huff

We are delighted by the popularity of THE MICROCOMPUTING SERIES. We appreciate your support, and look forward to your suggestions and comments. Please write to us at this address:

West Publishing Company, College Division
50 West Kellogg Blvd., P.O. Box 64526, St. Paul, MN 55164

ABOUT THE AUTHOR

Steven C. Ross holds a B.S. degree in History from Oregon State University, and M.S. and Ph.D. degrees in Business Administration from The University of Utah. Currently he is an Assistant Professor of Management at Marquette University in Milwaukee, Wisconsin. At Marquette, he has been responsible for the introduction of microcomputers into the primary computer course and for the integration of computer applications throughout the curriculum. Dr. Ross also consults with businesses of all sizes to integrate microcomputers into the managerial operations of those organizations. His teaching and consulting experiences have provided ample material for this book.

PREFACE

With a true view all the data harmonize,
but with a false one the facts soon clash.
Aristotle, *Ethics*

Understanding and Using dBASE III Plus is about the management of data on personal computers—specifically, the use of the popular program dBASE III Plus. Data are the lifeblood of an organization, and the business student and professional must know how to manage data if he or she is to be a successful manager. Not only is the dBASE package a powerful data manager in its own right, it is also a good tool for learning about data management concepts in general.

WHY THIS BOOK?

There are many books available that discuss dBASE III Plus. Why then would anyone write another book? I decided to do so because both my students and my colleagues at several universities desired a book tailored to the way personal computing is taught at the college and professional level. We felt that there was no book designed for use in academic or workshop settings. We felt a need for a book that would present concepts and skills as well as provide activities, applications, and questions for practice and teaching purposes. *Understanding and Using dBASE III Plus* is such a book.

This book is designed to support the efforts of the instructor by providing the essential facets of the software combined with activities and exercises designed to reinforce and evaluate the student's learning experience. Examples are drawn from the fields of business administration and economics to illustrate how the software may be used in other course work and in the daily tasks performed by business professionals. The instructor's manual provides supplementary materials and suggestions for integrating this book with other course materials.

This book serves a different role than the reference manuals furnished with the dBASE software. These manuals are quite comprehensive, but often are difficult to read and fail to provide adequate examples. This book is designed for instruction in fundamental, intermediate, and advanced operations, supported with substantial reference material. When more detailed information is required, the user will have a significant foundation.

Finally, *Understanding and Using dBASE III Plus* serves as a member of THE MICRO-COMPUTING SERIES published by West Publishing Company. It may be used alone, in combination with other books in the series (listed on the back cover), or to supplement any other book in a course where a knowledge of dBASE III Plus is required.

HOW TO USE THIS BOOK

You should complete the first four units in the order presented. With that background, the material in the remainder of the book may be covered in the order that suits you best. The more work you do on the computer, the better you will learn the topics. As a minimum, you should complete the Guided Activities with each unit. I strongly encourage you to work through the Applications Exercises also. Each activity and exercise is designed to illustrate points made in the previous units, and many contain additional material that is best presented during a computer session.

Each unit includes the following features:

Learning Objectives: the knowledge and skills addressed in the unit.

Important Commands: the commands to be covered, which will later serve as a quick reference to the contents of the unit.

Computer Screens: full-screen figures depicting the steps and results of most commands.

Guided Activity: a step-by-step, hands-on illustration of the operations discussed in the unit. The activities contain ✔ Checkpoints, which ask you questions as you work to further develop your knowledge and skill level. The answers to the Checkpoints are found in Appendix B.

Review Questions: questions designed to test your understanding of the material presented. The answers to selected review questions are contained in Appendix B.

Documentation Research: exercises that require you to use the software publisher's documentation to learn more about the commands and functions discussed in the unit.

Additional features of *Understanding and Using dBASE III Plus* are as follows:

Application Exercises: six exercises spread throughout the book which provide additional practice using the material presented. These are designed to be more challenging than the Guided Activities.

Getting Started on Your Microcomputer: this appendix is provided as a quick reference for those who need a refresher or minimal reference for the computer hardware and the disk operating system.

Two Indexes: the Symbols Index and Alphabetic Index are designed to allow you to quickly locate the relevant information.

Keyboard Diagram, Common dBASE Error Messages and Remedies, and **Quick Reference:** these references are placed at the back of the book, where you can easily refer to them.

Data Disk: a disk available to instructors which contains both student files (such as files needed as input for the Guided Activities and Applications) and instructor files (such as solutions to Guided Activities and Applications, and files for tests). If you need additional information about this data disk, a demonstration data disk is available which includes files from each of the initial software lab manuals in THE MICROCOMPUTING SERIES. Instructors wishing to request a copy should write to: College Department, West Publishing Company, 50 West Kellogg Boulevard, P.O. Box 64526, St. Paul, MN 55164-1003, or contact their West sales representative. *For classes using the Student Version of dBASE III Plus:* A special data disk is available that contains modified MIX.DBF, ACCOUNTS.DBF, and MAILING.DBF for use with the Student Version of dBASE III Plus. Contact your West sales representative or call 1-800-329-9424 if you need this disk.

A NOTE OF THANKS . . .

to my father, who taught me the importance of organization and management of data;

to my friends at the bank and the printers, who motivated me to learn the virtues and the vices of dBASE III Plus;

to the students and faculty at the many universities and colleges who have used the first edition of this book;

to Rich Wohl, Sharon Walrath, Jayne Lindesmith, and Cheryl Wilms of West Publishing who guided me in the development of a presentable manuscript;

to the reviewers, James Clifford of New York University, Paul Dravillas of Moraine Valley Community College, Gary Gora of Northern Alberta Institute of Technology, Paula Saunders of Royal Business School, Steven Schlindler of Kent State University, and Glenn Thomas of Kent State University, whose numerous specific and insightful comments have increased the accuracy and readability of this work;

to the reviewers of the first edition, Eileen Bechtold Dlugoss of Cuyahoga Community College, Charles Fromme of Queensborough Community College, and Kathleen Tesker of St. Louis Community College, whose many helpful comments have laid a firm foundation for this edition; and

to Meredith, Kelly, and Shannon, who continue to provide love and encouragement as we traverse life's hills and valleys.

I hope each of you is pleased with the final product.

S.C.R.
Milwaukee
April 1987

1 FUNDAMENTAL DATA BASE OPERATIONS

This is the first of three parts in this manual. In this part, we cover fundamental information that you must know to operate dBASE III Plus and that will allow you to construct useful data bases. We will discuss the diskettes that are a part of the dBASE package, how dBASE uses the keyboard, the screen display, and the data base concept.

With that background, we will learn how to create a data base file, how to enter data into that file, how to view the information in the file, how to edit the information in the file, and how to change the structure of the file.

The exercise at the end of this part will guide you through the development of a simple data base. At the conclusion of the exercise, you will have a good introduction to working with dBASE III Plus. The remainder of the manual will prepare you for more sophisticated tasks.

Which Version of dBASE Are You Using? This manual is written specifically for dBASE III Plus. You may use it with the Student Version of dBASE III Plus as well as the unabridged version (the major difference is that the Student Version uses smaller data files). dBASE III Plus is the most recent of the dBASE family which also includes dBASE III and dBASE II. If you are using dBASE II or dBASE III (*not* Plus), you should obtain *Understanding and Using dBASE III (Including dBASE II)*, which is written specifically for those versions of dBASE.

Compatibility between the Versions of dBASE III. Most commands and concepts are the same in dBASE III Plus and the original dBASE III, so data files and indexes created under one version may be used by the other. The only problems occur with some commands and functions that have been added in dBASE III Plus and are not a part of dBASE III. Where necessary, footnotes will be used to alert you to features that are different or absent in the original dBASE III. We will use the terms *dBASE* and *dBASE III* to refer to both versions, and *dBASE III Plus* and *original dBASE III* to refer to the specific versions.

Installing the Student Version of dBASE III Plus

There are two versions of this manual. One version includes two disks that have a *Student Version* (also called *DEMO* version, *Sampler Version*, and *Limited Use Version*) of dBASE III Plus. If you purchased a copy of the manual that includes software, you must take a few minutes to install the software. Once installed, you never have to install the software again unless you change computer configuration.

Before starting the installation process, you must obtain the answers to a few questions:

I. Does the computer you will be using have more than 256 kilobytes of random-access memory (RAM)? If you do not know the answer and no one else is available to answer the question, use the CHKDSK command described on page A-12 in Appendix A of the manual. The next to the last line of the results is entitled "bytes total memory." If that number is greater than 262144, then you have more than 256K total memory.
[ ] yes   [ ] no

II. Does the computer you will be using have a hard disk? [ ] yes   [ ] no

III. Do you own your own copy of DOS, or does your organization own the DOS you use to start the computer? [ ] yes   [ ] no

With the answers to these three questions, you may proceed with installation. You need the two disks that came with this manual and a DOS disk (your own or the organization's). If you are *not* using your own DOS, you also need a blank, formatted disk.

1. Start the computer as usual. Enter the date and time if asked. (If this is your first encounter with a personal computer, read Appendix A before performing this installation process.)

2. Place the System Disk #1 that came with this package in drive A. Type **install**<CR>.

3. You are given four choices. Your response should be as follows:

   A if your answers to the questions above were I: "no" and II: "no." If you answered "no" to question III, put your blank disk in Drive B instead of the organization's DOS disk. (dBASE will copy a file named CONFIG.SYS to that disk, which you may later delete.) If you answered "yes" to question III, then put your DOS disk in Drive B.

   B if your answers to the questions above were I: "yes" and II: "no." If you answered "no" to question III, put your blank disk in Drive B instead of the organization's DOS disk. (dBASE will copy a file named CONFIG.SYS to that disk, which you may later delete.) If you answered "yes" to question III, then put your DOS disk in Drive B.

   C if your answers to the questions above were I: "no" and II: "yes."

   D if your answers to the questions above were I: "yes" and II: "yes."

dBASE will complete the steps necessary to install the program and instruct you further.

UNIT

1

THE DATA BASE CONCEPT

This unit is an intellectual exercise only; no computer is needed! In this unit we will discuss the terminology of data base management and important factors to consider before you sit down at the computer to begin creating a data base system. This discussion is intended as an elementary introduction to data base design, for a more thorough treatment of the topic, ask your instructor to recommend additional references.

LEARNING OBJECTIVES

1. At the completion of this unit, you should know

   a. the definitions of data base management terms,

   b. important considerations before you begin to create a data base system.

2. At the completion of this unit, you should be able to describe a simple data base system on paper.

DATA BASE SYSTEM TERMINOLOGY

Since the language of data base management is probably new to you, this section contains brief definitions of some terms, which will be illustrated in the following section.

A *data base management system* (DBMS) is a package of computer programs and documentation that lets you establish and use a data base. The dBASE III package is a popular personal computer DBMS. A DBMS is a set of programs; it is not the data in the system.

A *data base* is a collection of interrelated data; the complete collection of data, pointers, tables, indexes, dictionaries, and so forth. A data base contains data, it is not the programs which manage the data (which are called the DBMS).

A *table* is a part of a data base. It is similar to a two-dimensional table in which the rows are records and the columns are fields, and it is usually stored on a disk as a file. In dBASE, a table is stored in a .DBF file plus associated .NDX files.

A *file* is a collection of data on disk accessed by a unique name. It is generally a sequence of records of identical format, and it may contain data, an index, a screen format, or a report format.

A *record* is a group of related fields of information treated as a unit. The *rows* of a table are usually analogous to a record.

The *fields* of a record contain the data items. You might think of a field as being the location in a record where a data item is stored. A field has certain characteristics such as length and data type (e.g., number, character, date, memo, and logical types are found in dBASE III). Fields correspond to *columns* in tables.

A *byte* is usually one character, letter, digit, or symbol. Field width is measured in bytes.

The *data dictionary* contains a full description of the fields in a data base or a table. It describes the relationships among various fields.

An *index* contains a table of record numbers, called *pointers*, which are arranged to permit the rapid location of a particular record.

The *key* is a unique identifier for each record. It may be a single field or a group of fields.

DATA BASE SYSTEM EXAMPLE

With the preceding definitions as a basis, let us consider an example of a data base. Assume that you are the operator of a fast-food restaurant. In your restaurant, you combine raw materials (hamburger patties, buns, lettuce, ice cream, etc.) to produce finished goods (hamburgers, milk shakes, etc.).

Like many manufacturers, you are concerned about your inventory of raw materials. You want to minimize the amount of raw materials on hand because keeping inventory is expensive. You are also worried about spoilage. Before you started using a computer, you kept your inventory on index cards that looked like Figure 1-1.

As a first step in data base development, you transferred your inventory data to a sheet of paper with a result that looked like Table 1-1. Many of the key data base concepts can be illustrated by considering the example in Table 1-1.

Each character in each entry in the table occupies one *byte*. For instance, each of the date entries is eight bytes wide. When designing a data base, you need to know the maximum width in bytes of the entries in a given field.

```
Stock Number      0014

Description       12 oz. cup

Cost Each         0.03

Quantity on Hand     300

Date of Last Order  10/4/87
```

FIGURE 1-1 Inventory Card

TABLE 1-1 The Inventory in Tabular Form

Stock Number	Description	Unit Cost	Quantity on Hand	Date of Last Order
0014	12 oz. cup	0.03	300	10/04/87
0015	16 oz. cup	0.05	400	09/28/87
0018	4 oz. fry pack	0.02	332	10/19/87
0019	6 oz. fry pack	0.03	500	10/15/87
0013	8 oz. cup	0.02	600	10/06/87
0011	Coca Cola (oz.)	0.05	800	10/13/87
0012	Sprite (oz.)	0.05	700	10/12/87
0001	all-beef patty	0.10	100	10/01/87
0016	apple pie	0.16	346	08/15/87
0009	catsup (oz.)	0.04	386	10/10/87
0006	ch. onion (oz.)	0.06	876	10/10/87
0004	cheese slice	0.02	255	10/09/87
0017	cherry pie	0.14	200	09/19/87
0010	fren. fry (oz.)	0.01	999	10/12/87
0003	lettuce leaf	0.01	90	10/03/87
0005	pickle slice	0.03	900	09/15/87
0008	regular bun	0.10	200	10/03/87
0007	sesame seed bun	0.12	400	10/08/87
0002	sp. sauce (oz.)	0.01	400	09/30/87

Each entry on the card and each column in the table is called a *field*. Notice that the type of data is consistent as you read down the column: either numbers, text, or date data. Fields are identified by *field names* such as Stock Number, Description, Unit Cost, Quantity on Hand, and Date of Last Order. (dBASE will require us to use shorter names than these illustrations.) As you design a database, consider the types of information you will want to keep as a start toward field definition.

Each card is a separate *record*. Reading across the rows of the table, we also see what a record is: a group of related fields of information treated as a unit. Read across the top row: 0014, 12 oz. cup, 0.03, 300, and 10/04/87 are all related to each other; we have 300 12-oz. cups that cost 3 cents each and were last ordered on October 4. We will need one record for each unique unit, and we must make sure that the data base system we use has sufficient capacity.

All this information is stored in a *data file*. Without a computer, a file is typically a box of index cards or a manila folder in a cabinet. With a computer, a file is a portion of the disk with a unique name. At this point, we may want to start thinking of appropriate filenames for our data files.

The Stock Number field is a *key* field; a number or text string that is unique for each record. If our inventory were large, we would build an *index file*, a table that would allow us to rapidly locate a particular record once we know its key number. As you become more familiar with how your data are arranged, consider how you will want to search for items (e.g., by stock number, perhaps also by description).

The data file, along with index files such as the Stock Number index discussed earlier, is a *table*.

We might have other databases, such as a list of suppliers and a list of the items we sell (the menu). Collectively these databases constitute the *data base* of the business. Recall that the data base is a collection of interrelated data.

Finally, the *data base management system* is the method by which we manage all this data. Before computers, people used an amazing collection of colored index cards, notes to themselves, and Mrs. MacNamara to keep track of their information. While no computer will ever replace Mrs. MacNamara, a DBMS such as dBASE III Plus does enhance your ability to manage large amounts of data. But dBASE needs your help to manage data, which is what the remainder of this book is about.

DATA BASE SYSTEM DESIGN

Designing a good data base system is a lot like writing a good newspaper story: it involves the questions who, what, when, where, why, and how. In designing a database system, however, these questions are generally asked in a different order.

The most important question is *why*? (Ignoring the possibility that your teacher has provided the why . . .) If you have all your important information on a 3x5 card, then you probably do not need to spend $4000 on a computer and DBMS to manage that information. On the other hand, a DBMS will help you if you have a lot of items (i.e., records), several elements of information for each item (i.e., fields), changing attributes which must be accounted for, multiple repetitive computations that you perform, or the need to rapidly locate a given item.

If you start your design process by listing the whys, then you will have a useful guide as you build the elements to manage the data. Be prepared for your list of whys to expand, however, as you realize the potential of your system.

What is really two questions. What data do you have to put into the system, and what output do you want from the system? *What data* is needed in the system will be determined to a large extent by *what output* which is in turn a derivative of *why*.

Sometimes the desired output will be a list, such as a set of mailing labels; sometimes the desired output will be a single item, such as the magazine that certain people regularly read. For instance, if you are a salesperson and wish to have a data base that will provide you with a list of potentially good customers, then you will need data that defines customer goodness (e.g., income, age, previous purchases) as well as data that will enable you to contact the customer (e.g., address, publications normally read).

Timing is important. *When* will the output be required, and when will the data be updated? If you need daily lists, then you need to update data daily. You may have a system that can collect data continuously, such as a computerized cash register, or your input may be based on periodic reports from others, such as monthly sales reports. Update as often as possible, and at least as often as you expect to extract useful data.

Now is a good time to ask *where* the data will come from. Do you have or can you collect the necessary data using current organizational resources, or must you buy the data from elsewhere? The salesperson may have a record of previous purchases and addresses, but may not know the customers' income or age.

Now you are ready to address *how* the computer will provide the output given the available data. Are there calculations that need to be made? Are there decisions that must be made? Are there criteria for selection? Must the output be sorted in a particular order? Must the data be summarized? Our salesperson may want mailing labels, sorted in zip code order, of all persons who have made purchases in the past two years, whose household income is more that $20,000. He or she does not want to send more than one copy to a household, so duplicate addresses must be avoided.

One challenging facet of data base design will be forging the link between input and output, the how. While you are in this phase, make notes as to how you would do the job by hand. For instance, how would you eliminate duplicate addresses if you had a pile of index cards containing names and addresses?

Finally, you must decide *who* will build the system; who will write the programs and who will input the data; and, once the data base is established, who will be responsible for maintaining it: adding, deleting, or changing data and ensuring that the programs continue to function as required. Do not treat this question lightly; maintenance of data is a critical, though usually dull, task.

Once you have answered the why, what, when, where, how, and who questions, you are ready to proceed with data base development.

Capacity Considerations

Several aspects of DBMS capacity are important. First, the DBMS must allow enough fields to accommodate our needs (see Table 1-2 for a summary of dBASE capacity constraints). Second, the DBMS will impose a certain maximum number of bytes per record. Third, the DBMS must be capable of maintaining the required number of records. Finally, the DBMS will impose a limit on how many databases may be in use at one time.

TABLE 1-2 dBASE III Capacity Constraints

number of fields	128
bytes per record	4000
number of records	one billion (31 in the Student Version)
number of open databases	10

The specific computer system may also impose capacity limitations. A standard PC (personal computer) disk drive will hold about 360,000 bytes of data, which is less than the maximum capacity of a dBASE III data file. Personal computers with hard disks have much more capacity, however, and most organizations maintaining data base systems will use these machines to store their data.

REVIEW QUESTIONS

The answers to questions marked by an asterisk may be found in Appendix B.

1. Define the following terms:

   a. Data Base Management System

   b. Key

   c. Index

   d. Field

   e. Record

   f. Byte

2. What is the difference between a data base and a table?

3. What is the difference between a field and a record?

*4. If each field were ten bytes wide, what would be the maximum number of fields in a dBASE III record?

5. Consider the example in Table 1-1. What is the minimum width in bytes necessary for each of the following fields?

   *a. Stock Number

   b. Description

*c. Unit Cost

*d. Quantity on Hand

e. Last Order Date

6. Put yourself in the position of the restaurant manager discussed in this unit. Using why, what, when, where, how, and who, describe a useful data base system. Be creative!

UNIT

2 THE dBASE ENVIRONMENT

Before the fun of database management can begin, we must know which disks to use, how to start the program, how dBASE uses the keyboard, and the various menus offered by the **ASSIST** feature.

LEARNING OBJECTIVES

1. At the completion of this unit, you should know

   a. the use of the dBASE disks,

   b. how dBASE III uses the keyboard,

   c. the various menus offered by the **ASSIST** feature,

   d. how to use the **HELP** feature.

2. At the completion of this unit, you should be able to load the dBASE III program.

IMPORTANT COMMANDS

> DBASE
> ASSIST
> HELP

THE dBASE DISKETTES

Each version of dBASE III comes with a different number of diskettes; two of the disks are of primary importance and two others are of occasional importance. The two most important disks are *System Disk #1* and *System Disk #2*, which contain the dBASE III program. These disks are all you need for most operations.

11

Your organization may put the *disk operating system* (MS-DOS or PC-DOS) and a special configuration file on System Disk #1, which will allow you to use that disk to start the computer. In some cases, the disk operating system (DOS) will not fit on System Disk #1, and you will have to start the computer with a separate DOS disk. (This is the case with the Student Version.) The separate DOS disk is supplied by your organization. It must contain the disk operating system and a special configuration file placed on the disk by whomever is in charge of the software. This file is called CONFIG.SYS, and it allows twenty files and twenty-four buffers. The system disks are used as noted in the "Startup Procedure" section of this unit.

Two other dBASE III disks are the *Sample Programs and Utilities Disk*, and the *On-disk Tutorial Disk*. (Neither is included with the Student Version.) As you might expect, these contain sample programs and data files, as well as ancillary programs. You will not need these disks for the material discussed in this manual, but you will need them if you decide to do the tutorials in the dBASE manual.

THE dBASE KEYBOARD

We will describe the "typical" IBM keyboard, which is illustrated in the back of this manual. Other keyboards are similar, although placement and color of specific keys and the text or characters used to identify the key may vary slightly. The IBM and other personal computers have over eighty keys, about forty more than most typewriters. Many of the "extra" keys have symbols or mnemonics rather than characters. To minimize confusion, the following conventions will be used in this manual to refer to specific keys:

Keys with multiple character names will have those names spelled out in Small Type, usually followed by the word *key* (e.g., F1 key, Home key, Del key).

Keys with symbols only will have the key name enclosed in < > (less-than and greater-than signs), as follows:

<TAB>	The gray key just below the Esc key, with two arrows on it.
<SHIFT>	Two gray keys: one between Ctrl and Alt keys, the other just above the Caps Lock key.
<BACKSPACE>	A gray key at top of keyboard, with an arrow pointing left.
<CR>	A gray key between the <BACKSPACE> and PrtSc keys.
<ARROW KEYS>	A set of white keys on the right of keyboard, also called <UP>, <LEFT>, <DOWN>, and <RIGHT>. Note that <LEFT> and <BACKSPACE> are two different keys and that they do different things.

Keys that yield a single character (such as Aa, $4, and >.) are represented in plain text, assuming that you know when to use the <SHIFT> key (e.g., A$>).

Function Keys

These keys are on the left side or across the top of the keyboard. Two are discussed here, the remainder are presented as appropriate throughout this manual.

F1   Starts you through a series of Help screens. When you have had enough help, press the Esc key to get back to dBASE operations.

F2   Starts you into the dBASE III **ASSIST** menu, which is a *command-building* support function. Much of the initial work in this manual will show you how to use the **ASSIST** menu.

The other function keys will be discussed as needed in later units. See Table 2-1 for a complete list.

TABLE 2-1 dBASE III Function Key Assignments

F1	Help;	F2	Assist;
F3	List;	F4	Dir;
F5	Display Structure;	F6	Display Status;
F7	Display Memory;	F8	Display;
F9	Append;	F10	Edit;

Ctrl-key Combinations

Most people know how to use the <SHIFT> key on a typewriter to produce a capital letter: hold down the <SHIFT> while pressing the letter key. On a computer, the Ctrl and Alt keys work like the <SHIFT> key. To type Ctrl-M, hold down the Ctrl key and press M. In the following text, a Ctrl-key combination is indicated by preceding the letter with a circumflex:

    ^N = Ctrl-N

Full-Screen Operations

Many dBASE operations are in *full screen* mode, where you are allowed to move the cursor over all or a part of the screen using the following keys. Data input, report creation, and command file creation all operate in full screen mode. We will discuss the relevant numeric keypad and other keys here, and remind you of them as appropriate in later units.

Numeric Keypad Keys

These white keys are found on the right side of the keyboard. There are Ctrl-key substitutes for most of the keypad keys, and these are listed below the keypad key.

<ARROW KEYS>   Move the cursor up, left, right, or down depending on the specific application. <UP> and <DOWN> move a line or field at a time; <LEFT> and <RIGHT> move a character at a time.

Home
^A   Moves the cursor one word to the left.

End
^F   Moves the cursor one word to the right.

^End ^W	To exit and save from most editing situations.
PgUp ^R	Moves to the previous record or screen display.
PgDn ^C	Moves to the next record or screen display.
Del ^G	Deletes the character under the cursor.
Ins ^V	Toggles the *insert mode* on or off. When it is on, characters typed will be inserted and succeeding characters on the line will be pushed to the right. When it is off, a character typed will replace the character under the cursor.

Other Keys

<BACKSPACE>	Erases the character to the left of the cursor.
Esc ^Q	Exits without saving changes.
^N	Inserts a new line or field definition.
^T	Erases one word to the right of the cursor.
^U	Marks a record for deletion, removes a field definition during **CREATE** or **MODIFY STRUCTURE**, removes a report field (column) during **MODIFY REPORT**.
^Y	Erase to end of field, or entire line.
Num Lock	Puts keypad in numeric mode. To use the <ARROW> keys, you must hold down the <SHIFT> key.
^Num Lock	The combination of Ctrl and Num Lock will pause the display; use this to momentarily stop a list of data going by on the screen. Press the <SPACE> bar to resume the display.
Break	*Break* is the combination of the Ctrl and Scroll Lock keys; hold down Ctrl and press Scroll Lock. This will stop most printing and calculating processes.
PrtSc	The combination of <SHIFT>PrtSc will send a snapshot of the screen to the printer. Most of the figures in this book are modified screen prints. This capability is especially useful when you are having problems and no one is available to help you. Make a *screen print* and take that print to your instructor or friend.

```
                    dBASE III PLUS  Version 1.1
                    This Software is Licensed to:
                         Steven C. Ross
                          Personal Copy
                           3288591-36


        Copyright (c) Ashton-Tate 1985, 1986.  All Rights Reserved.
    dBASE, dBASE III PLUS and Ashton-Tate are trademarks of Ashton-Tate

    You may use the software and  printed materials in  the dBASE III
    PLUS package under the  terms of the  Software License Agreement;
    please  read it.   In summary,  Ashton-Tate grants you a paid-up,
    non-transferable,  personal license to use dBASE III  PLUS on one
    computer  work  station.   You  do  not become  the owner  of the
    package nor do  you have  the  right  to  copy  (except permitted
    backups  of  the  software)  or  alter  the  software  or printed
    materials.   You are legally accountable for any violation of the
    License Agreement and copyright, trademark, or trade secret law.
```

```
Command Line    |<C->|
```

```
    Press <┘ to assent to the License Agreement and begin dBASE III PLUS.
```

FIGURE 2-1 The dBASE III Plus, Version 1.1, Opening Screen
(Copyright (C) Ashton-Tate, printed with permission.)

STARTUP PROCEDURE

The exact procedure for starting dBASE III will vary from place to place, and perhaps from computer to computer.[1] Because of the size of the program, using dBASE III requires that you start the computer using two different disks. For most versions of dBASE III, *System Disk #1* will contain a copy of the disk operating system (DOS), and *System Disk #2* will contain help and program overlay files needed to execute the various commands.

Floppy Disk Systems

1. Put a formatted disk in Drive B. This disk will hold the files that you create. Insert the disk with DOS in the Drive A; this is usually System Disk #1. (With the Student Version, you must use a separate DOS disk.)

---

[1] If your copy of dBASE III has not been configured, you or the person responsible for the software must perform the steps detailed in the "Installation" or "Setting Up" section of the manual that came with the software. If you are using the Student Version of the software, see page 2 of this manual for installation instructions.

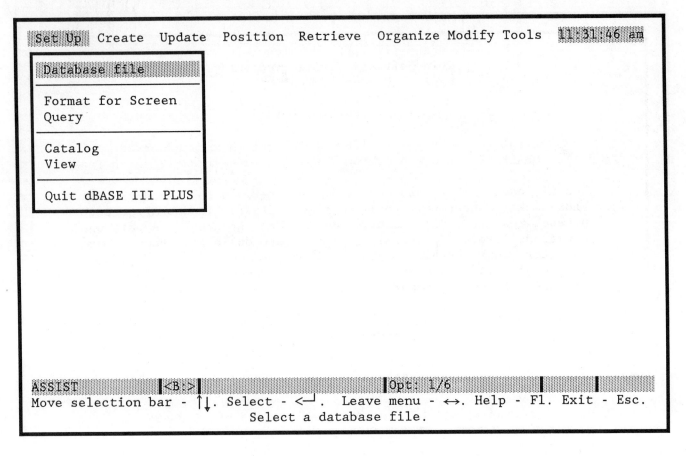

FIGURE 2-2 The Initial **ASSIST** Screen, Set Up Menu

2. Reset or turn on the machine, as appropriate. Remember to enter the date and time as prompted. Entering the current date and time will allow DOS and dBASE to *date-stamp* your files when you save them, providing useful information if you later need to determine when a file was last used.

3. Once the system is loaded (or reloaded) and the date and time are set, put System Disk #1 in the computer if necessary, then type the command **dbase** to load the program.

4. You should now see the Opening Screen (Figure 2-1). After a few moments, you will be instructed to remove System Disk #1 and insert System Disk #2. The remainder of the program will be loaded.

5. Most versions of dBASE III Plus and some versions of the original dBASE III move directly to the **ASSIST** menu, which is illustrated in Figure 2-3. If your screen looks like Figure 2-3, you have moved directly to the command level. Near the bottom of the screen, you see a period; that is the command or dot prompt. dBASE awaits your command. If you have a dot prompt and you want to use the **ASSIST** feature, press the **F2** key.

```
                    dBASE III PLUS  version 1.0  IBM/MSDOS
        Copyright (c) Ashton-Tate 1984, 1985, 1986.  All Rights Reserved.
             dBASE, dBASE III, dBASE III PLUS, and Ashton-Tate
                       are trademarks of Ashton-Tate


        You may use the dBASE III PLUS software and  printed materials in
        the dBASE III PLUS software package under the terms  of the dBASE
        III  PLUS  Software  License Agreement.   In summary, Ashton-Tate
        grants you a paid-up,  non-transferable,  personal license to use
        dBASE III PLUS on one  microcomputer or workstation.   You do not
        become the owner of  the package,  nor do  you have  the right to
        copy or alter the software or printed materials.  You are legally
        accountable  for any violation of  the  License  Agreement  or of
        copyright, trademark, or trade secret laws.




                        Press the F1 key for HELP.
   Command Line      |<C:>|
                 Type  a  command (or ASSIST) and press the ENTER key (<─┘).
                      Enter a dBASE III PLUS command.
```

FIGURE 2-3 The dBASE III Plus, Version 1.0, Opening Screen with Dot Prompt
Copyright (C) Ashton-Tate, printed with permission.

Hard Disk Systems

Most hard disk systems will have the dBASE programs installed on the hard disk. You will be able to start dBASE III directly from the hard disk. (With version 1.0 of the original dBASE III, you will have to use the System Disk in the disk drive so the program can verify that you are using a legitimate copy.)

1. Reset or turn on the machine, as appropriate. Remember to enter the date and time as prompted. Entering the current date and time will allow DOS and dBASE to *date-stamp* your files when you save them, providing useful information if you later need to determine when a file was last used.

2. Once the system is loaded (or reloaded) and the date and time are set, type the command

       dbase

   to load the program.

3. You should now see the Opening Screen (Figure 2-1). After a few moments, most versions of dBASE III Plus and some versions of the original dBASE III move directly to the **ASSIST** menu, which is illustrated in Figure 2-2. If your screen looks like Figure 2-3, you have moved directly to the command level. Near the bottom of the screen, you see a period; that is the command prompt. dBASE awaits your command. If you have a dot prompt and you want to use the **ASSIST** feature, press the F2 key.

4. Put a formatted disk in the disk drive. This disk will hold the files that you create.

THE STATUS BAR

A highlighted bar near the bottom of the screen is called the *status bar*. This line informs you of several features of the environment in which you are operating. Look at the status bars in the figures in this unit to see how the line can change as you do your work. For instance, the status bar in Figure 2-1 looks like this:

```
Command Line    |<C:>|                    |         |         |
```

Press <⏎ to assent to the License Agreement and begin dBASE III PLUS.

which informs you that you are at the dBASE command level (dBASE is waiting for you to enter something from the keyboard, in this case a <CR> to continue); and that Drive C is the default disk drive.

In Figure 2-2, the status bar changes to reflect the fact that we are now in an **ASSIST** menu. The default drive in this figure is B. Notice the two lines below the status bar:

```
ASSIST          |<B:>|                |Opt: 1/6        |         |
Move selection bar - ↑↓. Select - <⏎.  Leave menu - ↔. Help - F1. Exit - Esc.
                        Select a database file.
```

The line immediately below the status bar is called the *navigation line*, telling us what effect the various <ARROW> and other keys will have. The bottom line on the screen is called the *message line*, normally informing us what will happen if we select the highlighted choice.

Once we have started to use a database file, the status bar changes to inform us what file is in use and where we are in that file, as illustrated in the status bar in Figure 2-5:

```
ASSIST          |<B:>|DATEBOOK          |Rec: 1/4        |         |
Move selection bar - ↑↓. Select - <⏎.  Leave menu - ↔. Help - F1. Exit - Esc.
              Add new records to the bottom of this database file.
```

dBASE will also inform us if the Ins, Caps Lock, or Num Lock keys have been pressed by displaying messages on the right side of the status bar:

```
ASSIST          |<B:>|DATEBOOK          |Rec: 1/4        |Ins     |NumCaps
```

THE ASSIST MENUS

dBASE III Plus is provided with a set of menus collectively called the **ASSIST** menus. Normally, the *Set Up* menu is your point of entry into dBASE III Plus (Figure 2-2). Although you cannot use all of the power of dBASE from these menus, you may use them to perform many common dBASE functions. The purpose of this section is to provide you with a brief introduction to the menus, which will be elaborated upon in the remainder of this manual.

As you read across the top of Figure 2-2, you see the names of the eight **ASSIST** menus. We discuss each in turn.

The Set Up Menu

This menu (illustrated in Figure 2-2) allows you to make use of *previously defined* database files, screen formats, and so on. These must have been created previously (see the Create Menu).

Database File. *Select a database file.* A *database file* contains the data we wish to maintain and analyze (see Unit 1). We tell dBASE which file to use by this menu selection.

Format for Screen. *Select a screen design for updating with APPEND and EDIT.* dBASE provides a generic *format* for data entry and editing operations. We may develop a special form (see Unit 14), and we use this selection to inform dBASE of our special form.

Query. *Select a query file to filter records in this database file.* Sometimes, we wish to hide, or filter out, some of the records in the database. A *query* does just that; this selection informs dBASE of the query we wish to use. See Unit 5.

Catalog. *Select a catalog from which to choose files.* To dBASE, a *catalog* is a certain set of files. This selection limits our choices to a specific set of files, hiding others from our view.

View. *Select a view to use.* The *view* of the data defines which datafiles are in use, and how one file is related to another. We will discuss file interrelationships in Unit 16.

Quit dBASE III PLUS. *Finish this session of ASSIST and QUIT dBASE III PLUS.* This is the *only* way to leave the program from the **ASSIST** menus. This selection will close (and save) all open datafiles and indexes.

The Create Menu

This menu (illustrated in Figure 2-4) allows you to define database files, screen formats, and so on. These are later activated by the Set Up Menu, and changed through the Modify Menu.

Database File. *Create a database file structure.* Used to define the structure of the database file. Once the structure is defined, you may input data immediately or add data later (see the Update Menu, Append selection). See Unit 3.

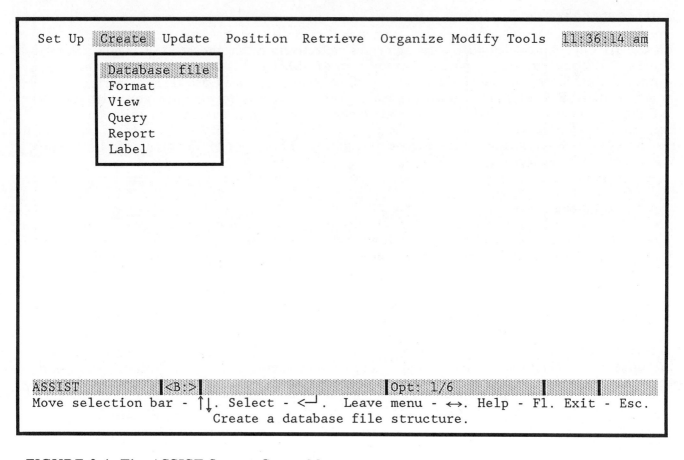

FIGURE 2-4 The **ASSIST** Screen, Create Menu

Format. *Create a screen design.* Used to specify a customized placement of data on the screen. See Unit 14.

View. *Create a view file.* Used to specify a number of files and how they are related to each other. See Unit 16.

Query. *Create a query to access specified records in this database file.* Limits available records to those that meet certain criteria. See Unit 5.

Report. *Create a report layout.* Defines the format of a report that will be run later from the Retrieve Menu. See Unit 9.

Label. *Create a label format.* Defines a layout for labels that will be run from the Retrieve Menu. See Unit 10.

The Update Menu

This menu (illustrated in Figure 2-5) allows you to add, change, and remove data in database files.

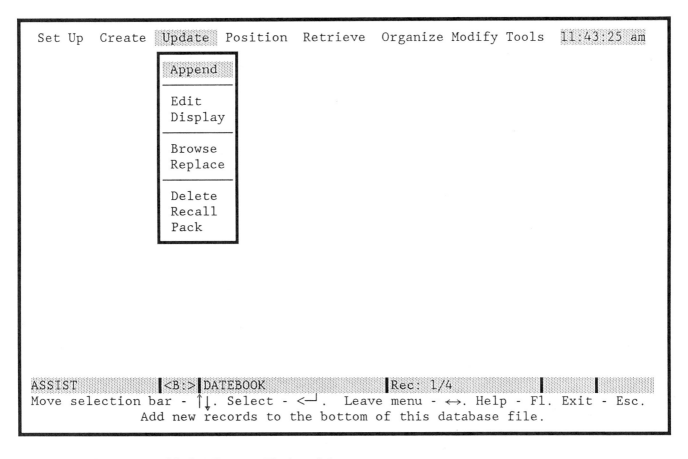

```
 Set Up   Create   Update   Position   Retrieve   Organize Modify Tools   11:43:25 am
                   ┌─────────────┐
                   │   Append    │
                   │─────────────│
                   │   Edit      │
                   │   Display   │
                   │─────────────│
                   │   Browse    │
                   │   Replace   │
                   │─────────────│
                   │   Delete    │
                   │   Recall    │
                   │   Pack      │
                   └─────────────┘




 ASSIST              │<B:>│DATEBOOK                    │Rec: 1/4              │        │
 Move selection bar - ↑↓. Select - <┘.  Leave menu - ↔. Help - F1. Exit - Esc.
                 Add new records to the bottom of this database file.
```

FIGURE 2-5 The **ASSIST** Screen, Update Menu

Append. *Add new records to the bottom of this database file.* Is the primary command for adding data to a datafile. Data can be put in all at once, or over a period of days, weeks, months, (years . . . centuries). See Unit 3.

Edit. *Edit the contents of this database file, one record at a time.* Allows you to make changes to data already in the datafile. See Unit 3.

Display. *Display the contents of this database file.* Shows you the contents of a specific record or group of records. This command does not allow you to make changes, but allows you to find records that need to be changed. See Units 3 and 4.

Browse. *Edit the contents of this database file, several records at a time.* Displays as much of your datafile as will fit on the screen, to allow you to make changes to existing records. See Unit 7.

Replace. *Update the individual fields of this database file.* Used to make systematic changes to a specific datafile field. See Unit 7.

Delete. *Mark specified records for deletion.* Used to place a temporary mark on some records so dBASE will not include them in operations. See Unit 7.

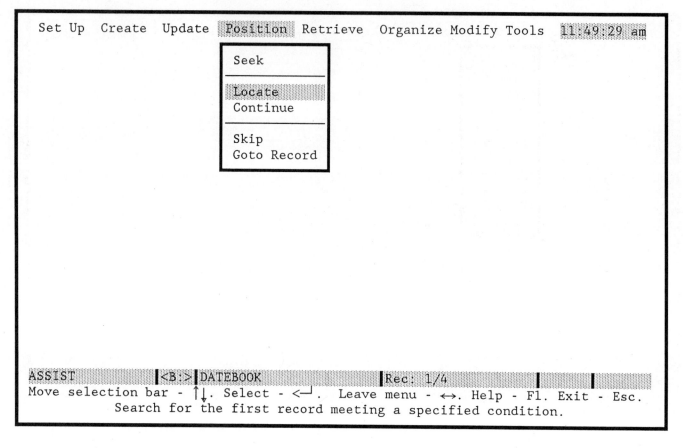

FIGURE 2-6 The **ASSIST** Screen, Position Menu

Recall. *Restore specified records marked for deletion.* Removes the deleted-record marks. See Unit 7.

Pack. *Permanently erase records marked for deletion.* Purges deleted records from the data file. See Unit 7.

The Position Menu

This menu (illustrated in Figure 2-6) allows you to move to a specific record in the database file. The *current record* is noted in the *status bar* near the bottom of the screen. In Figure 2-6, the notation `Rec: 1/4` indicates that we are currently positioned at the first record in a file of four records. We will discuss the concept of current record in Unit 3.

Seek. *Search for an index key that matches the specified expression.* Used to rapidly locate a specific record in a file that has been indexed. If the current datafile does not have an open index, you will not be able to select this option. See Unit 6.

Locate. *Search for the first record meeting a specified condition.* Moves through the datafile searching for a record that matches a criterion defined by you. See Unit 6.

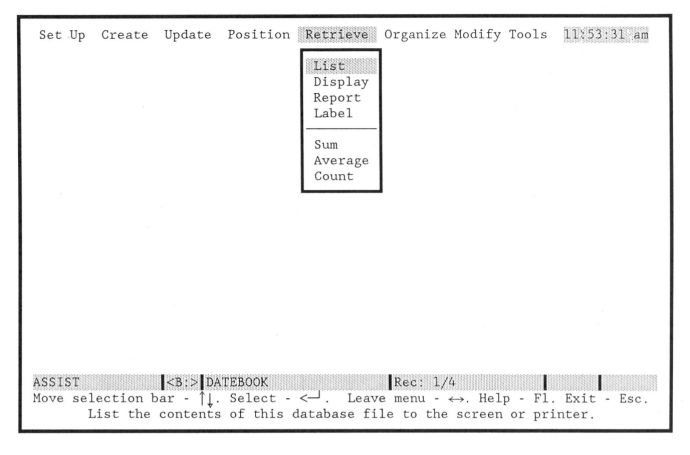

Set Up   Create   Update   Position   Retrieve   Organize Modify Tools   11:53:31 am

```
                              ┌──────────────┐
                              │    List      │
                              │  Display     │
                              │  Report      │
                              │  Label       │
                              │ ──────────── │
                              │  Sum         │
                              │  Average     │
                              │  Count       │
                              └──────────────┘
```

ASSIST   │<B:>│DATEBOOK   │Rec: 1/4   │   │
Move selection bar - ↑↓. Select - <┘. Leave menu - ↔. Help - Fl. Exit - Esc.
          List the contents of this database file to the screen or printer.

FIGURE 2-7 The **ASSIST** Screen, Retrieve Menu

Continue. *Search for the next record meeting the LOCATE condition.* Available only after the Locate selection has been used. Used to search for any other records that meet the condition. See Unit 6.

Skip. *Position the file pointer by skipping records.* Used to move among records, forwards or backwards, a specified number of records. See Units 12 and 13.

Goto Record. *Move the file pointer to a specific record number.* Takes you to the top or bottom record, or to any record by number. See Unit 13.

The Retrieve Menu

This menu (illustrated in Figure 2-7) allows you to obtain screen or printed output of your data, and to compute summary statistics.

List. *List the contents of this database file to the screen or printer.* Displays all or part of the datafile. See Units 3 and 4.

Display. *Display the contents of this database file.* Used for screen display. See Unit 3.

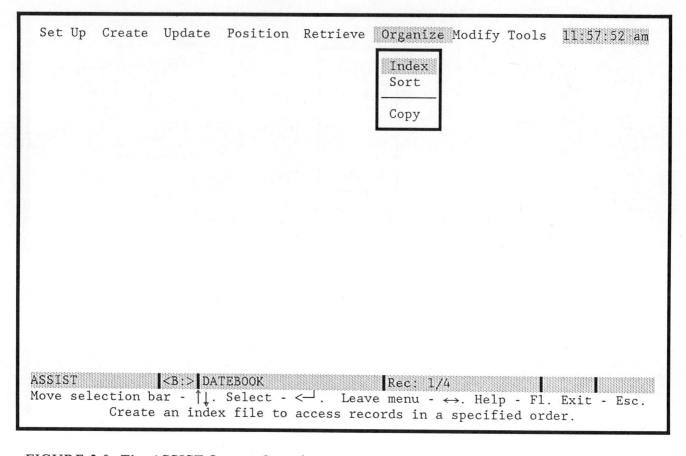

FIGURE 2-8 The **ASSIST** Screen, Organize Menu

Report. *Display this database file using an existing report layout.* Uses a report layout that has been previously created (Create Menu) to display the data in the file. See Unit 9.

Label. *Display this database file using an existing label format.* Uses a label format that has been previously created (Create Menu) to display the data in the file. See Unit 10.

Sum. *Display the totals of the specified numeric fields.* Adds contents of numeric fields for all or a select group of records. See Unit 5.

Average. *Display the averages of specified numeric fields.* Computes averages of numeric fields for all or a select group of records. See Unit 5.

Count. *Display the record count of this database file.* Determines how many records are in the file, or how many meet a criterion you specify. See Unit 5.

The Organize Menu

This menu (illustrated in Figure 2-8) is used to change the order of the records in the file, and to build an index.

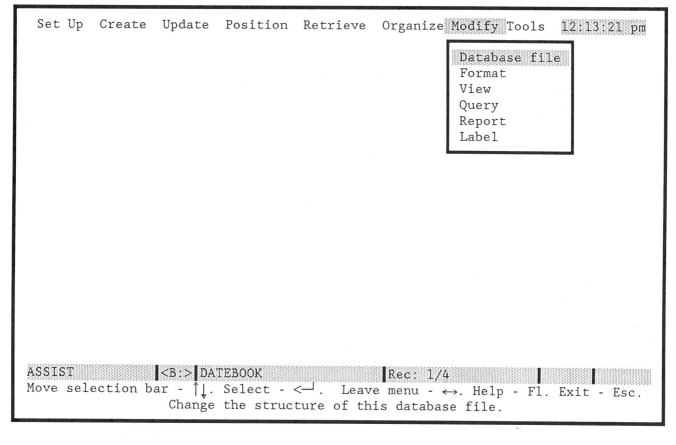

FIGURE 2-9 The **ASSIST** Screen, Modify Menu

Index. *Create an index file to access records in a specified order.* Creates an index, which changes the apparent order of the records for operations such as those on the Position and Retrieve Menus. See Unit 6.

Sort. *Create a sorted database file.* Creates a new copy of the file, with the records in a different order. See Unit 6.

Copy. *Copy records from one database file to another.* Often used to make a backup copy of the database, or to make a copy of only certain records or with the records in a different order. See Unit 8.

The Modify Menu

This menu (illustrated in Figure 2-9) is used to change the database files, screen formats, and so on, which you specified through the Create Menu.

Database file. *Change the structure of this database file.* Allows you to change the structure of a file without losing data already input. See Unit 7.

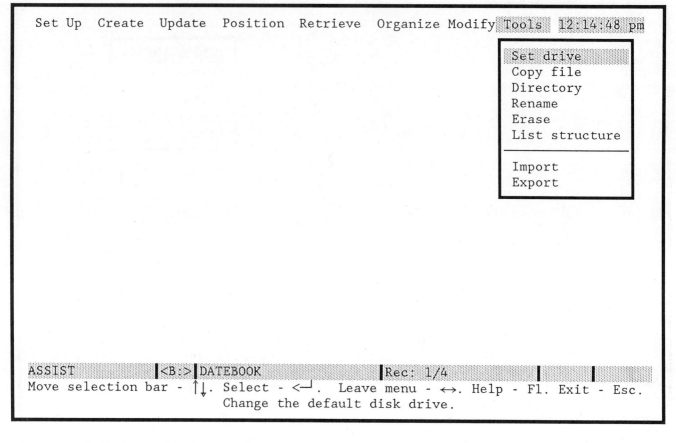

FIGURE 2-10 The **ASSIST** Screen, Tools Menu

Format. *Change the structure of an existing screen design.* See Unit 14.

View. *Change the structure of an existing view file.* See Unit 16.

Query. *Change the structure of an existing query file.* See Unit 5.

Report. *Change the structure of an existing report layout.* See Unit 9.

Label. *Change the structure of an existing label format.* See Unit 10.

The Tools Menu

This menu (illustrated in Figure 2-10) is the "catchall" menu, containing functions that do not fit any of the other menu headings.

Set drive. *Change the default disk drive.* Tells dBASE which disk drive to search for data and other files. See Unit 8.

Copy file. *Duplicates the contents of an existing file to create a new file.* See Unit 8.

Directory. *Display the contents of a disk directory.* Displays all files or those of a certain type (e.g., database files). See Unit 8.

Rename. *Rename an existing file.* See Unit 8.

Erase. *Remove an existing file from the disk directory.* See Unit 8.

List structure. *Display the structure of this database file.* See Unit 3.

Import. *Import a PFS file into dBASE III PLUS.* Used for conversion of PFS data (PFS is a popular file management program) to dBASE format. See Unit 8.

Export. *Export a dBASE III PLUS file to a PFS file.* Converts dBASE data for the PFS program. See Unit 8.

HELP

Pressing the F1 key will invoke the Help feature. Help in dBASE is *context-sensitive*, which means that dBASE will attempt to provide helpful information based on what you are currently doing. If you press the F1 key while you are working in **ASSIST**, Help will give you information about the selection which is currently highlighted. In Figure 2-11, we see the result of pressing F1 when *Set Up* and *Database file* are highlighted.

If you press F1 (or enter the command **HELP**) at the dot prompt, dBASE will give you a general help menu (illustrated in Figure 2-12). Use the <UP> and <DOWN> keys to select a topic, and dBASE will provide additional choices. Press the Esc key to exit from Help.

Help is very useful once you know a little bit about dBASE, and experienced users will often turn to Help when they do not remember exactly how to use a command, or to learn more about a command. If you get into Help by accident, remember that you can always escape by pressing the Esc key.

REVIEW QUESTIONS

1. List the dBASE diskettes, and describe the uses of each.

2. How does dBASE use the following keyboard keys?

   *a. F1

   b. F2

   c. End

   d. Home

   *e. PgUp

```
 Set Up  Create  Update  Position  Retrieve  Organize Modify Tools    04:08:46 pm

                                      USE

       USE selects  the  active database file  and its index files from existing
       files.    Subsequent commands operate on this database file until another
       one is selected.   If a new file is needed,  use the Database File option
       in the Create menu.

            Command Format:   USE [<database file name>/?]
                              [INDEX <index file name>] [ALIAS <alias name>]




 ASSIST             <D:>                          Opt: 1/6
                 Press any key to continue work in ASSIST.
                        Select a database file.
```

FIGURE 2-11 A Specific Help Screen

*f. Del

*g. ^End

h. Esc

i. <BACKSPACE>

3. How do you load dBASE into the computer? Make note of any steps that differ in your organization from what is described in this unit.

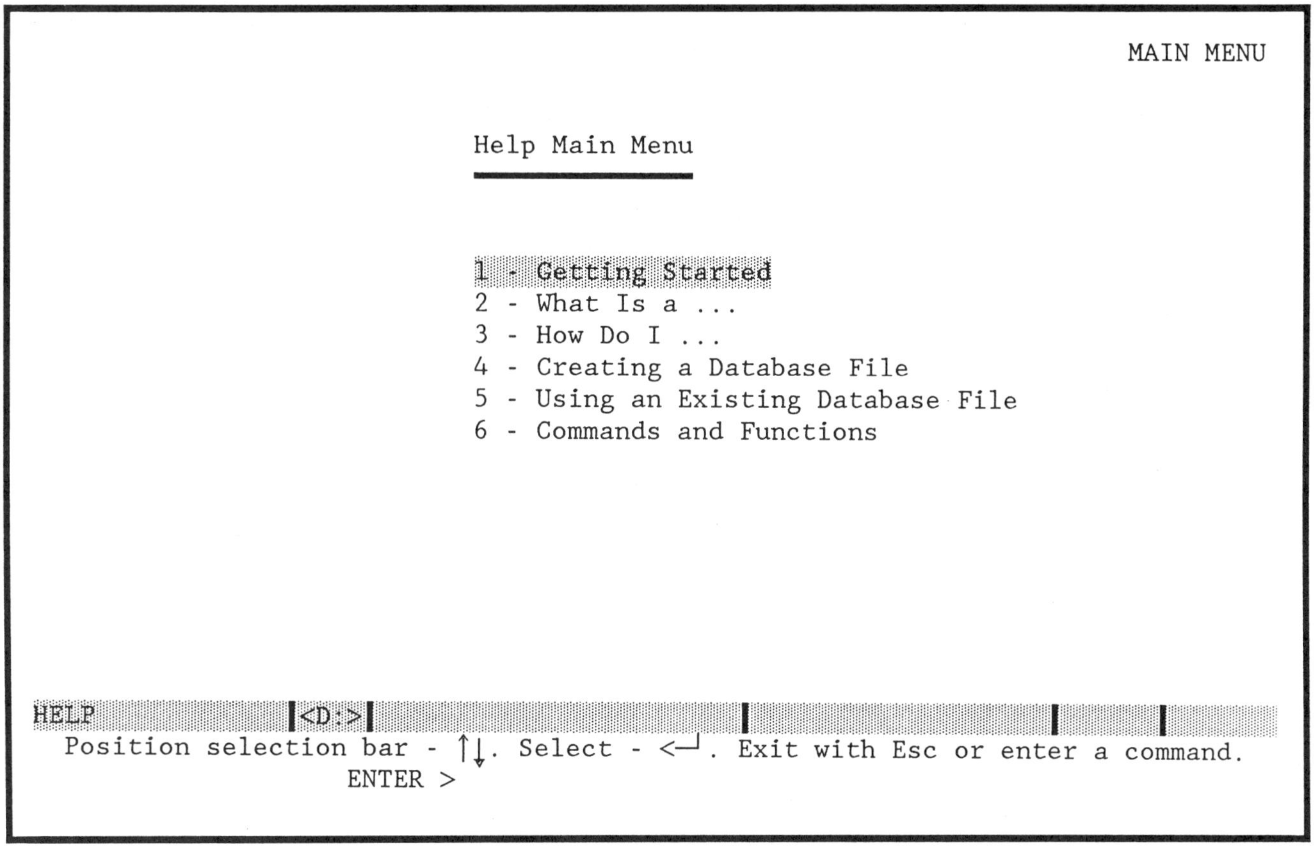

```
                                                                 MAIN MENU


                        Help Main Menu
                        _____



                     1 - Getting Started
                     2 - What Is a ...
                     3 - How Do I ...
                     4 - Creating a Database File
                     5 - Using an Existing Database File
                     6 - Commands and Functions










HELP               |<D:>|                    |              |        |
     Position selection bar - ↑↓. Select - <┘. Exit with Esc or enter a command.
                        ENTER >
```

FIGURE 2-12 The General Help Menu

DOCUMENTATION RESEARCH

The dBASE III Plus documentation is contained in two three-ring binders. Book 1 is entitled *Learning and Using dBASE III Plus* and contains a tutorial section ("Learning") and a reference section ("Using"). This volume is sufficient for most users, and we will use the term "reference manual" to refer to this book. Book 2 is entitled *Programming with dBASE III Plus* and contains advanced information about writing programs and using the software in a computer network. You will not need the second book for this manual.

One of the most useful skills you can develop in this course is the ability to use the documentation supplied by the software manufacturer. If your school or organization makes that documentation available for your use, then use the documentation to determine the answers to the following questions. You will find **DOCUMENTATION RESEARCH** sections at the end of most units.

1. Look at the dBASE III Reference Manual. What are the keywords and symbols used in command descriptions?

2. Turn to the index of the dBASE III Reference Manual and locate the following topics. On which page of the manual is each topic discussed?

   a. Numeric accuracy

   b. Search condition

   c. Technical specifications

3. Turn to the index of this book and locate the topics listed in question 2. On which page in this book is each topic discussed?

UNIT

3

DATA FILE CREATION

It is time to move from the discussion of data base concepts to the use of data base concepts. In this unit, you will learn how to create a data file, how to enter data into the file, how to view the data in a file, how to edit entries in the file, and how to backup your data files. At the conclusion of this unit, your first activity on the computer will be to build a simple data file.

LEARNING OBJECTIVES

1. At the completion of this unit, you should know

   a. the various types of fields,

   b. how to structure a data file.

2. At the completion of this unit, you should be able to

   a. create a data file,

   b. enter data into the file,

   c. display the file contents,

   d. change entries in the file,

   e. backup your data files.

IMPORTANT COMMANDS

CREATE {filename}
USE {filename}
DISPLAY STRUCTURE
APPEND
DISPLAY
LIST
EDIT
QUIT

COMMANDING dBASE

dBASE commands consist of a *command verb*, usually followed by *command parameters* that may be nouns and conditional expressions. Only a portion of the many command variations are discussed in this manual, but those that are presented will serve in most situations and will provide a foundation for more sophisticated variations. To assist you, "Quick Reference" and "Common dBASE Error Messages and Remedies" sections are provided inside the back cover of this book.

Commands via the ASSIST Menu

The easiest method for entering common dBASE commands is to use the **ASSIST** menu, which is the normal starting place for dBASE III Plus (see Figure 3-1). The key word is *common*, because not all commands are available from **ASSIST**. Where the command is available, the method for issuing the command is as follows:

1. Using the <LEFT> and <RIGHT> arrow keys, move the highlight in the top row to the menu you wish. As you move left and right, the text in the *pull-down menu* below the highlight changes. (You may also press the first letter of the menu (e.g., S for *Set Up*.)

2. When you have highlighted the proper menu, use <UP> and <DOWN> to select the activity you wish to perform. The bottom line on the screen will present a short explanation of what that activity will accomplish. For instance, in Figure 3-1, we see that *Set Up* and *Database file* are selected, and the bottom line of the screen tells us that this selection will allow us to "Select a database file."

3. Once the selection is highlighted, press <CR>. Normally, you will be prompted through one or more submenus to achieve the desired result. This series of menus and submenus is called a *menu tree*. If you get going down the wrong branch, press <LEFT>, <RIGHT>, or the Esc key to return to a previous menu or submenu.

In this book, we will illustrate the progression through the **ASSIST** menus using *italic* type to indicate menu options, a box (■) to indicate a choice (i.e., where you press an <ARROW> or <CR>), and **BOLDFACE** type to indicate information that you must type. Thus, the series of commands to create a database file, named DATEBOOK on the disk in Drive B, will be given as

■ *Create* ■ *Database file* ■ *B:* ■ **DATEBOOK** ■

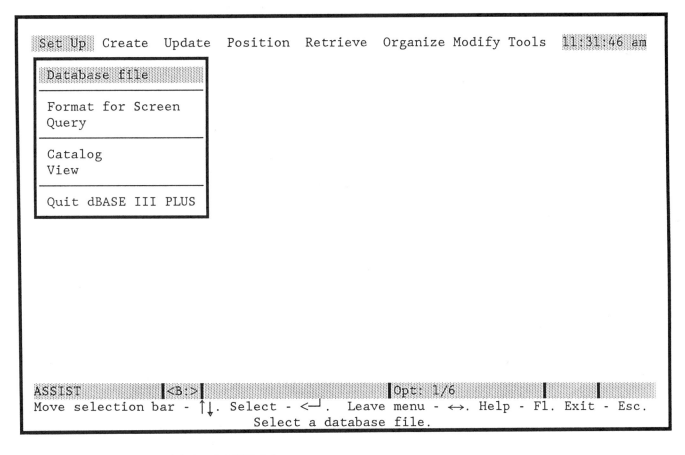

FIGURE 3-1 The Initial **ASSIST** Menu

As you use the **ASSIST** menu to enter commands, the command will be displayed on the screen just above the status bar. If you look at the commands being built while you use the **ASSIST** menu, you will learn the dBASE command language much faster.

Commands via the Dot Prompt

Commands may be issued at either the *dot prompt*, which is obtained by pressing the Esc key when at the **ASSIST** main menu level; or they may be included in command or program files, which will be discussed in Part 3. In either case, the command is entered by typing the command verb followed by any necessary parameters, and is terminated by pressing the <CR> key. Commands may be entered in upper- or lowercase. If you make a mistake entering a command at the dot prompt, press the <BACKSPACE> key to back up and correct a character, or press the Esc key to start again.

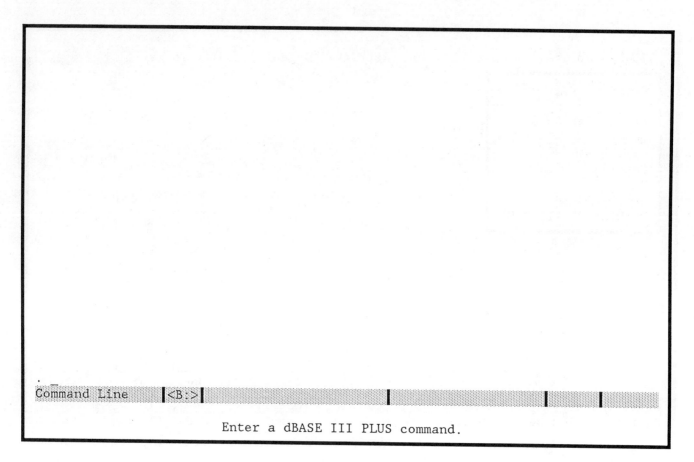

Command Line |<B:>| | | | |

Enter a dBASE III PLUS command.

FIGURE 3-2 The dBASE III Dot Prompt

Many command verbs and parameters may be abbreviated to the first four letters of the command, and may be capitalized or not. For instance, **DISPLAY STATUS** may also be entered as **DISP STAT**, **display stat**, or **disp status**. In this manual, full-length versions of commands will be used in most examples, and commands contained within paragraphs will be printed in **BOLDFACED CAPITAL** letters. Braces ({ }) are used to indicate where a command requires you to enter situation-specific information such as a parameter. For instance, the **CREATE** command requires you to enter a **{filename}**. In some instances, dBASE will prompt you for additional information if you fail to enter it with the command.

History

dBASE III Plus offers a feature called *history* which allows you to access, edit, and repeat any of the last twenty commands. At the dot prompt, press the <UP> arrow one or more times, and your most recent commands will come into view. To repeat a command, press <CR> when it is displayed. To change the command, or to correct a typing error, display the command and use <RIGHT> and <LEFT> arrow keys to move to the point to be changed. Press the Ins key if you need to insert text; use <BACKSPACE> or Del to delete text. When the command is proper, press <CR> to execute. (You do not need to move the cursor to the end of the command before pressing <CR>.) Although this feature must be used from the dot prompt, you are presented with the last twenty commands issued from both dot prompt and **ASSIST** menu.

Moving between ASSIST and the Dot Prompt

Pressing the Esc key at the top level of the **ASSIST** menu will clear that menu and present you with the dot prompt (Figure 3-2). Pressing the F2 key or typing ASSIST<CR> at the dot prompt will reinstate the **ASSIST** menu. As you become more familiar with dBASE III, you will spend less time in **ASSIST** and more time at the dot prompt. In this book, we will give both **ASSIST** and dot prompt command sequences. As you use **ASSIST**, you will see the command being created near the bottom of the screen. This is a good way to learn the dBASE command language, which you will need in Part 3 to build command files.

QUITTING

When using dBASE, it is very important to exit to the operating system before turning off the computer. Proper exit will ensure that your work is saved. Failure to exit properly may result in the loss of some or all of the data in any open file.

The **QUIT** command will close (i.e., save) all open data files, terminate any programs in operation, and exit to the operating system. The command is given by typing **QUIT** at the dot prompt. *Always use* **QUIT** *to exit dBASE.*

From the ASSIST Menu. **QUIT** is found as part of the ■ *Set Up* ■ menu:

■ *Set Up* ■ *Quit dBASE III PLUS* ■

CREATING A DATA FILE

The **CREATE** command allows you to specify the field structure of a new file. The file will have a .DBF extension added automatically by dBASE. The command is given from the **ASSIST** menu or the dot prompt, and the filename is specified when you give the command. The general form of the **CREATE** command is

    create {filename}

The {filename} can be any legal DOS filename of eight or fewer characters from the set A through Z, 0 through 9, and the _ (underscore) character. Examples:

    create oklahoma
    create utah_dat

Once the **CREATE** command is entered, the screen will clear and look like Figure 3-3. dBASE expects you to define each field in the file using four characteristics: Field name, Type, Width, Decimal places. If you make a mistake, you can use the <ARROW> keys to move around on the screen and correct the mistake before exiting the create process. If you do not notice the mistake before you exit the create process, you will have to use the

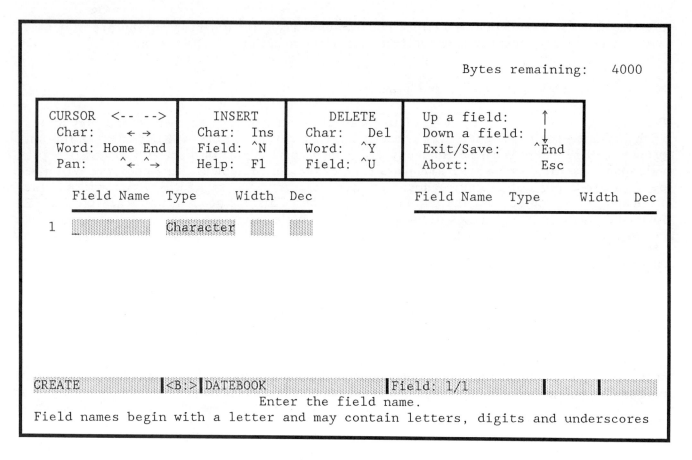

FIGURE 3-3 Creating a Data File (I)

MODIFY STRUCTURE command discussed in Unit 7 to change the file structure. See Figure 3-4 for an example of the data file creation process in dBASE III Plus.

From the ASSIST Menu. **CREATE** is found as part of the ■ *Create* ■ menu:

    ■ *Create* ■ *Database file* ■ *B:* ■ {FILENAME} ■

Note that most of the examples in this book assume you are working with a two-floppy-disk system and that Drive B is the disk drive which contains your data disk. If you are using a hard-disk system, the drive will normally be A (the floppy disk drive) or C (the hard disk). The person who sets up the system should establish the proper drive as the default drive: the drive which dBASE will automatically offer you when it needs a drive specified.

Field Name

The *field name* begins with an alphabetic character, and may consist of up to ten characters from the set A through Z, 0 through 9, and the _ (underscore) character. All letters will be converted to uppercase. Each field name must be unique within a database, but different data-bases may have fields with identical names. To specify a field name, type the name in the

```
                                            Bytes remaining:    3962

 ┌─────────────────────┬──────────────────┬──────────────────┬────────────────────────┐
 │ CURSOR  <-- -->     │    INSERT        │    DELETE        │ Up a field:      ↑     │
 │ Char:      ← →      │ Char:  Ins       │ Char:   Del      │ Down a field:    ↓     │
 │ Word: Home End      │ Field: ^N        │ Word:   ^Y       │ Exit/Save:      ^End   │
 │ Pan:      ^← ^→     │ Help:  F1        │ Field:  ^U       │ Abort:          Esc    │
 └─────────────────────┴──────────────────┴──────────────────┴────────────────────────┘

       Field Name   Type     Width  Dec         Field Name   Type     Width  Dec
       ──────────────────────────────────         ──────────────────────────────────
   1   NAME         Character   15
   2   AGE          Numeric      2    0
   3   PHONE        Character   13
   4   LAST_DATE    Date         8
   5                Character

 CREATE          <B:> DATEBOOK              Field: 5/5                          Caps
                         Enter the field name.
 Field names begin with a letter and may contain letters, digits and underscores
```

FIGURE 3-4 Creating a Data File (II)
Note: Items entered by the user are in **boldface**.

column below Field Name. If the name is fewer than ten characters, press the <CR> key to move to the next column, Type.

Field Type

The field *type* tells dBASE what type of data will be stored in the field. In dBASE III, type may be one of the following:

C   *Character string* (anything printable).
N   *Numeric* (numbers, decimal point, leading - [minus] sign).
L   *Logical* (True or False, Yes or No).
D   *Date* (in form 12/31/86).
M   *Memo*.

The choice of field type is often confusing to novices. Use these guidelines:

» If the field represents yes/no or true/false data, then choose logical type.

» If the field contains a date, then choose date type.

» If the field contains numeric data that you will be performing arithmetic calculations on or with, then choose numeric type.

» If the field contains a large amount of text (generally, more than fifty characters up to 5000 characters), then choose memo type.

» If none of the above apply, then choose character type.

Many fields that contain numbers should not be numeric type fields. If the number contains characters other than digits 0 through 9, . (period), or a leading - (minus sign), dBASE will not let you store it in a numeric field. Thus, social security numbers (e.g., 531-66-2876) and telephone numbers (e.g., 447-5996) must be character fields. Also, numbers with required leading zeros such as zip codes, (e.g., 02142) must be stored as character fields, or the leading zero will be lost (yielding 2142 instead of 02142). Finally, numbers that will be used as index keys should be stored as character type data.

dBASE III will assume that you want Character type. If that is your choice, press <CR> and the cursor will move to the Width column. If you need a different type, press the key corresponding to that type. The cursor will move to the Width column if you have specified character or numeric, or to the next field name if you have specified date, logic, or memo.

Field Width

For character and numeric types, the field *width* must be specified. This is the total width of the field. Character data may be up to 254 bytes, numeric data is accurate to 15.9 digits. Three field types have fixed width (logical data is of width 1, date data is width 8, and memo data is width 10), and dBASE III will not ask you to specify width for fields of those types.

Decimal Places

If the field type is numeric, you must specify the number of *decimal places*. Warning: The width must be greater than or equal to the number of decimal places *plus two*; dBASE requires room for a leading zero and the decimal point. Decimal places are optional and are not recommended for integer-only data.

Terminating the Process

Pressing the <CR> key as the first character of a field name terminates the create process. You will be asked if you wish to "Input data records now?" Generally you should answer N (no), so you can check the structure before entering data.

Check

Before inputting data, it is wise to check the structure of the file you have created. Do so with the **DISPLAY STRUCTURE** command. The result is illustrated in Figure 3-5.

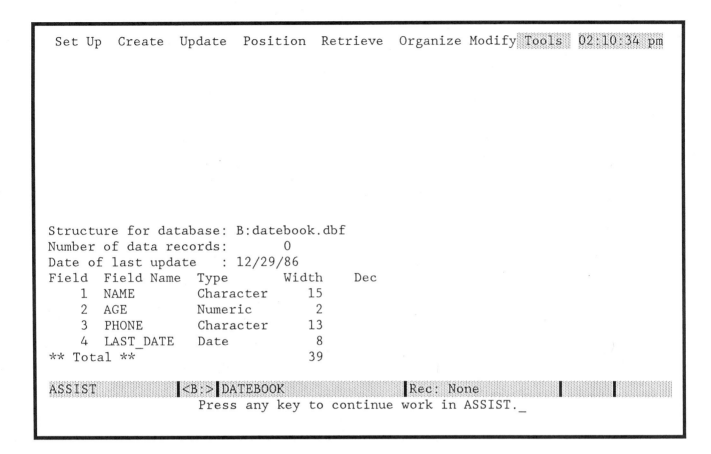

FIGURE 3-5 Checking the Structure of a Data File

Note that the structure displayed in Figure 3-5 is the same as the structure created in Figure 3-4. The total length of the structure is the sum of the field widths plus one; the extra character is used to indicate *end of record* and whether or not the record is marked as *deleted* (see Unit 7). The **DISPLAY STRUCTURE** command may be given by pressing the F5 key at the dot prompt.

If you notice a mistake in the structure of the file, use the **MODIFY STRUCTURE** command discussed in Unit 7 to make corrections.

From the ASSIST Menu. DISPLAY STRUCTURE is found as part of the ■ *Tools* ■ menu:

■ *Tools* ■ *List structure* ■

You will be asked "Direct the output to the printer? [Y/N]" which you may answer as appropriate.

DATA ENTRY

Once the structure is verified, you may enter data into the file. All the data may be put in at one time, or data may be entered over several sessions. In either case, the process is the same: first the file is opened, then the data are entered.

Opening a File

The **USE** command is used to open a data file for subsequent dBASE operations. Before any operations can be performed on a previously created data file, the file must be opened. This command may be given from the **ASSIST** menu or the dot prompt, and you must specify the filename. The basic form of the **USE** command is

  use {filename}

Examples:

  use oklahoma
  use utah_dat

The **USE** command, from either the dot prompt or the **ASSIST** menu, is also a method for saving your work, because **USE** will close the previously open file before it opens a new one, saving work-to-date to the disk. This happens even if the file you use next is the same as the file you were using. It is a good idea to reopen the file every so often to make sure your work does not get lost.

From the ASSIST Menu. USE is found as part of the ■ *Set Up* ■ menu:

  ■ *Set Up* ■ *Database file* ■ *B:* ■ *DATEBOOK.DBF* ■ N ■

dBASE will list all .DBF files on the default drive, and you need only <ARROW> to the one you choose. The N is in response to the question "Is the file indexed? [Y/N]". Indexing will be discussed in a later unit.

Adding Data to a File

The **APPEND** command will position you at the end of the data file and allow you to enter data into a new record (which then becomes the last record). The **APPEND** command may be given by pressing the F9 key.

From the ASSIST Menu. APPEND is found as part of the ■ *Update* ■ menu:

  ■ *Update* ■ *Append* ■

Entering the Data. Once the **APPEND** command is issued, the screen will clear and you will be presented with a blank form (see Figure 3-6). Enter the information into the highlighted blocks on the form. If you try to enter nonnumeric characters into numeric fields, dBASE will beep at you. If you enter an invalid date (such as 02/31/84), dBASE will print the message "Invalid Date" and require you to reenter the date.

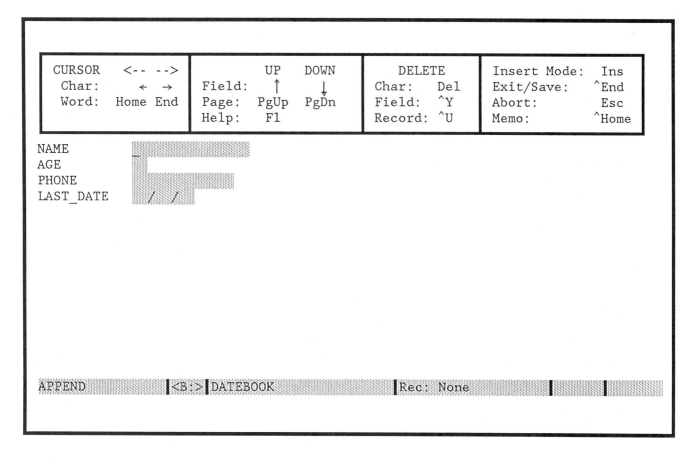

FIGURE 3-6 Entering Data (I)

If the item you are entering completely fills the field width, dBASE will beep and move to the next field. If the item does not fill the field, press <CR> to move to the next field. It is a good idea to watch the screen as you enter the first few records to see if you are getting what you want. See Figure 3-7 for an example of a completed record.

If you make a mistake, you may correct that mistake without leaving the append process. Use the <ARROW> keys to move around in the current record to the point of error, then use the Del, Ins, and <BACKSPACE> keys as necessary to correct. If the mistake is on a previous record, use the PgUp key to move to that record. Once the mistake is corrected, the PgDn key will take you to the point where you may continue appending.

Once the record is completed (i.e., the last field is filled in), you will be presented with a new blank record. You can append ad infinitum. Press <CR> at the first character of the first field of a new record to exit the append process. You may also exit the append process by pressing Ctrl-End.

```
┌──────────────────────────────────────────────────────────────────────────────┐
│ ┌──────────────────┬──────────────────────┬──────────────────┬──────────────┐ │
│ │ CURSOR  <-- -->  │        UP   DOWN     │   DELETE         │ Insert Mode: Ins │
│ │ Char:    ←   →   │ Field:   ↑    ↓      │ Char:   Del      │ Exit/Save: ^End │
│ │ Word: Home End   │ Page: PgUp PgDn      │ Field:  ^Y       │ Abort:     Esc │
│ │                  │ Help:  F1            │ Record: ^U       │ Memo:    ^Home │
│ └──────────────────┴──────────────────────┴──────────────────┴──────────────┘ │
│                                                                                │
│ NAME         Grouch, Oscar                                                     │
│ AGE          21                                                                │
│ PHONE        (801)581-1234                                                     │
│ LAST_DATE    11/27/84                                                          │
│                                                                                │
│                                                                                │
│ APPEND          |<B:>|DATEBOOK              |Rec: 4/4        |        |        │
└──────────────────────────────────────────────────────────────────────────────┘
```

FIGURE 3-7 Entering Data (II)
Note: Items entered by the user are in **boldface**.

Another command for adding data to a data file is the **INSERT** command, which allows you to insert a new record immediately after the current record (which may be first, last, or intermediate). **INSERT BEFORE** places the new record immediately before the current record. Only one record at a time is inserted. *I do not recommend using the* **INSERT** *command* because, under some circumstances, the last record in the data file is lost. The **INSERT** command is not provided on the **ASSIST** menu.

SAVING YOUR WORK

The **USE** command is one method for saving your work because **USE** will close the previously open file (i.e., write all data to a disk file) before it opens a new one. This happens even if the file you use next is the same as the file you were using when you gave the command. It is a good idea to **USE {filename}**, or ■ *Set Up* ■ *Database file* ■, every so often to make sure your work does not get lost. **USE** without a {filename} will close the file in use without opening another. (This latter version of the command can be given only from the dot prompt.)

The **QUIT** command, or ■ *Set Up* ■ *Quit dBASE III PLUS* ■, also saves your work by closing all open files before exiting to the operating system.

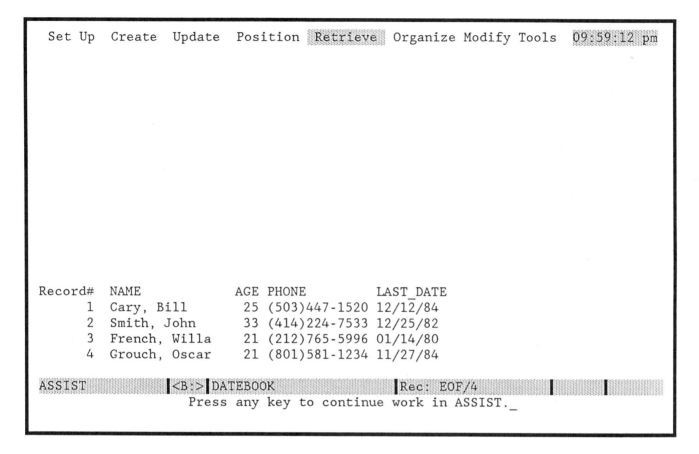

FIGURE 3-8 Listing Data

VIEWING THE DATA IN A DATA FILE

Two commands allow you to view data from the dot prompt. You will find use for both during your dBASE experience.

Viewing All Records

The **LIST** command is used for a quick glance at your data file. The **LIST** command is illustrated in Figure 3-8. The **LIST** command may be given by pressing the F3 key at the dot prompt.

   The list may be limited to certain fields, with the form **LIST** {list}:

   list name, salary

To make a printed copy of your data file, add **TO PRINT** to the command:

   list to print
   list name, salary to print

You may also add a logical condition to the **LIST** command to cause it to show you only some of the records. We will discuss conditions and constrained lists in Unit 4.

From the ASSIST Menu. LIST is found as part of the ■ *Retrieve* ■ menu. The easy method is to move directly through the default commands:

■ *Retrieve* ■ *List* ■ *Execute the command* ■

You will be asked "Direct the output to the printer? [Y/N]" which you may answer as appropriate.

Viewing a Limited Set of Records

The **DISPLAY** command shows all or part of the data file in use:

display	*Shows the current record.*
display next 10	*Will show the current record and the nine succeeding records (see Unit 6).*
display all	*Shows all records, one screenful at a time.*

The **DISPLAY** command may be given by pressing the F8 key. The **DISPLAY** command is similar to **LIST**. **DISPLAY** is oriented more toward screen display, however, and will pause after it fills the screen with information, waiting for you to press a key to continue. You may also display only records that meet some specified criterion, and you may limit the display to specific fields.

From the ASSIST Menu. DISPLAY is found as part of the ■ *Retrieve* ■ menu. The easy method is to move directly through the default commands:

■ *Retrieve* ■ *Display* ■ *Execute the command* ■

This will display the current record (which is indicated in the *status bar* at the bottom of the screen). If you are at the end of file (EOF), this command will display nothing.

The Current Record

As dBASE manipulates a data file, there is always one record which is the *current record*. The current record is indicated in the status bar (the highlighted line near the bottom of the screen) with a notation such as Rec: 2/4 (in Figure 3-9) or Rec: EOF/4 (in Figure 3-8). The notation 2/4 means that dBASE is at the second record, and that there are four records in the file. EOF/4 means that dBASE is at the end of the file: no record is current because you have moved past the last record in the file.

A command such as **LIST** will normally take you to the end of the file, while a command such as **DISPLAY** will leave you at the current record and show the contents of that record on the screen. The **APPEND** command adds one record to the length of the file and makes that (last) record the current record for data entry. The **EDIT** command (discussed in the next section) deals with the current record.

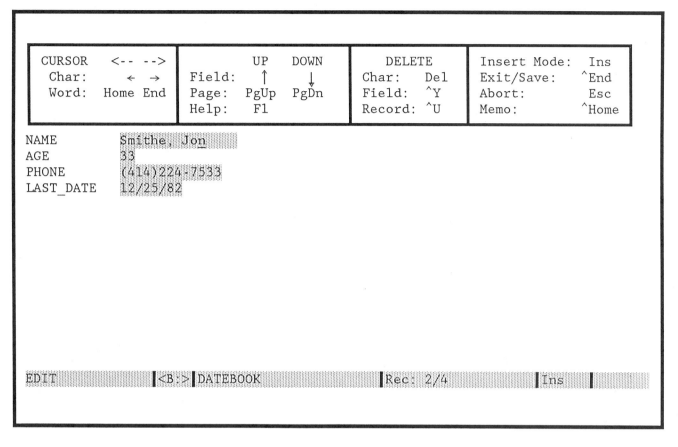

CURSOR	<-- -->		UP	DOWN	DELETE		Insert Mode:	Ins
Char:	← →	Field:	↑	↓	Char:	Del	Exit/Save:	^End
Word:	Home End	Page:	PgUp	PgDn	Field:	^Y	Abort:	Esc
		Help:	F1		Record:	^U	Memo:	^Home

NAME   Smithe, Jon
AGE   33
PHONE   (414)224-7533
LAST_DATE   12/25/82

EDIT |<B:>|DATEBOOK |Rec: 2/4 |Ins |

FIGURE 3-9 Editing Data

EDITING DATA

One of the main reasons for listing data is for proofreading. To correct errors, use the **EDIT** command which allows you to selectively change the data in a data file field. Initiate editing by entering either **EDIT** (to edit the current record) or **EDIT {record number}** to edit any other specific record. In either case, you may then selectively change data. (See Figure 3-9)

Use the <ARROW> keys to move around in the record to the point of error, then use the Del, Ins, and <BACKSPACE> keys as necessary to correct. If there is an error on another record, use the PgUp or PgDn key to move to that record. Once all mistakes are corrected, type ^End (Ctrl-End) to terminate the process and save changes, or press the PgDn or PgUp keys to move to the next or previous record in the file, which you may then edit. To terminate editing, press ^End.

To abort editing, press the Esc key, which will not save the changes made to the current record (but changes made to other records will normally be saved, even if you press Esc). The **EDIT** command may be initiated by pressing the F10 key.

From the ASSIST Menu. **EDIT** is found as part of the ■ *Update* ■ menu:

■ *Update* ■ *Edit* ■

This allows you to edit the current record (listed in the status bar). Use the PgUp and PgDn keys to move to other records. If you have a large file, you may wish to move to the record *before* giving the ■ *Update* ■ *Edit* ■ command. The following ■ *Position* ■ menu sequence moves you to record 2:

> ■ *Position* ■ *Go to Record* ■ *RECORD* ■ 2 ■

Example. For instance, to change John Smith to Jon Smithe, type **EDIT 2** (or use the two **ASSIST** commands listed above), which will put you at the beginning of the NAME field in the second record. <RIGHT ARROW> to the , (comma) in the name, press the Ins key, then press the **e** key, which will insert an *e* before the comma. Next <RIGHT ARROW> to the *h* and press the Del key, which will delete the *h* and move the *n* to the left. Press Ctrl-End to terminate editing.

BACKUP

Backup is one of those computer words that is a noun, an adjective, and a verb. A backup is a copy of the original file, usually stored in a safe place in case something happens to the original to render it unusable. Backup disks contain backups. To backup is to make backup copies.

There are a multitude of gremlins lurking out there that will ruin your day if you are not prepared. You may inadvertently ruin a file by making the wrong changes and saving it. Disks occasionally develop bad spots that make previously saved files unreadable. Spills (coffee, soda) and ashes may ruin a disk. Someone may steal your briefcase (backpack) or you may misplace your box of disks. Unexpected electromagnetic radiation may erase disks (telephones, magnetic paper clip holders, and library security systems all look innocent, but any of these may damage your disks). Disks left in cars may be damaged by extreme heat or cold.

Become obsessive about making backup copies of your work. I recommend that you make a backup every time you finish a session at the computer. There are several levels of backup:

Same disk, different filename.
Different disk, same location.
Different disk, different location.

Same Disk, Different Filename

This method saves the file under two different names. If something goes wrong with one version of the file, the other may be OK.

To implement, use the **COPY** command (discussed in more detail in Unit 8) to copy the file to another database with a different name, for example:

copy to raw2

This provides a minimal level of protection. It does protect you from random failures that affect single data files, and it may provide you a previous version if you make unwanted changes. It will not help, however, if something (like a spilled cup of coffee) destroys the entire disk.

Different Disk, Same Location

This method saves the file on two different disks, under the same filename. If one disk gets destroyed, the other is available. This provides additional protection. Keep the backup disk in the box except when you are using it, so that most local disasters (such as the spilled coffee) will not affect it. You are still at risk, however, for disasters such as theft of your backpack, fire, or electromagnetic fields.

To implement on a floppy-disk system, **QUIT** from the dBASE. When you have the DOS command prompt (A>__), put the backup disk in Drive A, leaving your data disk in Drive B. (The backup disk must have been formatted previously, and may contain other files.) Type the command

copy b:*.* a:

which will copy all files from the B: disk to the A: disk. Be careful: If you type the command incorrectly, or put the disks in the wrong drives, you may copy old versions of files over new versions. I recommend putting a tab over the write-protect notch of the original disk to prevent wrong-way copying.

To implement this backup method on a hard-disk system, where you have been storing your data files on a floppy disk, you may use the same command as above. DOS can treat one physical disk drive as two logical disk drives, and will instruct you to change disks as necessary to accomplish the copy. Again, be careful, and use a write-protect tab on the original to prevent wrong-way copying.

To implement this backup method on a hard-disk system where you have been storing your data files on the hard disk, place your backup (floppy) disk in the disk drive and use the **COPY** command to copy the files. Because the hard disk can hold many more files than your floppy disk, you must specify each file, or each type of file, with a series of commands such as the following:

copy c:*.dbf a:
copy c:*.prg a:

and so on. Your instructor may suggest additional methods which have been developed in your particular organization.

Different Disk, Different Location

This method saves the file on two different disks, under the same filename. The disks are stored in separate locations, so that if the disk box gets destroyed, the backup is available.

This is implemented in the same manner as the previous version, except that you have to find a place to store the backup. If you have a desk or locker at work or school, you could leave a copy there and take the other copy home. You might ask a friend to take your backup disk. Some computer areas have a place to store disks, and you could leave the backup there.

This provides the greatest protection. It is very unlikely that the same disaster would destroy both of your disks.

GUIDED ACTIVITY

This activity requires you to use the data file creation commands. It includes two ✔CHECKPOINT questions, the answers to which are found in Appendix B.

1. Follow the startup procedure for your version of dBASE, as outlined in Unit 2.

2. We want to create a file that will replace our personal address book, the one in which we keep the names and numbers of our friends. The first step in the process is to look at a list of the data to determine the file structure. Such a list appears in Table 3-1.

TABLE 3-1 List of Friends

NAME	AGE	PHONE	LAST_DATE
Cary, Bill	25	(503)447-1520	12/12/84
Smith, John	33	(414)224-7533	12/25/82
French, Willa	21	(212)765-5996	01/14/80
Grouch, Oscar	21	(801)581-1234	11/27/84

3. We will name the file DATEBOOK. Looking at the data, we decide to name the fields NAME, AGE, PHONE, and LAST_DATE. (Why the _ [underscore] in LAST_DATE?) For type, we choose character for NAME and PHONE, numeric for AGE, and date for LAST_DATE. Widths are 15, 2, 13, and 8, respectively.

4. Give the command **CREATE DATEBOOK**, or ■ *Create* ■ *Database file* ■ *B:* ■ **DATEBOOK** ■. The screen will look like Figure 3-3. Enter the structure information, until the screen looks like Figure 3-4. When dBASE asks for the description of the fifth field, press <CR> to exit the create process. Answer N to the "Input data records now?" question.

5. Give the command **DISPLAY STRUCTURE**, press the F5 key, or ■ *Tools* ■ *List structure* ■. The structure should look like Figure 3-5. If the structure is different, ask your instructor what to do, or read "Modifying the Structure of a Data File" in Unit 7.

6. If the structure is acceptable, the next step is to enter the data. Type the command **USE DATEBOOK**, or ■ *Set Up* ■ *Database file* ■ *B:* ■ *DATEBOOK.DBF* ■ N ■, to ensure that the file is open, then **APPEND**, the F9 key, or ■ *Update* ■ *Append* ■. The screen will now look like Figure 3-6. Enter the data from Table 3-1 into each record. (You may wish

to review the section "Adding Data to a File" before you start entering data.) As you are entering data, the screen will look like Figure 3-7.

7. After entering Oscar Grouch's data, you will be presented with a blank form for Record No. 5. Press <CR> before typing anything, and dBASE will terminate the append process.

8. To proofread, type the command **LIST**, the F3 key, or ■ *Retrieve* ■ *List* ■ *Execute the command* ■. Check what you see on the screen against Table 3-1 or Figure 3-8. If there are differences, make a note so they can be corrected in the next step.

9. To complicate things, John Smith joined a rock group and changed his name to *Jon Smithe*. Using the command **EDIT 2**, or ■ *Update* ■ *Edit* ■, and the example in the section "Editing Data," make the change. Also correct any errors in other entries. Remember to type Ctrl-End to exit editing.

10. List the data again to check the results of your editing. If the file is correct, and if a printer is available, make a list on the printer to obtain a printed (also known as a *hardcopy*) listing of your file.

11. *For Additional Practice*: If you would like additional practice using the commands discussed in this unit, do the following.

    a. From the dot prompt, give the command **USE** without a {filename} to save your current file.

    b. Create a database, named TOURNEY, which will hold the results of the league baseball tournament. You must determine, from the data presented below, how to structure the database.

    c. Enter the following data into your database. Once the data are entered, check, and edit if necessary.

Date	Home Team	Score	Visiting Team	Score
8/9/87	Buffalo	5	Stony Brook	6
8/9/87	Moscow	12	Pullman	8
8/23/87	Stillwater	1	Corvallis	3
8/16/87	Stillwater	5	Moscow	4
8/8/87	Stillwater	4	Norman	3
8/16/87	Stony Brook	3	Corvallis	4
8/8/87	Westwood	3	Corvallis	4

12. When you have completed the preceding steps, give the command **QUIT**, or ■ *Set Up* ■ *Quit dBASE III PLUS* ■, to exit dBASE. From the DOS (A>_) prompt, give the command **DIR B:** (or **DIR A:** if you are using a hard disk PC) to make sure that you have a file named DATEBOOK.DBF on your disk.

13. Make a *different-disk* backup copy of your work.

✔ **CHECKPOINT**
What must you do before you make a different-disk backup copy?

_____

✔ **CHECKPOINT**
What command will you give to make a different-disk backup copy?

_____

14. If everything is proper, turn off the computer and return the dBASE software to the Lab Supervisor.

REVIEW QUESTIONS

1. List the types of fields in dBASE III, state the maximum or default width, and indicate a use for each.

2. What field name, type, width, and decimals would be most appropriate for each of the following:

    *a. Stock market ticker symbols (e.g., IBM, APPL, T, DEC, X)

    *b. Stock prices (e.g., 8.125, 108.0, 16.35)

    *c. Telephone numbers (e.g., (414)224-1440, (212)667-7329)

    d. Social security numbers (e.g., 543-55-2786)

    *e. Smoker or nonsmoker category

    *f. Dates (e.g., 1/1/86, 7/4/76)

    g. Zip codes (e.g., 06981, 97701, 53234)

    h. Zip+4 codes (e.g., 06981-2258, 97701-1143, 53234-5011)

3. Look at Table 1-1 (on page 5). What structure would you create for the data in that table? Specify field name, type, width, and decimals for each field needed.

4. Why should you backup your data?

5. Develop a backup system that will work for you. Consider most likely hazards to your data, organization policies about using data, and access to computers. Describe the system.

DOCUMENTATION RESEARCH

Using the reference manual, determine the answers to the following questions which deal with the commands discussed in this unit. I recommend you also write the reference manual page number by the discussion of the command in this unit.

1. CREATE — how can you delete a field during the creation process?

2. USE — if a file extension is not specified (the usual case), what extension is assumed by dBASE?

3. APPEND — how do you enter data into a memo field?

4. DISPLAY — what type of field is not normally displayed?

5. LIST — what is the major difference between this command and **DISPLAY**?

6. EDIT — how do you abort editing?

7. QUIT — what may happen if you reset the computer without using this command?

8. Look up the section of the reference manual entitled "Entering Commands and Using History," and determine what to do if you make a typing error when entering a command.

CHEZ JACQUES (I)

In this exercise, you will create one file and edit two others that will be used in subsequent exercises. You will be given the dot commands for many of the steps, but you must determine the **ASSIST** menu equivalents if you wish to use that menu.

1. Start by signing out the dBASE manual and software, as well as the *Exercises Disk*. (The Exercises Disk is a special disk prepared by your instructor which contains files needed for this book and others in this series. At your organization, the disk may be called a different name.)

2. Insert the Exercises Disk in Drive A. Insert a formatted disk in Drive B.[1] This disk will hold the files that you create and edit.

3. Reset or turn on the machine, as appropriate. Remember to enter the date and time as prompted.

4. Once the system is loaded and the date and time are set, you should see the DOS command prompt (A>__). Give the commands

    copy fin_good.dbf b:
    copy mix.dbf b:

    which will copy two database files from the Exercises Disk to your disk.[2]

5. Once the copying is finished, remove the Exercises Disk and insert the dBASE III disk. Follow the startup procedure for your version of dBASE as outlined in Unit 2.

---

[1] If you are using a fixed-disk PC, your instructor will give you instructions for accomplishing steps 2 through 4.

[2] Note to Instructors: A special data disk is available that contains a modified MIX.DBF for use with the Student Version of dBASE III Plus. Contact your West Sales Representative or call 1-800-329-9424 if you need this disk.

6. You have been hired by Jacques LaFayette to establish a data base for the Chez Jacques Hamburger Chateau. The first step is to create files that contain a list of the raw materials, the menu, and the mix of ingredients in the menu items. You decide to create the raw materials file yourself, and to hire someone else to create the other two files.

7. To begin the process, you must determine the structure for the raw materials file, which you will name RAW_MATL. Look at Table 1-1 (on page 5). Note that there are five columns of information; therefore, five fields will be needed. Appropriate field names would be RMID (raw materials identification, called "stock number" in Table 1-1), DESC (description), COST (unit cost), INVENTORY (quantity on hand), and LAST_ORDER (date of last order).

   To complete the determination of the structure, consider each field in turn. For RMID, the type should be Character because leading zeros are important and no arithmetic is to be performed. (As we will see later, this field will also be an index key.) The minimum necessary field width is four bytes.

   For DESC, the type must be Character. What is the minimum field width?

   For COST, the type should be Numeric because we anticipate that we will be doing mathematics on this field. How many decimal places are needed, and what is the minimum field width?

   For INVENTORY, the type should be Numeric because we anticipate that we will be doing mathematics on this field. How many decimal places are needed, and what is the minimum field width?

   For LAST_ORDER, the type should be Date because this field contains date data. The field width defaults to eight bytes.

Therefore, the structure should be as follows:

Field	Field name	Type	Width	Dec
1	RMID	Character	4	
2	DESC	Character	15	
3	COST	Numeric	8	2
4	INVENTORY	Numeric	3	
5	LAST_ORDER	Date	8	

8. Give the command **CREATE RAW_MATL** and create the file as defined in Step 7.

9. Once the file is created, give the commands **USE RAW_MATL** and **DISPLAY STRUCTURE** to determine whether or not you have defined all fields correctly. If there are errors, consult with your instructor or refer to the section "Modifying the Structure of a Data File" in Unit 7.

10. If the structure is acceptable, give the **APPEND** command and input the data from Table 1-1. Type the data exactly as it appears, including punctuation and capitalization, because any differences may frustrate you as you do later activities and exercises.

11. When data for all nineteen records have been input, exit the append process by typing <CR> when presented with the form for Record No. 20. Type the command **LIST** to see the data on the screen. Make a note of any discrepancies. The field names will be different in your list from those in Table 1-1.

12. If there are discrepancies, give the command **EDIT #**, where # is the record number with the error, and correct the data.

13. When you are happy with RAW_MATL, you must check the FIN_GOOD and MIX files against Tables A-1 and A-2. If the data in the file does not agree with the data in these tables, edit the file so that the data does match the data in Tables A-1 and A-2. *Note: MIX.DBF for the Student Version of dBASE III Plus contains fewer records. Only those records with a FGID of 1006* or greater *are included.* You will note that the person who entered the FIN_GOOD data apparently got the restaurants mixed up. The procedure for each is the same:

use fin_good	*Open the file.*
display all *or*	*List on screen*
list to print	*or printer.*
	Proofread.
edit #	*Correct records with errors (# is the number of a record with an error).*

14. When all files are perfect, type the command **QUIT** to exit dBASE. From the DOS (A>) prompt, give the command **DIR B:** to make sure that you have files named RAW_MATL.DBF, MIX.DBF, and FIN_GOOD.DBF on your disk. Remember to backup your work. If everything is proper, turn off the computer and return the dBASE software and the Exercises Disk to the Lab Supervisor.

TABLE A-1 Data in the Finished Goods File

Record#	FGID	DESC	SELL_PRICE	INVENTORY
1	1016	Apple Pie	0.79	0
2	1001	Big Jac	1.35	0
3	1007	Cheese Burger	0.69	0
4	1017	Cherry Pie	0.79	0
5	1010	Giant Coke	0.99	0
6	1013	Giant Sprite	0.99	0
7	1006	Hamburger	0.59	0
8	1011	Large Coke	0.79	0
9	1008	Large Fries	0.67	0
10	1014	Large Sprite	0.79	0
11	1002	Jac Meal /Co/Ap	2.25	0
12	1003	Jac Meal /Co/Ch	2.25	0
13	1004	Jac Meal /Sp/Ap	2.25	0
14	1005	Jac Meal /Sp/Ch	2.25	0
15	1012	Regular Coke	0.49	0
16	1009	Regular Fries	0.43	0
17	1015	Regular Sprite	0.49	0

TABLE A-2 Data in the Mix File
If you are using the Student Version of dBASE III Plus, see Note below.

Record#	FGID	RMID	RM_QTY	Record#	FGID	RMID	RM_QTY
1	1001	0001	2	42	1004	0018	1
2	1001	0002	2	43	1004	0016	1
3	1001	0003	1	44	1005	0001	2
4	1001	0004	2	45	1005	0002	2
5	1001	0005	4	46	1005	0003	1
6	1001	0006	1	47	1005	0004	2
7	1001	0007	1	48	1005	0005	4
8	1002	0001	2	49	1005	0006	1
9	1002	0002	2	50	1005	0007	1
10	1002	0003	1	51	1005	0012	11
11	1002	0004	2	52	1005	0014	1
12	1002	0005	4	53	1005	0010	4
13	1002	0006	1	54	1005	0018	1
14	1002	0007	1	55	1005	0017	1
15	1002	0011	11	56	1006	0001	1
16	1002	0014	1	57	1006	0005	2
17	1002	0010	4	58	1006	0008	1
18	1002	0018	1	59	1006	0009	1
19	1002	0016	1	60	1007	0001	1
20	1003	0001	2	61	1007	0005	2
21	1003	0002	2	62	1007	0008	1
22	1003	0003	1	63	1007	0009	1
23	1003	0004	2	64	1007	0004	1
24	1003	0005	4	65	1008	0010	6
25	1003	0006	1	66	1008	0019	1
26	1003	0007	1	67	1009	0010	4
27	1003	0011	11	68	1009	0018	1
28	1003	0014	1	69	1010	0011	15
29	1003	0010	4	70	1010	0015	1
30	1003	0018	1	71	1011	0011	11
31	1003	0017	1	72	1011	0014	1
32	1004	0001	2	73	1012	0011	7
33	1004	0002	2	74	1012	0013	1
34	1004	0003	1	75	1013	0012	15
35	1004	0004	2	76	1013	0015	1
36	1004	0005	4	77	1014	0012	11
37	1004	0006	1	78	1014	0014	1
38	1004	0007	1	79	1015	0012	7
39	1004	0012	11	80	1015	0013	1
40	1004	0014	1	81	1016	0016	1
41	1004	0010	4	82	1017	0017	1
[continued in right column]							

Note: For the Student Version of dBASE III Plus, this file has fewer records. Only items with a FGID of 1006 or higher are included; therefore Record #56 in this Table corresponds to Record #1 in the Student Version file.

PART
2 INTERMEDIATE DATA BASE OPERATIONS

In this part, we begin to use the computer to accomplish data base inquiry operations. Because most inquiry operations require selection or computation, the first unit in this part deals with the operators and functions available in dBASE. Summary statistics and query files are covered in the second unit. The third unit in this part discusses methods for ordering data in a file and for locating specific records, followed by units dealing with system interface and data file modification.

We will also learn several ways to extract data from our data files and to output that data in the format we desire. Possible output formats include Reports, Labels, and Lists. You may also send data to other applications programs that will format it as necessary.

The exercises in this part will provide practice in using the operations discussed.

UNIT

4 CONDITIONS AND EXPRESSIONS

dBASE allows you to perform simple mathematic operations as well as complex search routines. This unit provides the basis for those procedures: operators that join components of an expression and functions that modify the meaning of an expression.

Do not try to memorize this material. Skim the unit to see how the material is arranged and work the review problems at the end of the unit. You will need to refer to this unit often, but you do not need to memorize everything that follows.

LEARNING OBJECTIVES

1. At the completion of this unit, you should know

   a. the difference between logical conditions and computed expressions,

   b. what *order of precedence* means,

   c. how each operator is used in expressions and conditions,

   d. what the various categories of functions are.

2. At the completion of this unit, you should be able to

   a. write expressions and conditions using the various operators,

   b. write expressions and conditions using functions.

IMPORTANT COMMANDS

?
LIST

LOGICAL CONDITIONS VERSUS COMPUTED EXPRESSIONS

We will make use of two general types of expressions. One type will be called *logical conditions*, the other will be called *computed expressions*. Logical conditions are used with dBASE commands to limit the scope of a command. For instance, in the command **LIST <u>FOR SALARY>10000</u>**, the underlined portion is a logical condition. Logical conditions are usually preceded by the preposition **FOR**, and consist of one or more logical and comparison operators and logical-type data, usually combined with computed expressions, functions, and character, date, or numeric data.

Computed expressions are used as index keys, in lists and reports, for computation of values, and as part of a logical condition (e.g., **LIST FOR <u>COST*INVENTORY</u>>10**, where the underlined portion is the computed expression). Computed expressions consist of functions, arithmetic and string operators, and character, date, and numeric data.

One common difficulty experienced by novice dBASE users is the confusion of logical conditions and computed expressions. *Remember: If you wish to limit the scope of an operation, use a logical condition. If you wish to obtain a result, use a computed expression.*

We will discuss the use of the **LIST** command from the dot prompt and from the **ASSIST** Menu later in this unit.

THE CALCULATOR

dBASE provides a very handy command (available *only* from the dot prompt) that is called the *calculator* or *what-is* command. The command itself is simple:

  ? {expression list}

The {expression list} may be any computed expression consisting of mathematical formulas, field names, memory variables, or a combination. In its simplest form, this command may be used as a calculator: **? 65-18** will display **47.00** on the screen. When field names are included in the {expression list}, the contents of the fields in the current record will be used: **? NAME** will display the contents of the name field of the current record (the concept of current record was discussed in Unit 3). A command such as **? SALARY*1.25** will tell you what the salary would be after a 25% raise. The current contents of the field (NAME, SALARY) is not changed.

OPERATORS

Operators are the glue that binds elements of expressions, the *operands*, together. Most of us are familiar with operators such as the + (plus) sign:

  2 + 2

In dBASE, the operands may be data file field names, memory variables (discussed in Part 3), or values contained within the expression itself.

Order of Precedence

Order of precedence refers to the priority of calculation. Expressions are evaluated from left to right, with sub-expressions enclosed by ( ) (parentheses) evaluated first, and with operators higher in the list evaluated before operators lower in the list.

For instance, from algebra we remember that

$$\frac{6^2}{12} = \frac{36}{12} = 3$$

and not

$$\frac{6^2}{12} = \frac{1}{2}^2 = \frac{1}{4}$$

The same situation will occur in dBASE, where

    6^2/12 = 3

(The ^ sign, when used in a numeric formula, means exponentiation.)

Arithmetic Operators

Arithmetic can be performed on numeric and date fields or variables, and on values in expressions.

Arithmetic operators, in order of precedence, are as follows:

unary +, -	The *sign* (positive or negative) of a numeric expression.
**, ^	*Exponentiation.*
*, /	*Multiplication* and *division.*
binary +, -	*Addition* and *subtraction.*

Using Arithmetic Operators in Expressions. Arithmetic operators are used to perform operations on the contents of fields (represented by field names), memory variables, values, and functions within expressions. In the following examples, assume that fields named FIELD1, FIELD2, . . . FIELD6 all contain numeric values:

    FIELD1 = 4
    FIELD2 = 7
    FIELD3 = 3
    FIELD4 = 5
    FIELD5 = 8
    FIELD6 = 9

? field1+field2   *Adds field* FIELD1 *to field* FIELD2 *and displays the sum (*11*) on the screen.*

? field1*field3	*Displays the product of fields* FIELD1 *and* FIELD3: 12.
? field1^field4	*Displays* FIELD1 *to the* FIELD4[th] *power:* 1024.
? (field1+field2+field3)/field5	*Computes and displays the sum of fields* FIELD1, FIELD2 *and* FIELD3, *all divided by* FIELD5: 1.75.
? field4/field5+field6	FIELD4 *is divided by* FIELD5, *the result is added to* FIELD6: 9.62.
? field4/(field5+field6)	FIELD4 *divided by sum of* FIELD5 *and* FIELD6: 0.29.

String Operators

The term *string* is used to denote a character field, a character variable, or a series of characters enclosed by ' . . . ' (single quotes), " . . . " (double quotes), or [. . .] (brackets) symbols. (If you start a string with one symbol, you must end it with the matching symbol. Note that you do *not* use the ` mark to open a single-quoted string; use the ' to open and close the string.) Just as we use arithmetic operators and functions with numeric- and date-type data, we use string operators and functions with character-type data.

The string operators have equal precedence, and are therefore evaluated left to right:

$ *Substring comparison*, if **A** and **B** are character fields, **A$B** will be true if and only if string **A** is equal to **B**, or is contained in **B**. This operator is used in logical conditions.

+   *Concatenation*, connects the strings end to end. Blanks in either string are retained. This operator is used in computed expressions.

-     *Concatenation*, connects the strings end to end. Blanks at the end of the string to the left of the - sign are moved to the (right) end of the combined expression. This operator is used in computed expressions.

Using String Operators in Expressions. String operators are used to tie together fields (represented by field names), memory variables, strings, and functions into expressions. In the following examples, assume that fields named FIELD7, FIELD8, and FIELD9 all contain character data:

FIELD7 = 'ABCDEF'
FIELD8 = "GHIJKL"
FIELD9 = [DEFGHI]

? field7+field8	*Displays* ABCDEFGHIJKL.
? field9$field7	*Displays* .F. *(false) because* 'DEFGHI' *is not in* 'ABCDEF'.

? field9$(field7+field8)   *Displays* **.T.** *(true) because 'DEFGHI' is in 'ABCDEFGHIJKL'.*

? field9$(field8+field7)   *Displays* **.F.** *(false) because characters are not in same order ('DEFGHI' is not in 'GHIJKLABCDEF').*

Comparison Operators

Comparisons can be performed between character, numeric and date fields or variables, and strings (in quotation marks) and numeric values in conditions. Both items being compared must be of the same type. These operators generate logical results (true or false) that are used primarily in data file search routines.

All comparison operators have equal precedence, and are therefore evaluated left to right:

<	*Less than.*
>	*Greater than.*
=	*Equal to.*
<>	*Not equal to.*
#	*Not equal to.*
<=	*Less than or equal to.*
>=	*Greater than or equal to.*
$	*Substring comparison* (discussed earlier).

Logical Operators

Logical operators are used to tie two logical conditions together. These operators generate logical results (true or false) that are used primarily in data file search routines.

Logical operators, in order of precedence, are as follows:

.NOT.	*True is changed to false and false is changed to true.*
.AND.	*Both conditions must be true for the total to be true.*
.OR.	*If either condition is true, then the total is true.*

Important: The periods on either side of .NOT., .AND., and .OR. must be included; otherwise, dBASE will think these words are field names.

Using Comparison and Logical Operators. You may recall the discussion of the **LIST** command in Unit 3, where we mentioned that a logical condition could be used to limit the number of records listed. This form of the command is **LIST FOR {condition}**. Comparison and logical operators are used to build the **{condition}**.

The following are example commands using logical conditions. Each command will list or display all records for which the logical condition is true.

```
list for (field1 = field2)
display for (field1 <= field3)
list for .not. (field3 >= field5) to print
```

```
display field2, field3 for ((field7 $ field8) .or. .not. (field3 > field1))
list field8 for (field4 < 10000) to print
```

When the *field type* is logical, then the logical {condition} may consist simply of the name of the field. For instance, if we have a field named SMOKER that is true if the person smokes and false otherwise, then

list for .not.smoker

will provide a list of all who do not smoke.

The comparison operators may also be used to compare character-type data. One character string may be less than or greater than another string based on the character order. (Character order is displayed in Table 6-1, in Unit 6.) Also, two strings may be tested for equality. The strings are equal if they are exactly the same, or if the right-hand character string is identical to the starting characters of the left-hand character string:

? 'Rose' = 'Rose'   *Yields* **.T.** *because the two strings are the same.*

? 'Rose' = 'rose'   *Yields* **.F.** *because the capitalization is different.*

? 'Rosenbaum' = 'Rose'   *Yields* **.T.** *because the string on the right matches the beginning characters of the string on the left.*

? 'Rose' = 'Rosenbaum'   *Yields* **.F.** *because the string on the right is longer.*

Order of Precedence of Operators

When the various types of operators are combined in a logical condition, they have the following order of precedence:

» Expressions containing mathematical and string operators (+, -, *, /, and ^) are evaluated (computed) first; yielding a computed expression.

» Comparisons are then made between expressions joined by comparison operators (=, <, >, <=, >=, <>, $); yielding a logical result (true or false).

» Logical results are combined by the logical operators (.NOT., .AND., .OR.) to yield another logical result.

It is not uncommon for a logical condition to be rather complex:

list for .not.smoker .and. mo_income>35000/12 .or. state="CA"

FUNCTIONS

Functions are used to form all or part of an expression. What follows is a partial list. See the appropriate reference manual if you need a complete list and more detailed explanations. dBASE III Plus provides more functions: these are noted in the lists that follow.

The terms in parentheses that follow a function are called arguments of the function. Some functions do not require arguments and are followed by empty parentheses — i.e., ( ) — to differentiate them from field names. For the other functions, the argument must be a specific type, either character string, numeric, or date.

Character String Functions

Functions in this group deal with character and text strings.

AT(char string 1,char string 2) *Substring search function*, yields an integer whose value is the character number in char string 2 that begins a substring identical to char string 1.

> **? at('ross','across')**   *Yields the result* 3.

CHR(numeric expression) *Number to character function*, yields the ASCII character equivalent of the numeric expression. Usually used to send a control code to a printer or a special graphics character on the screen. (See discussion of **SET PRINT ON** in Unit 8.)

> **? chr(3)**   *Displays a heart on the screen.*

> **? chr(15)**   *Shifts some printers into compressed type style.*

LEFT(char expression,length) *Substring selection from left*, forms a character string from the left part of another string. (dBASE III Plus only.)

> **? left('William',4)**   *Will yield* Will.

> **list for left(desc,2) = 'ch'**   *Will list those items whose DESC field begins with the characters* ch. *(If the raw material file were in use, this would list three records.)*

LEN(char string) *Length function*, this function yields an integer whose value is the number of characters in the string.

> **? len('Mike')**   *Yields the result* 4.

LOWER(char string) *Lower case function*, yields the same string as the char string except all letters are converted to lower case. Often used when we do not remember how data are capitalized in the data file. Note that this function does not permanently convert the letters; it only converts them for the duration of the command and leaves the original text as it was.

> **? lower('Ross')** *Yields* ross.

> **list for lower(desc) = 'sp'** *Will list those items whose DESC field begins with the characters* sp, *regardless of capitalization. (If the raw material file were in use, this would list two records.)*

LTRIM(char string) *Trim leading blanks*, removes leading blanks from a character string. Usually used when the contents of a field is shorter than the length of the field. (dBASE III Plus only.)

REPLICATE(char string,number) *Replicate function*, repeats the char string a number of times; useful to create simple bar graphs. (dBASE III Plus only.)

> **? replicate('*',10)** *Will yield* **************.

> **list cost, replicate('*',cost*100)** *Will list all costs and a* ***** *for each cent the item costs.*

RIGHT(char expression,length) *Substring selection from right*, forms a character string from the right part of another string. This can be combined with the STR( ) and LTRIM( ) functions to provide specially-formatted numeric output. (dBASE III Plus only.)

> **? right('Stevenson',3)** *Will yield* son.

> **list right('********'+ltrim(str(cost,8,2)),8)** *Will yield a list of costs with leading* ***** *characters. Try this with the raw material file to see the result.*

RTRIM(char string) *Trim function*, removes trailing blanks from a character string. Usually used when the contents of a field is shorter than the length of the field. (dBASE III Plus only.) Same as TRIM( ).

STR(numeric expression,length,decimals) *String function*, evaluates a numeric expression and yields a character string, decimals specifier is optional. This function is further illustrated in Unit 10.

> **? str(95.6,6,2)** *Yields* 95.60. *Because the* length *is specified as 6 and there are only five digits in the number (including the decimal point and 0 added at the end), there is a blank space preceding the 9.*

STUFF(char string 1,start,number,char string 2) *Replace portion of string,* changes char string 1 starting at start character, removing number of characters, and inserting char string 2. (dBASE III Plus only.)

> **? stuff('Super Model',4,2,'reme')**   *Will yield* **Supreme Model.**

SUBSTR(char expression,start,length) *Substring function,* forms a character string from the specified part of another string.

> **? substr('across',2,5)**   *Will yield* **cross.**

TRANSFORM(numeric or character expression,format) *Format function,* converts a numeric or character expression to a specified format. Most useful to display numbers with embedded commas and decimal point. The formats are discussed in more detail in Unit 14. (dBASE III Plus only.)

> **? transform(1234567.89,"###,###,###.##")**   *Will yield* **1,234,567.89.**

> **list transform(cost,"##,###.##")**   *Will yield a formatted list of costs.*

TRIM(char string) *Trim function,* removes trailing blanks from a character string. Usually used when the contents of a field is shorter than the length of the field.

> **list trim(first_name)+' '+last_name**   *Will list the FIRST_NAME field, a space, and the LAST_NAME field. The first and last names will be separated by only one space, regardless of whether or not the first name fills the FIRST_NAME field.*

UPPER(char string) *Upper case function,* yields the same string as the char string except that all letters are converted to upper case. Often used when we do not remember how data are capitalized in the data file. Note that this function does not permanently convert the letters; it only converts them for the duration of the command and leaves the original text as it was.

> **? upper('Ross')**   *Yields* ROSS.

> **list for upper(desc) = "SP"**   *Will list those items whose DESC field begins with the characters SP, regardless of capitalization. (If the raw material file were in use, this would list two records.)*

> **list for upper(desc) = 'sp'**   *Will not list anything since the lowercase letters sp will never match the DESC field after it has been converted to uppercase.*

Numeric Functions

dBASE III Plus contains a few numeric functions that are not available in the original dBASE III. For the examples in this section, assume that we have a database with fields named NAME and BALANCE, which contain the name of a customer and the amount that he or she owes on a charge account.

ABS(numeric expression) *Absolute value*, returns a positive number regardless of the sign of the numeric expression. (dBASE III Plus only.)

? abs(5-7) *Yields* **2.**

list abs(balance) *Will list the BALANCE field of all records, converting negative balances to positive (for the list only).*

EXP(numeric expression) *Exponential function*, returns the value of e^x. This function would be used in calculations by financial analysts.

INT(numeric expression) *Integer function*, evaluates the numeric expression and discards the fractional part to yield an integer value. Truncates, does not round.

? int(6.75) *Yields* **6.**

list name, int(balance) *Use to list the whole-dollar amount of the balance due, without rounding.*

LOG(numeric expression) *Log function*, returns the natural logarithm ($\log_e$) of a given number. This function would be used in calculations by financial analysts.

MAX(numeric expression 1, numeric expression 2) *Maximum value*, returns the larger of the two numbers. (dBASE III Plus only.) This function is often used to set a *lower limit*. If, for instance, we have a minimum payment of $20 or 20 per cent of the balance due, whichever is greater, the lower limit is 20. We would use the following function to display all names and minimum payments due:

list name, max(20, .2*balance)

MIN(numeric expression 1, numeric expression 2) *Minimum value*, returns the smaller of the two numbers. (dBASE III Plus only.) Continuing the example started with MAX, we realize that some customers may have a balance of less than $20. Therefore, the payment should be the minimum of (1) the balance due, (2) $20, or (3) 20 per cent of the balance due if the balance due is greater than $20. The list is generated by the following command:

list name, min(balance, max(20, .2*balance))

MOD(numeric expression 1, numeric expression 2) *Modulus*, returns the remainder of the first number divided by the second. This function is often used in conjunction with the INT( ) function when converting numbers from one metric to another (e.g., from months to years and months). (dBASE III Plus only.)

list int(months/12), mod(months,12) *Yields two columns of numbers: years on the left and months on the right.*

ROUND(numeric expression,decimal) *Rounding function*, rounds the numeric expression to specified number of decimal places.

? round(236.56,1) *Yields* 236.60.

? round(236.54,1) *Yields* 236.50.

? round(-236.56,1) *Yields* -236.60.

list name,round(balance,0) *Yields a list of names and balances rounded to the nearest dollar.*

SQRT(numeric expression) *Square root function*, returns the square root of a positive number.

VAL(char string) *String to numeric function*, forms a number from a character string made up of digits, signs, and up to one decimal point. The conversion to a number stops when a nonnumeric character is encountered.

? val('236.50 miles') *Yields* 236.50.

list for val(desc)>0 *Provides a list of those records whose DESC field starts with a number.*

Date and Time Functions

dBASE III has ten date and time functions, the most useful of which are discussed below. Both DATE( ) and TIME( ) must be followed by empty parentheses so dBASE will not confuse them with field names.

DATE( ) *Date function*, returns the system date in the form MM/DD/YY. This is date-type data, and may be compared with date-type fields in the database. If you set the date properly when loading the system, this will be today's date.

If the system date is 01/01/87, then
? date( ) *Yields* 01/01/87.

CDOW(date variable) *Character day of week function*, returns the name of the day of the week from a date variable.

If the system date is 01/01/87, then
? cdow(date( )) *Yields* Thursday.

CMONTH(date variable) *Character month function,* returns the name of the month from a date variable.

> *If the system date is 01/01/87, then*
> **? cmonth(date( ))**   *Yields* **January**.

CTOD(char expression) *Character to date function,* creates a date-type data from a character string. This is the only way to enter date-type expressions from the keyboard. Used as precursor to date arithmetic.

> *If I want to know how long it is to New Year's Day 1988, I would use the following:*
> **? ctod('01/01/88')-date( )**

DTOC(date expression) *Date to character function,* creates a character string from a date variable. Used to create a text string for headings and in other places where only character-type data is permitted. This function is illustrated in Unit 10.

TIME( ) *Time function,* returns the system time as a character string in the form hh:mm:ss. If you set the time properly when loading the system, this will be the current time.

> **? time( )**   *Yields the current time, e.g.,* **12:04:46**.

Input, Output, Record, and Environment Functions

Functions in these groups are primarily used in command (program) files, and will be discussed in Part 3 of this manual.

Functions Not Discussed

To save space, only the most useful Character, Numeric, and Date functions are discussed in this unit. The list below contains those not presented, with a brief description. More detail can be found in the dBASE III manuals.

Function	Description
ASC(char string)	Character to ASCII Code Conversion
DAY(date variable)	Day of Month
DOW(date variable)	Day of Week
MONTH(date variable)	Month of Year
SPACE(number)	Generates Blank Spaces
YEAR(date variable)	Year

```
. list for cost>.10
Record#   RMID DESC            COST INVENTORY LAST_ORDER
      9   0016 apple pie       0.16       346 08/15/87
     13   0017 cherry pie      0.14       200 09/19/87
     18   0007 sesame seed bun 0.12       400 10/08/87


. list off for cost>.10
RMID DESC            COST INVENTORY LAST_ORDER
0016 apple pie       0.16       346 08/15/87
0017 cherry pie      0.14       200 09/19/87
0007 sesame seed bun 0.12       400 10/08/87

. set heading off
. list off for cost>.10
0016 apple pie       0.16 346 08/15/87
0017 cherry pie      0.14 200 09/19/87
0007 sesame seed bun 0.12 400 10/08/87

. list off desc,cost for cost>.10
apple pie           0.16
cherry pie          0.14
sesame seed bun     0.12

. set heading on
. list desc,cost,(1.15*cost) for cost>.10
Record#   desc            cost  (1.15*cost)
      9   apple pie       0.16      0.1840
     13   cherry pie      0.14      0.1610
     18   sesame seed bun 0.12      0.1380

.
```

Command Line |<B:>|RAW_MATL |Rec: EOF/19

Enter a dBASE III PLUS command.

FIGURE 4-1 Variations of the **LIST** Command
Note: Items entered by the user are in **boldface**.

CONSTRAINED LISTS

There are many methods for extracting data from dBASE files and presenting that data in a report format. The quickest method is to use the **LIST** command, from either the dot prompt or the **ASSIST** Menu, to produce a list of the data. The normal list output includes all records, field names, and record numbers. In this section, we discuss how to eliminate some aspects of lists that you may consider extraneous. Look at Figure 4-1, which contains a series of commands given from the dot prompt. First, the command **LIST FOR COST>.10**, was given which produced a standard list with record numbers and field names, but limited to items that cost more than ten cents.

In many cases, the record numbers will be unnecessary. The second listing was created with the command **LIST OFF FOR COST>.10**. The **OFF** keyword works with both **LIST** and **DISPLAY** commands to suppress record number information.

Standard list format includes field names. To suppress field names on lists and displays, give the command **SET HEADING OFF**, which will remain in effect until you exit dBASE, or give the command **SET HEADING ON**.

If field names are specified with the command, then only those fields will be listed. For instance, the command **LIST OFF DESC,COST FOR COST>.10** listed only those fields.

Lists may also contain computed expressions. To list these raw materials, with present costs and costs plus fifteen percent, the command **LIST OFF DESC, COST, (1.15*COST) FOR COST>.10** was given.

The listing may be sent to the printer by adding the phrase **TO PRINT** to any of the commands.

From the ASSIST Menu. **LIST** is found as part of the ■ *Retrieve* ■ menu. Instead of moving directly through the default commands, you may choose to specify only certain fields or a condition. For instance, in Figure 4-2, the menu sequence

   ■ *Retrieve* ■ *List* ■ *Construct a field list* ■

has been given. dBASE lists all fields on the left of the screen and a description of the highlighted field in the center of the screen. Use <UP> and <DOWN> to highlight the desired field, then press <CR> to select the field. Repeat as often as necessary. When all desired fields are included, press <LEFT> or <RIGHT>.

After completing the field list, we build a search condition and execute the command. Observe the progress through the menus in Figures 4-3 through 4-7. Notice that the command is displayed immediately above the status bar as it is being constructed.

The **OFF** and **SET HEADING OFF** options are not readily available in this mode. Also, a computed expression may not be included in a list generated from the **ASSIST** menu. (We will discuss the *scope* options in Unit 6.)

GUIDED ACTIVITY

This activity requires you to conduct simple inquiry operations using the operators and functions discussed in this unit.

1. Follow the startup procedure for your version of dBASE as outlined in Unit 2.

2. **USE RAW_MATL**, which you created in Application A. (If your instructor did not assign Application A, a copy of RAW_MATL will be provided.)

3. List, on the printer, all materials for which the cost is less than 0.10.

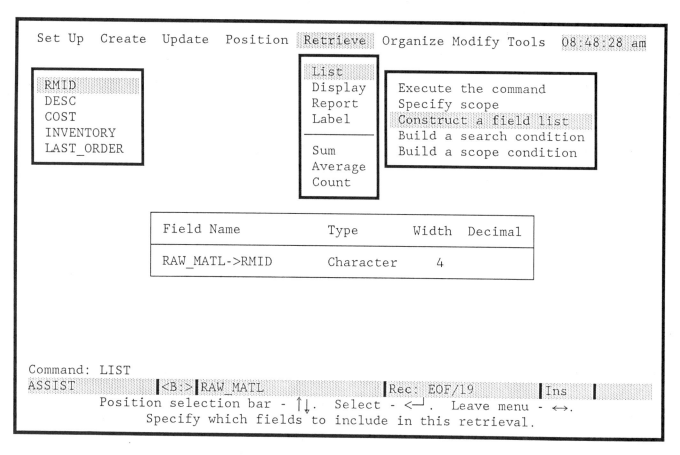

FIGURE 4-2 Constructing a Field List

This requires that you know a few things. First, how to direct a list to the printer (Unit 3). Second, how to write a condition that is true only when the cost is less than 0.10. Finally, how to use the condition with the **LIST** command. Your screen will look similar to the top of Figure 4-1 if you have executed this command from the dot prompt. You may also give this command from the **ASSIST** Menu.

✔ **CHECKPOINT**
What command do you use to accomplish this list?

_____

4. Inventory value is defined as the product of the cost per unit and the inventory quantity. List, on the printer, all materials for which the inventory value is greater than 10.00.

✔ **CHECKPOINT**
What command do you use to prepare this list?

_____

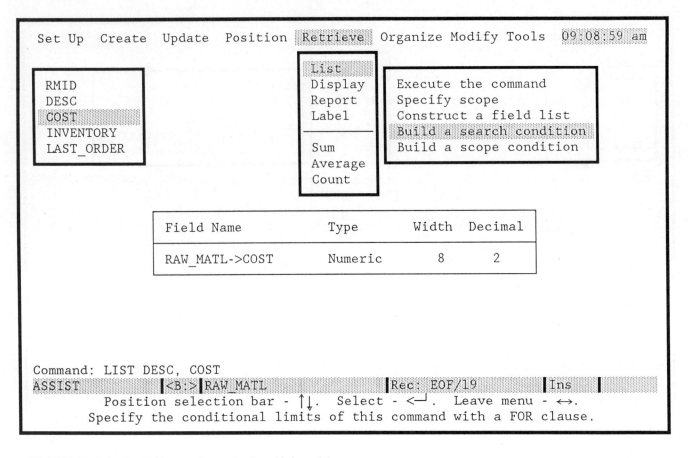

FIGURE 4-3 Building a Search Condition (I)

5. List, on the printer, all materials that are inventoried by the ounce (oz.). You will have to use the substring comparison operator.

✔ **CHECKPOINT**
What command do you use to develop this list?

6. Print a list of all raw material items in which Chez Jacques has more than fifty dollars invested. The list should not include record numbers or field names.

✔ **CHECKPOINT**
What commands do you use to print this list?

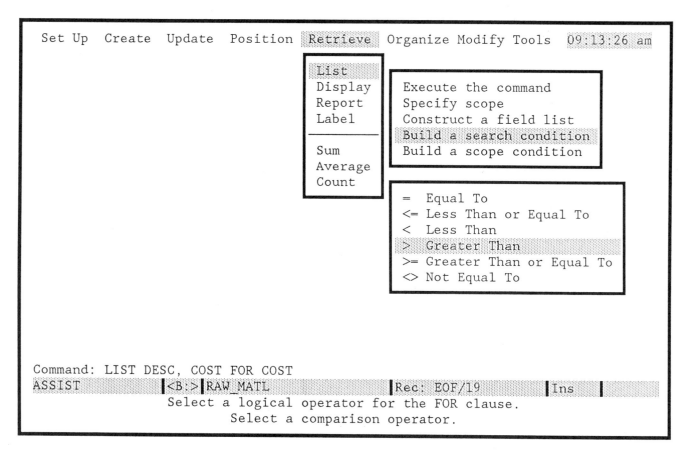

FIGURE 4-4 Building a Search Condition (II)

7. *For Additional Practice*: If you would like additional practice using the command and functions discussed in this unit, do the following.

a. From the dot prompt, give the command **USE TOURNEY** to save your current file and open the additional-practice file you created in Unit 3.

b. Generate a list of the games, plus the total score for the game.

c. Generate a list of winners. This will take two commands, one to list the name of the home team if the home team score is greater than the visiting team score, and a second command to do the opposite.

d. Generate a list of the games, with an additional column which is .T. if the home team won and .F. if the visiting team won. Your command will take the basic form

    list hometeam, homescore, visteam, visscore, homescore>visscore

You must, of course, use the field names you assigned when you created the database.

e. Repeat the list from step d, converting all team names to upper case.

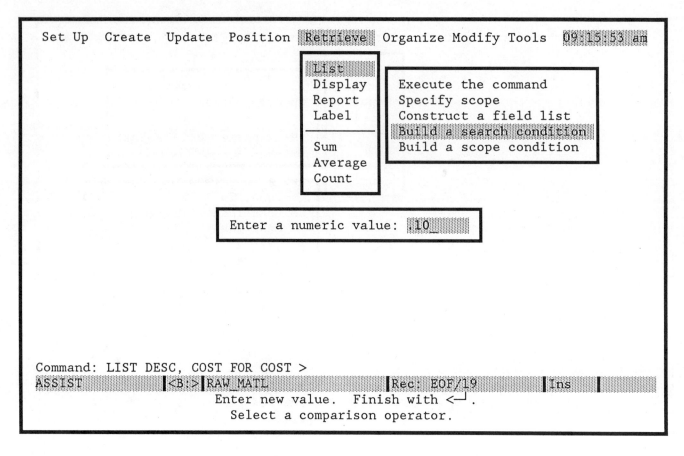

FIGURE 4-5 Building a Search Condition (III)
Note: Item entered by the user is in **boldface**.

f. Generate a list of the games without record numbers or field names.

g. Generate a list of the winning scores, using the MAX( ) function.

h. Do each of the steps again, printing the results.

8. When you have completed all of the above, give the command **QUIT** to exit dBASE. Turn off the computer and return the dBASE software to the Lab Supervisor.

REVIEW QUESTIONS

1. What is the difference between logical conditions and computed expressions?

*2. What does *order of precedence* mean?

3. What are the various categories of functions?

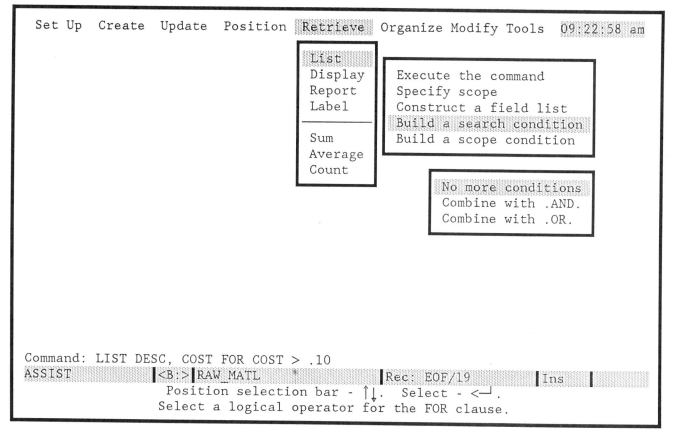

FIGURE 4-6 Building a Search Condition (IV)

4. Assume that the following fields have the values indicated. Determine whether the conditions are true or false.

Field	Type	Value
NAME	C	Fred
COLOR	C	RED
AGE	N	25
SIZE	N	46

*a. (name $ color)

*b. (color $ name)

*c. (color $ upper(name))

*d. (age < size)

 e. (age # size)

```
 Set Up   Create   Update   Position   Retrieve  Organize Modify Tools    09:25:37 am




















Record#  DESC                COST
      9  apple pie           0.16
     13  cherry pie          0.14
     18  sesame seed bun     0.12

ASSIST              |<B:>|RAW_MATL                    |Rec: EOF/19           |Ins     |
                    Press any key to continue work in ASSIST.
```

FIGURE 4-7 The Resulting List

   *f. .not. (age > size)

   *g. (color $ name) .and. (age < size)

   *h. (color $ name) .or. (age < size)

    i. (lower(color) $ name)

   *j. (age < 25)

    k. (name = 'Fred') .and. (size > 40)

*5. What commands would you use to print a list of all raw material items in which Chez Jacques has more than fifty dollars invested? The list should not include record numbers or field names. Remember that investment in inventory is the product of unit cost and quantity on hand.

*6. When may you use the = (equal sign) when comparing strings, and when must the $ operator be used?

DOCUMENTATION RESEARCH

Using the reference manual, determine the answers to the following questions which deal with the functions discussed in this unit. I recommend you also write the reference manual page number by the discussion of the function in this unit.

1. ? command — what will a single ? without a following {expression} do?

2. AT(char string 1,char string 2) — what value will be returned if char string 1 is not contained in char string 2?

3. CHR(numeric expression) — what numeric expression will sound the *bell*?

4. How are the LEN(char string) and TRIM(char string) functions combined to determine the number of characters in a character-type database field?

5. STR(numeric expression,length,decimals) — what will happen if the length is less than the number of digits in the number?

UNIT
5
SUMMARY STATISTICS AND QUERIES

dBASE provides commands that compute a limited set of summary statistics about all or a specified portion of the numeric fields in the data file. The purpose of this unit is to introduce you to these commands. This unit also contains an introduction to the filter command and query files, which cause the database to appear as if it contains only records that meet a certain condition.

LEARNING OBJECTIVE

At the completion of this unit, you should be able to

a. use each of the summary statistics commands,

b. use the filter command and query files.

IMPORTANT COMMANDS

    COUNT
    SUM
    AVERAGE
    SET FILTER TO {condition}
    CREATE QUERY {query filename}
    SET FILTER TO FILE {query filename}

COUNTS

The **COUNT** command counts the number of records in the file or in a selected portion of the file. The result of the command **COUNT** is the number of records in the file. **COUNT** *does not add up (i.e., sum) the contents of the fields.* To count the number of records for which a given {**condition**} is true, use the form

count for {condition}

COUNT is usually used with a logical {condition}. For instance, **COUNT FOR (STATE='ND')** will tell you how many people in your mailing list live in North Dakota, while **COUNT FOR .NOT.(STATE='NY')** will tell you how many live in places other than New York.

From the ASSIST Menu. COUNT is found on the ■ *Retrieve* ■ menu. The most direct method of counting is

    ■ *Retrieve* ■ *Count* ■ *Execute the command* ■

which will tell you how many records are in the data file. You may also build a search condition using the procedures discussed with the **LIST** command in Unit 4.

SUMS

The **SUM** command computes the sum of the values of numeric fields and expressions in the file or in a selected portion of the file. The sums are printed on the screen and may be stored in memory variables. The common forms of the command are as follows:

sum	*Sums each numeric field in all records.*
sum {list}	*Sums listed fields and expressions for all records.*
sum for {condition}	*Sums only those records for which {condition} is true.*
sum {list} for {condition}	*Sums listed fields and expressions in records for which {condition} is true.*

The {list} may be composed of field names or expressions. For instance, if you have a personnel file with hours worked and hourly rate in fields HOURS and RATE, you could use the command **SUM HOURS, HOURS*RATE** to yield the number of hours worked as well as the total wages earned. This command computes a sum for each field or expression in the {list} (or for every field if there is no {list}).

From the ASSIST Menu. SUM is found on the ■ *Retrieve* ■ menu. The most direct method of summing is

    ■ *Retrieve* ■ *Sum* ■ *Execute the command* ■

which will sum all numeric fields in the file. You may also construct a field list or build a search condition, using the procedures discussed with the **LIST** command in Unit 4. You cannot sum an expression through the **ASSIST** menu.

AVERAGES

The **AVERAGE** command computes the arithmetic mean of all or a subset of numeric fields. It is similar in form to the **SUM** command:

average	*Averages each numeric field in all records.*
average {list}	*Averages listed fields and expressions for all records.*
average for {condition}	*Averages only those records for which {condition} is true.*
average {list} for {condition}	*Averages listed fields and expressions in records for which {condition} is true.*

This command computes an average for each field or expression in the {list} (or for every field if there is no {list}).

From the ASSIST Menu. **AVERAGE** is found on the ■ *Retrieve* ■ menu. The most direct method of averaging is

■ *Retrieve* ■ *Average* ■ *Execute the command* ■

which will average all numeric fields in the file. You may also construct a field list or build a search condition, using the procedures discussed with the **LIST** command in Unit 4. You cannot average an expression via the **ASSIST** menu.

EXAMPLES

Examples of the use of the statistics commands are illustrated in Figure 5-1. First, the file RAW_MATL was opened with the **USE** command. Then **COUNT** determines the total number of records in the file. The second **COUNT** tells us that six records have an inventory in excess of 500.

SUM, without any logical condition, sums each numeric field (two in this case) and displays the results. The second **SUM** command is more selective; only items for which the cost is greater than 0.07 are chosen. Note that the second command sums a computed expression, not individual fields.

The third **SUM** command computes the sum for records that have '(oz.)' in the description field. Again, the sum computed is a computed expression composed of two numeric fields, and not the sum of the fields.

The first **AVERAGE** command simply averages each numeric field for all records. In the second instance, the average is of a computed expression. In the final case, only certain records are included in the average.

```
. use raw_matl
. count
      19 records
. count for (inventory>500)
       6 records
. sum
      19 records summed
         COST        INVENTORY
         1.05           8784
. sum cost*inventory for (cost>.07)
       5 records summed
      cost*inventory
              161.36
. sum cost*inventory for '(oz.)'$desc
       6 records summed
      cost*inventory
              156.99
. average
       19 records averaged
      COST INVENTORY
      0.06      462
. average cost*inventory
       19 records averaged
cost*inventory
         21.79
. average cost*inventory for 'cup'$lower(desc)
        3 records averaged
  cost*inventory
          13.67
.
```

| Command Line | \<B:\> RAW_MATL | Rec: EOF/19 | | |

Enter a dBASE III PLUS command.

FIGURE 5-1 Illustration of the Summary Statistics Commands
Note: Items entered by the user are in **boldface**.

FILTERS AND QUERY FILES

A *filter* is a logical condition that serves to limit the records that are available for processing in a datafile. Only records for which the filter condition is true will be listed, counted, and so on. You can achieve the same effect with **FOR {condition}** clauses in commands, but a filter condition is semipermanent and does not need to be repeated for each command. That is, once you set a filter condition, it remains in effect until you set another filter condition, turn off the filter, or close the file with which the filter is associated. Normally, you would use filters only when you intended to do a significant amount of work on a particular subset of the data in a file.

A filter condition is like any other condition: composed of field names, expressions, and logical and comparison operators. Filters may be established directly via a command, or they may be stored in a special *query file* for editing and subsequent re-use.[1]

The Filter Command

The file to be filtered must be in use before a filter is established. The basic commands for establishing a filter condition are

> **set filter to {condition}**
> **go top**

The **{condition}** may be any legitimate dBASE condition. For instance, if you wish to process records for a single state, use the commands

> **set filter to state='NY'**
> **go top**

The **GO TOP** command moves us to the first record for which the filter condition is true, making that record the current record. This command is necessary whenever a filter condition is set. Any command such as **LIST**, **COUNT**, or **SUM** will now use information from only records for which the STATE field is 'NY'.

Once we are finished with the filter, we may set another filter, or we may deactivate the filter with the command

> **set filter to**

with no **{condition}**.

Query Files

A *query file* is a file (with the extension .QRY) that contains a filter condition. The virtue of query files is that they may be created, saved, edited, and used again. The logic of the **SET FILTER** command is lost once another filter is established, but that logic is saved if a query file is created.

The process of establishing a query file begins with the command

> **create query {query filename}**

_____

[1] Query files are not available in the original dBASE III; you must use the **SET FILTER** command.

```
┌─────────────────────────────────────────────────────────────────────────┐
│ Set Filter          Nest            Display            Exit  02:26:09 pm  │
│ ┌─────────────────────────────────────────────────┐                      │
│ │ Field Name                                       │                      │
│ │ Operator                                         │                      │
│ │ Constant/Expression                              │                      │
│ │ Connect                                          │                      │
│ │ ─────────────────────────────────────────────── │                      │
│ │ Line Number          1                           │                      │
│ └─────────────────────────────────────────────────┘                      │
│                                                                           │
│ ┌──────┬────────┬──────────────────┬────────────────────────┬──────────┐ │
│ │ Line │ Field  │ Operator         │ Constant/Expression    │ Connect  │ │
│ ├──────┼────────┼──────────────────┼────────────────────────┼──────────┤ │
│ │ 1    │        │                  │                        │          │ │
│ │ 2    │        │                  │                        │          │ │
│ │ 3    │        │                  │                        │          │ │
│ │ 4    │        │                  │                        │          │ │
│ │ 5    │        │                  │                        │          │ │
│ │ 6    │        │                  │                        │          │ │
│ │ 7    │        │                  │                        │          │ │
│ └──────┴────────┴──────────────────┴────────────────────────┴──────────┘ │
│ CREATE QUERY    |<B:>|B:HIGHCOST.QRY          |Opt: 1/2       |         |  │
│        Position selection bar - ↑↓.  Select - <┘.  Leave menu - ↔.       │
│             Select a field name for the filter condition.                 │
└─────────────────────────────────────────────────────────────────────────┘
```

FIGURE 5-2 Creating a Query File (I)

The extension .QRY is added automatically if you do not supply an extension. Once the command is given, you will be presented with the full-screen display illustrated in Figure 5-2. The process begins by choosing a *Field Name* (Figure 5-3), *Operator* (Figure 5-4), and *Constant* or *Expression* (Figure 5-5). If there are multiple expressions, use *Connect* to link them (with **.AND.** or **.OR.**). The ■ *Nest* ■ menu lets you place parentheses.

■ *Display* ■ shows you the records in the database that meet the query condition (see Figure 5-6). Use the PgDn and PgUp keys to scan several records to ensure that you have set the condition you wanted. Once you are satisfied with the query, use ^End (Ctrl-End) or select ■ *Exit* ■ *Save* ■. The filter described in the query file is automatically activated.

To activate the query file filter in a later dBASE session, use the command

set filter to file {query filename}

An active query file is deactivated with the command

set filter to

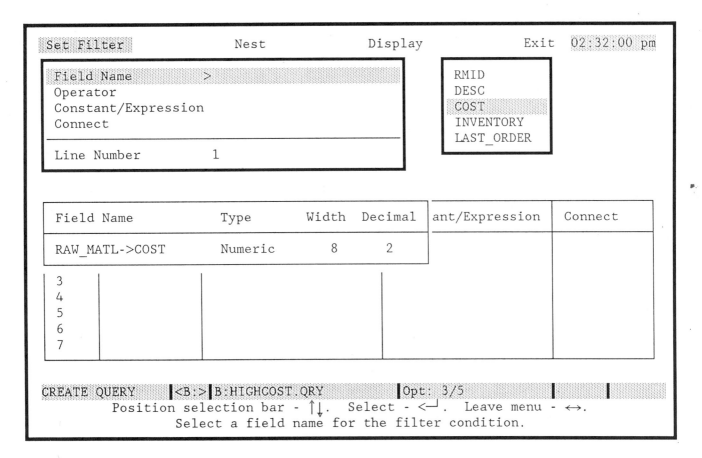

FIGURE 5-3 Creating a Query File (II)

If you wish to change the query file, use the command

modify query {query filename}

For multiple-line queries, move the selection bar to the Line Number line, press <CR>, and enter the number of the line you wish to edit.

From the ASSIST Menu. CREATE QUERY is found on the ■ *Create* ■ menu. The query creation process is the same regardless of whether or not it is initiated from the **ASSIST** menu. **MODIFY QUERY** is found on the ■ *Modify* ■ menu. **SET FILTER TO FILE** is found on the ■ *Set Up* ■ menu.

```
 Set Filter              Nest            Display              Exit  02:34:33 pm

  Field Name        COST                         =  Equals
  Operator            >                          >  More than
  Constant/Expression                            >= More than or equal
  Connect                                        <  Less than
 _____               <= Less than or equal
  Line Number       1                            <> Not equal to


  Line  Field      Operator         Constant/Expression      Connect

  1     COST
  2
  3
  4
  5
  6
  7


 CREATE QUERY    |<B:>|B:HIGHCOST.QRY         |Opt: 3/6          |           |
        Position selection bar - ↑↓.  Select - <┘.  Leave menu - ←→.
             Select a comparison operator for the filter condition.
```

FIGURE 5-4 Creating a Query File (III)

GUIDED ACTIVITY

This activity requires you to use the summary statistics commands. Before you go to the lab to work on this activity, answer the Review Questions for this unit. The results of using similar commands are illustrated in Figure 5-1. Some of the results may be obtained through the **ASSIST** menu, but others may be determined only through dot commands.

1. Follow the startup procedure for your version of dBASE as outlined in Unit 2.

2. Compute the following values:

✔ CHECKPOINT
What command must you give before you can compute values from the finished goods (menu) file?

_____

a. The number of Chez Jacques menu items that sell for less than 1.00.

```
┌─────────────────────────────────────────────────────────────────────────┐
│  Set Filter            Nest            Display            Exit  02:37:36 pm │
│  ┌──────────────────────────────────────────────────────────────┐        │
│  │ Field Name            COST                                     │        │
│  │ Operator              More than or equal                       │        │
│  │ Constant/Expression>.10_                                       │        │
│  │ Connect                                                        │        │
│  │ ────────────────────────────────────────────                  │        │
│  │ Line Number           1                                        │        │
│  └──────────────────────────────────────────────────────────────┘        │
│                                                                            │
│  ┌──────┬──────────┬─────────────────┬────────────────────┬───────────┐  │
│  │ Line │ Field    │ Operator        │ Constant/Expression│ Connect   │  │
│  ├──────┼──────────┼─────────────────┼────────────────────┼───────────┤  │
│  │ 1    │ COST     │ More than or    │                    │           │  │
│  │ 2    │          │ equal           │                    │           │  │
│  │ 3    │          │                 │                    │           │  │
│  │ 4    │          │                 │                    │           │  │
│  │ 5    │          │                 │                    │           │  │
│  │ 6    │          │                 │                    │           │  │
│  │ 7    │          │                 │                    │           │  │
│  └──────┴──────────┴─────────────────┴────────────────────┴───────────┘  │
│                                                                            │
│  CREATE QUERY      |<B:>|B:HIGHCOST.QRY         |Opt: 3/5      |      | Caps│
│   Enter a field name or an expression.  F10 for a field menu.  Finish with <┘. │
│            Enter an expression or constant for the filter condition.       │
└─────────────────────────────────────────────────────────────────────────┘
```

FIGURE 5-5 Creating a Query File (IV)

    b. The average selling price of the menu items. (The average selling price is probably a meaningless figure, but compute it anyway.)

✔ **CHECKPOINT**

    What command must you give before you can compute values from the raw materials file?

_____

    c. The total inventory value of raw materials. (Inventory value is defined as the product of quantity on hand and cost per unit.)

    d. The inventory value of raw materials that are measured by the ounce.

    e. The inventory value of raw materials that are not measured by the ounce.

3. Follow the examples of Figures 5-2 through 5-6 to create and test a query file. Then repeat the last three questions above (2c, 2d, and 2e). The results you obtain will probably be different because the query file allows only certain records to be processed.

```
Set Filter              Nest            Display           Exit   02:40:04 pm

RMID          0001
DESC          all-beef patty
COST             0.10
INVENTORY     100
LAST_ORDER    10/01/87
```

Line	Field	Operator	Constant/Expression	Connect
1	COST	More than or equal	0.10	
2				
3				
4				
5				
6				
7				

```
CREATE QUERY      <B:> B:HIGHCOST.QRY        Rec: 8/19
 Next/Previous record - PgDn/PgUp.  Toggle query form - F1.  Leave option - ↔.
        Display records in the database that meet the query condition.
```

FIGURE 5-6 Testing the Query File

4. *For Additional Practice*: If you would like additional practice using the commands discussed in this unit, do the following.

   a. From the dot prompt, give the command **USE TOURNEY** to save your current file and open the TOURNEY file.

   b. Determine the number of games won by the home team.

   c. Determine the total number of runs scored by the home team; by the visiting team.

   d. Determine the average winning margin (winner's score minus loser's score). Hint: You will need to use the ABS( ) function.

   e. Create a query which will limit the records to those played by *Stony Brook*, as either home or visiting team.

   f. With the query file in effect, repeat steps b, c, and d.

5. When you have completed all of the above, give the command **QUIT** to exit dBASE. If everything is proper, turn off the computer and return the dBASE software to the Lab Supervisor.

REVIEW QUESTIONS

What command or commands would you use to do the following?

*1. Count the number of Chez Jacques menu items that sell for less than 1.00.

2. Compute the average selling price of the menu items. (The average selling price is probably a meaningless figure, but compute it anyway.)

*3. Compute the total inventory value of raw materials. (Inventory value is defined as the product of quantity on hand and cost per unit.)

4. Compute the inventory value of raw materials that are measured by the ounce.

*5. Compute the inventory value of raw materials that are not measured by the ounce.

DOCUMENTATION RESEARCH

Using the reference manual, determine the answers to the following questions which deal with the commands discussed in this unit. I recommend you also write the reference manual page number by the discussion of the command in this unit.

1. COUNT — how can you avoid counting all records in the active database?

2. SUM — how can you avoid summing all fields of all records in the active database?

3. AVERAGE — how can you avoid averaging all fields of all records in the active database?

4. SET FILTER TO — when is the filter activated?

5. MODIFY QUERY — how can you delete a line of the query file?

UNIT

6

DATA FILE ORDER AND SEARCH

This unit deals with commands that allow you to specify the order in which data is presented and that allow you to search the data file for records with specific values in one or more fields. These are some of the most important DBMS commands.

With these commands, you will be able to determine ordinal position (e.g., who is first?, who is third?), to have your output appear in a certain order (e.g., in zip code order, alphabetical order) regardless of the order it was input, to quickly find a specific record (e.g., how many hamburger patties do we have?), or to locate and process records that meet a criterion (e.g., all materials inventoried by the ounce).

LEARNING OBJECTIVES

1. At the completion of this unit, you should know

   a. what the record pointer and current record are,

   b. the difference between sorting and indexing,

   c. what ASCII collating sequence means,

   d. the difference between finding and locating.

2. At the completion of this unit, you should be able to

   a. sort a file,

   b. index a file,

   c. find a record,

   d. locate records.

93

IMPORTANT COMMANDS

SORT TO {file} ON {field}
INDEX ON {expression} TO {index filename}
USE {data filename} INDEX {index filename}
REINDEX
GO TOP
GO BOTTOM
FIND {char string}
LOCATE FOR {condition}
CONTINUE

ORDERING THE DATA IN A FILE

There are two reasons for putting the data in a file into some specific order. First, if the data are in an order known to us (e.g., alphabetical), then we may quickly locate a specific record and answer questions about that record (e.g., "When is the last time we ordered cherry pies?"). Second, if the data are ordered according to some value, then we may determine rank-order (e.g., "Who are the ten best students?"). In the first case, we usually order the data using a character-type key (which may be a "number" such as RMID, or a descriptive field such as DESC). In the second case, we usually use a numeric key (such as grade-point average).

dBASE provides two methods for arranging the data in a file in some specific order. One, **SORT**, physically rearranges the data; the other, **INDEX**, builds a table of pointers that makes the data appear to have been rearranged. Although there are advantages to having a sorted file, you will generally use the index capability because indexing takes less time and is more flexible. Indexing can also be a first step in sorting.

Sorting

The **SORT** command is used to create a new file that is a reordered copy of the file in use. The records in the new file may be in either ascending or descending order. Ascending is the default. To achieve descending order (i.e., Z to A, 9 to 0) type /D after {field}. The file in use remains unaltered.

The general forms of the **SORT** command are

sort to {file} on {field}
sort to {file} on {field1}, {field2}, . . . , {field10}

where {file} is any legitimate filename and {field} is the field name of any one field in the database being sorted. If {field} is character type, then *ASCII collating sequence* is used (see Table 6-1). Therefore, *Smith* will follow *SMITH* and *SMYTHE*, *de Smet* will follow all of them, and *3D Cinema* will precede all. Typing /C after {field} instructs dBASE to ignore the case of alphabetic characters (which would put *SMYTHE* after *Smith*). Type /DC for descending order, regardless of case.

TABLE 6-1 ASCII Collating Sequence
(printable characters only)

<SPACE>	0	@	P	`	p
!	1	A	Q	a	q
"	2	B	R	b	r
#	3	C	S	c	s
$	4	D	T	d	t
%	5	E	U	e	u
&	6	F	V	f	v
'	7	G	W	g	w
(	8	H	X	h	x
)	9	I	Y	i	y
*	:	J	Z	j	z
+	;	K	[	k	{
,	<	L	\	l		
-	=	M	]	m	}
.	>	N	^	n	~
/	?	O	_	o	

Note: Ascending order proceeds down column, from left to right, for example, ? precedes @.

As a result of the sort operation, you will have two files with identical records, but the records will be in different order. You must **USE** the file you created by sorting before you will see the effect of the sorting.

Sorting is useful when you want to permanently alter the order of a file, and that order can be defined by one or more fields. A sorted file can be read from beginning to end faster than an indexed file. On the other hand, sorting takes more time, uses more disk space (because there are now two copies of the file), and is less flexible than indexing.

From the ASSIST Menu. SORT is found on the ■ *Organize* ■ menu. Once ■ *Organize* ■ *Sort* ■ is selected, you are prompted for the field or fields upon which to sort, then the file name for the sorted file. The process of sorting RAW_MATL on the DESC field is illustrated in Figures 6-1 and 6-2.

Indexing

The **INDEX** command is used to create an index file (with an .NDX extension) that contains pointers to records in the file currently in use. After indexing, the file appears to be sorted in ascending order of key values, but is not changed.

The general form of the **INDEX** command is

index on {expression} to {index filename}

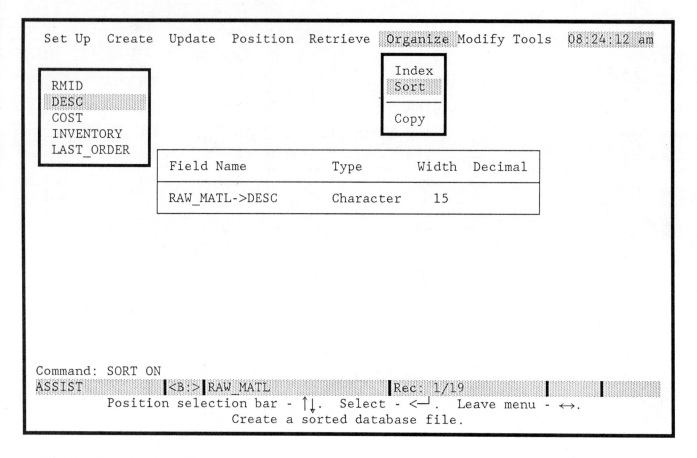

FIGURE 6-1 Sorting (I)

where {index filename} is a legitimate filename and {expression} is a dBASE expression formed of field names, operators, and functions. To keep life simple in situations with only one primary key in a file, I usually name the index file the same as the data file (e.g., **INDEX ON STOCK_NAME TO STOCKS** will create a STOCKS.NDX to go along with my STOCKS.DBF).

Key Expressions. The data in the {expression} may be Character, Numeric, or Date type. With **INDEX**, more than one field of the same type may be used to constitute the {expression}, the index *key*. Index keys are computed expressions, not logical conditions.

If {expression} is character type, then ASCII collating sequence is used. Therefore, *Smith* will follow *SMITH* and *SMYTHE*, and *de Smet* will follow all of them. To overcome this problem, key on **UPPER({expression})**, converting the key expression to all uppercase characters. For example, if NAME is the name of a character field, then **INDEX ON UPPER(NAME) TO INDXFILE** would place *Machinery* between *MacHenry* and *MacIlvenna*, instead of after them. This operation does not change the original file fields to *MACHENRY*, *MACHINERY*, and *MACILVENNA*; the data in the file stays as it was. The effect of the expression is only on the index key, not on the original data.

```
 Set Up  Create  Update  Position  Retrieve  Organize Modify Tools   08:28:41 am

                                          ┌─────────────┐
                                          │   Index     │
                                          │   Sort      │
                                          │ ─────────── │
                                          │   Copy      │
                                          └─────────────┘
              ┌──────────────────────────────────────────────────┐
              │ Enter a file name (consisting of up to 8          │
              │ letters or digits) followed by a period and       │
              │ a file name extension (consisting of up to 3      │
              │ letters or digits.)                               │
              │ Enter the name of the file: raw_sort_             │
              └──────────────────────────────────────────────────┘




 Command: SORT ON DESC TO B:
 ASSIST          │<B:>│RAW_MATL            │Rec: 1/19      │        │
                      Enter new value.  Finish with ←┘ .
                          Specify a file name.
```

FIGURE 6-2 Sorting (II)
Note: Item entered by the user is in **boldface**.

The {expression} may also be formed by the concatenation of two or more character fields. For instance, an {expression} such as **UPPER(LAST_NAME)+UPPER(FIRST_NAME)** would arrange a file of names in typical alphabetical order. You may use the STR( ) and DTOC( ) functions to combine numeric and date-type data with character-type data in the {expression}.

In some cases, you wish to index numeric type data in descending order. If NUMBER is the name of a numeric field, **INDEX ON NUMBER TO STOCKS** will create an index in lowest to highest order, while **INDEX ON -1*NUMBER TO STOCKS** will create an index in highest to lowest order of NUMBER field values.

The {expression} may also be formed as a function of two or more numeric fields. For instance, an {expression} such as **GRADEPTS/HOURS** would arrange a file of student information in ascending GPA (grade-point average) order.

From the ASSIST Menu. **INDEX** is found on the ■ *Organize* ■ menu. Once ■ *Organize* ■ *Index* ■ is selected, you are prompted for the expression upon which to index, then the file name for the index file. The process of indexing RAW_MATL on the RMID field is illustrated in Figures 6-3 and 6-4. The **INDEX** command is one of the few that allow you to enter an {expression} through the ASSIST menu. When the ■ *Organize* ■ *Index* ■ selection is

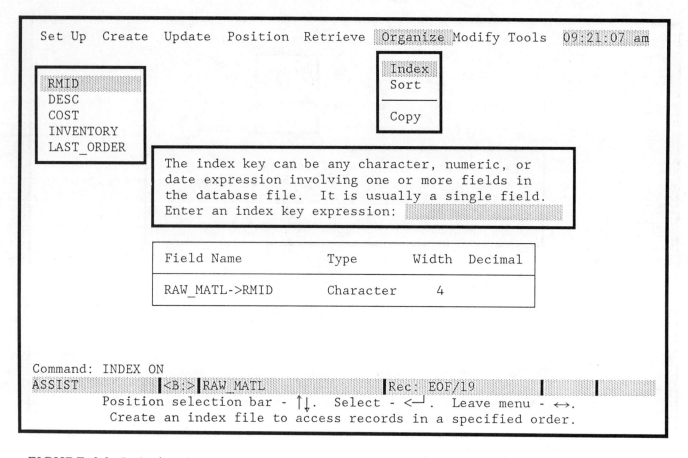

Set Up   Create   Update   Position   Retrieve   Organize Modify Tools   09:21:07 am

RMID
DESC
COST
INVENTORY
LAST_ORDER

Index
Sort

Copy

The index key can be any character, numeric, or
date expression involving one or more fields in
the database file. It is usually a single field.
Enter an index key expression:

Field Name	Type	Width	Decimal
RAW_MATL->RMID	Character	4	

Command: INDEX ON
ASSIST |<B:>|RAW_MATL |Rec: EOF/19 | |
         Position selection bar - ↑↓. Select - ⏎. Leave menu - ↔.
         Create an index file to access records in a specified order.

FIGURE 6-3 Indexing (I)

made, you must press the F10 key to see a list of field names (which was done in Figure 6-3).
Otherwise, you may directly enter field names and other components of the index key
{expression}.

Opening a Previously Indexed File. Once indexed, the file will continue to be accessed in key
order until closed (by **QUIT** or **USE** . . .). In later sessions, reopen the file with the command

   use {data filename} index {index filename}

A file need be indexed only once if all subsequent uses of that file include the **INDEX**
parameter. **APPEND, EDIT, REPLACE**, and many other commands will automatically update
the index file. *Important*: If you do not open the file with its index, then changes which
affect the key expression will not be made in the index. When you later use the file with the
index, the logical order of the index is no longer proper and you will not obtain the results
you expect. The **REINDEX** command, discussed later in this unit, provides a way to insure
that an index file reflects the current key expression values.

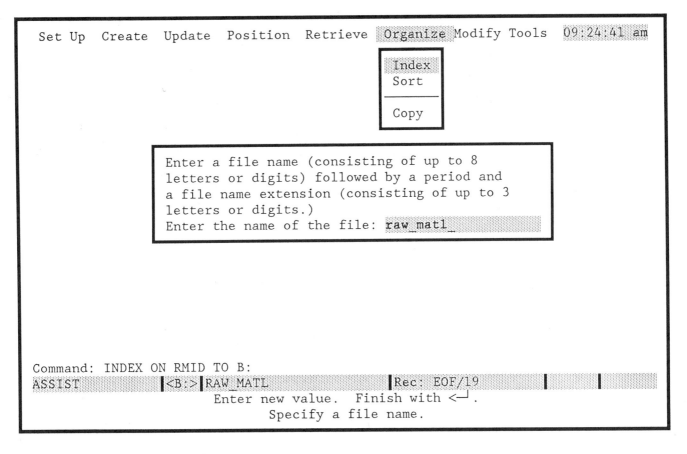

FIGURE 6-4 Indexing (II)
Note: Item entered by the user is in **boldface**.

It is possible to create *multiple indexes* (by giving several **INDEX** commands), all of which will be updated by **APPEND**, etc. The **USE** command necessary to open multiple indexes is as follows:

use {file} index {index1}, {index2}, . . . , {index7}

In this case, only {**index1**} (the first index file listed) affects the apparent order of the records, but {**index2**} . . . {**index7**} will be updated by changes to their respective keys. A maximum of seven index files may be opened with any one data file.

From the ASSIST Menu. The ■ *Set Up* ■ *Database file* ■ sequence always asks "Is the file indexed? [Y/N]" If you answer **Y**, you will be presented with a list of all index files on the disk. Point to the index file and press <CR> to open the database file with an index. If you select more than one index file, the first is the *master index*, the one that affects the apparent order of the records, and all others are *secondary indexes*, which are updated as changes are made to the data file but do not affect the apparent order of the data. The process of opening RAW_MATL with its index file is illustrated in Figure 6-5. (My disk has several index files that your disk will not have.)

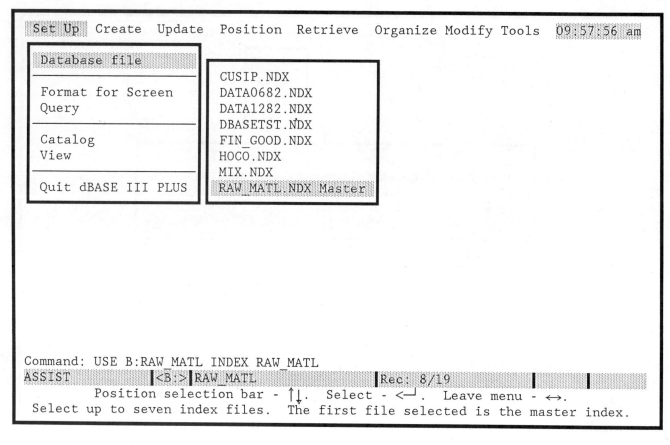

FIGURE 6-5 Opening a File with an Index

Rebuilding an Index. Most of us will forget on occasion to include the **INDEX** parameter when we use a file. If we make changes to the key field of the file, the index will probably become useless. dBASE has a command called **REINDEX** that will rebuild all active indexes.

To use this command, **USE** the data file with relevant indexes (**USE {file} INDEX {index1}, {index2} . . . {index7}**), then issue the command **REINDEX**. dBASE will read each index file to see what the key expression is, then perform the index operation again using the data file as it now exists. This command must be given from the dot prompt.

The Index/Sort. If you have a large indexed file on a floppy disk, you will notice that sequential access of indexed records takes some time. To speed up the process, you may want to *index/sort* that file. The procedure is as follows:

use bigfile	
index on name to bigindex	*Creates* BIGINDEX.NDX.
copy to bigsort	*Copies records to* BIGSORT.DBF *in* NAME-*order.*
use bigfile	*Opens* BIGFILE.DBF *without index.*
delete all	*These two commands remove all records*
pack	*from* BIGFILE.DBF, *see Unit 7.*
append from bigsort	*Appends records in* NAME-*order.*
index on name to bigindex	*Creates* BIGINDEX.NDX *for subsequent work.*

Make sure you have a backup copy of BIGFILE.DBF before trying this one. These commands may be given from the **ASSIST** menu, but it is probably easier to enter them from the dot prompt.

Temporary Indexes. On some occasions, you may wish to make an *ad hoc inquiry* (i.e., an inquiry designed to answer a specific question). For instance, you may need to determine which is the most expensive raw material. The easiest way to answer this question is to arrange the data in order from lowest to highest COST, then list the file to see which is the last record.

To accomplish such an operation, I usually build a temporary index, one that is used only for the moment and will not be maintained. To determine which is the most expensive raw material in the RAW_MATL file, the sequence is as follows:

```
use raw_matl
index on cost to temp
list
use raw_matl index raw_matl
```

The first command opens the RAW_MATL.DBF file. In the second command, an index file named TEMP.NDX is created. (I always use the name TEMP for temporary index files so I know that they are temporary.) In TEMP.NDX, the record pointers will be in ascending order of the COST field; thus, the highest cost will be last. The **LIST** command shows me the entire data file with the highest cost being the last record displayed. I make a note to myself of what the highest-cost raw material is, then, with the last command, reopen the file with its permanent index (which you will build in Application B). These commands may be given from either the dot prompt or the **ASSIST** menu.

dBASE III has a feature called *safety* that is designed to protect you from inadvertent erasing of a file. If you have done this procedure before, and a file called TEMP.NDX appears on the disk, dBASE III will ask you

```
TEMP.NDX already exists, overwrite (Y/N)?
```

before it destroys the old TEMP.NDX. In this case, it is safe to answer Y because the old file is no longer needed.

Benefits of Indexing. Indexing a file does two very useful things. First, the file will appear to be in index key order during operations such as **LIST** and when writing reports. Second, you can quickly find a particular key value in an indexed file (the topic of the next section). Although sorting the file will yield the first benefit, indexing is faster and more flexible because it permits multiple fields and computed results in the key expression.

SEARCHING THROUGH A FILE

There are two methods for searching through a data file. If the file is indexed and the key is unique for each record, then **FIND** is extremely fast, even on large floppy disk data files. If the file is not indexed, or if the key is not unique, then **LOCATE** must be used.

The Record Pointer

With the exception of **APPEND** and **EDIT** commands, we have not been concerned with the contents of a specific record, but rather with all records or a group of records that match a criterion (such as the **LIST FOR** . . . examples). The reason for a file search, however, is often to locate a specific record that will be displayed, edited, or used in a computation.

When a file is first used without an index (with either the **USE** dot command or the ■ *Set Up* ■ *Database file* ■ **ASSIST** menu sequence), dBASE will point at the first *physical record*, the first record you entered after the **APPEND** command. When a file is first used with an index, dBASE will point at the first record in index-key order, that is the first *logical record*. As you move through the file by searching for specific records, the *record pointer* also moves. Unlike most computer languages, dBASE does not require you to use an explicit command (such as **INPUT**) to read data from the file; moving the record pointer to a record automatically reads the contents of each field of the record. The record at which the record pointer is pointing is called the *current record*, and is indicated in the status bar near the bottom of the screen.

For the moment, we will use the **DISPLAY** command to show us what is in the current record. **DISPLAY** may be entered at the dot prompt by typing **DISPLAY** or **DISP**, or by pressing the F8 key. The command also may be entered with the following **ASSIST** menu sequence:

■ *Retrieve* ■ *Display* ■ *Execute the command* ■

The First or Last Record

If we are interested in viewing the data in the first or last record, we may use the command **GO TOP** or **GO BOTTOM**. If the file is indexed, then the first record will be the record with the lowest value of the index key, and the last record will have the highest value of the index key.

This capability is especially useful when we want to know the extreme values, such as *most costly* or *least quantity*, in our data. We index on the value of interest, then go to the top or bottom of the file to find the record with the extreme value.

From the ASSIST Menu. **GO TOP** and **GO BOTTOM** are part of the ■ *Position* ■ menu:

■ *Position* ■ *Goto Record* ■ *Top* ■
■ *Position* ■ *Goto Record* ■ *Bottom* ■

Finding a Particular Record

The **FIND** command causes dBASE to find the first record in the indexed data file in use whose key is the same as {char string}. **FIND** will work only if the data file has been indexed and opened (with the **USE** command) with the index.

The general form of the **FIND** command is

find {key}

where {key} is a character string or a number, depending on the index key. A character string need not be enclosed in quotation marks, except when the string contains leading blanks. **FIND** may be used with both character and numeric keys.

If the index key is character type, then **FIND** will operate when given the first few characters of the key (e.g., **FIND Ros** will find *Ross*, unless *Rosenbaum* is also in the file). **FIND** always finds the first occurrence, regardless of where the record pointer was before the issuance of the command. Therefore, a second **FIND Ros** will still find *Rosenbaum*, even if *Ross* is the next record.

The {char string} must match the index {expression}. If you used **UPPER(NAME)** as the index {expression}, then **FIND Ros** will fail because all key values are in uppercase. In such a situation, the {char string} also would have to be in uppercase, e.g., **FIND ROS**, even if the data in the field itself is in upper- and lowercase. This is because **FIND** goes to the index file and searches for a match; if a match is found, it refers to the record number of the match in the data file.

The text to be found must start in column 1 (the first byte) of the index key. **FIND Andrew** will not find *McAndrew*.

If there is no match, the message "No find" will be displayed on the screen.

The SEEK Command. A variation of the **FIND** command is the **SEEK** command. The general form is

seek {expression}

where {expression} can be Character, Numeric, or Date-type data. With **SEEK**, a character string must be enclosed in quotation marks if the key is character-type data. If the key is numeric, then a number or expression is used. If the index key is a date-type field, then the **SEEK** command combined with the **CTOD( )** function must be used:

seek ctod('10/12/87')

From the ASSIST Menu. **SEEK** is part of the ■ *Position* ■ menu. For instance, if we had indexed the RAW_MATL file on the RMID field and wished to position the record pointer to the record with RMID of 0012, we would enter the sequence

■ *Position* ■ *Seek* ■ '0012' ■

as is illustrated in Figure 6-6. The RMID must be enclosed in quotation marks because it is character-type data.

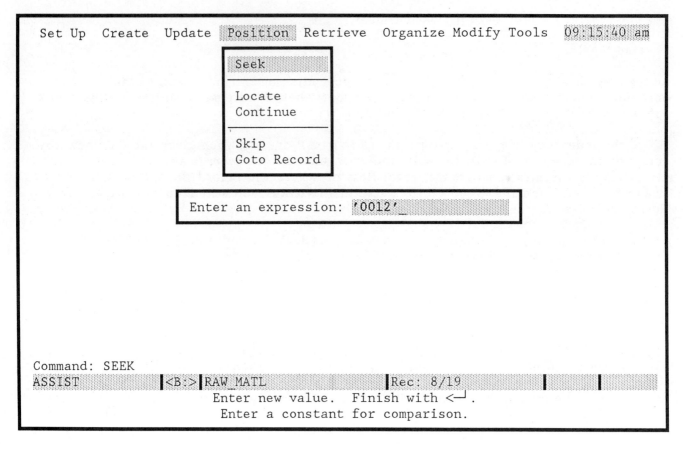

FIGURE 6-6 The **SEEK** Command
Note: Item entered by the user is in **boldface**.

The Scope Options

When you wish to list a series of records, but not necessarily all records, a *scope* option must be used. We have used simple scopes in our illustrations thus far, such as **DISPLAY ALL** or **LIST NEXT 10**. In most cases, you will use a {scope} or {scope condition} when the data are in a particular logical or physical order to list (or display, count, sum, average, delete, report) only records of interest. Properly done, a {scope condition} will work much faster than a {search condition} in a large file.

Scope. There are five methods of specifying {scope} to dBASE commands:

default scope *Whatever the command normally does: the current record for **DISPLAY** and the entire file (i.e., **ALL**) for other commands.*

all *The entire database, in either physical or logical order.*

next *n* *The current record and the* n - 1 *records that follow, in physical or logical order.*

record *n*   The record with physical number *n (regardless of whether or not the file is indexed).*

rest   *From the current record to the end of the file, in either physical or logical order.*

Scope Conditions. A {scope condition} uses the preposition **WHILE**, instead of the **FOR** used by a {search condition}. Other than the initial preposition, the construction of the condition is the same for both. Generally, a {search condition} will inspect all records in the database and list (or sum, etc.) all for which the condition is true. A {scope condition}, on the other hand, will start at the current record and will only list (or sum, etc.) while the condition remains true. As soon as the condition becomes false, the listing stops *even though the condition may be true for a later record.* The records are inspected in logical order if there is an active index; otherwise they are inspected in physical order.

To illustrate the difference, look at the data in the MIX.DBF file (see Table A-2 in Application A, on page 56). Notice that the file is sorted into ascending FGID number order. If you start at the first record, the command **LIST FOR FGID='1001'** will list seven records. If you start at the first record, the command **LIST WHILE FGID='1001'** will also list seven records. If you start at the first record, the command **LIST FOR FGID='1002'** will list twelve records. If you start at the first record, the command **LIST WHILE FGID='1002'** will list no (zero) records, because the condition is not true for the first record. If you start at the first record, the command **LIST FOR RMID='0001'** will list seven records. If you start at the first record, the command **LIST WHILE RMID='0001'** will list only one record, because the condition is not true when dBASE inspects the second record (even though it is true later in the file). Try these examples on your own. Remember to **GO TOP** (or ■ *Position* ■ *Goto Record* ■ *TOP* ■) before each command.

From the ASSIST Menu. The option to ■ *Specify scope* ■ or ■ *Build a scope condition* ■ is available on many menus. As with the option to ■ *Build a search condition* ■, dBASE will ask you the questions necessary to guide you through the process.

Illustration of INDEX and FIND

The **INDEX** and **FIND** commands are illustrated in the example in Figure 6-7. First, the RAW_MATL file is opened with the **USE** command. Then the file is indexed with RMID as the key expression. Note that dBASE tells us how many records are indexed.

We move to the first record of the file with **GO TOP**, then display the next ten records. Recall that **DISPLAY NEXT** shows the current record as the first record. In this case, the records with RMID numbers of 0001 through 0010 are displayed. The physical record numbers are also displayed in the left column, which provides a reference should we need to edit one of the records.

The next command is **FIND 0013**, which will move the record pointer to the first record that has the index key of 0013. We use the **DISPLAY** command to view the contents of the record. Finally, when we attempt to **FIND 0030**, we discover that there is no record with that RMID (i.e., index key) in our file, and are presented with a "No find" message.

```
. use raw_matl
. index on rmid to raw_matl
  100% indexed           19 Records indexed
. go top
. display next 10
Record#  RMID DESC              COST INVENTORY LAST_ORDER
      8  0001 all-beef patty     0.10       100 10/01/87
     19  0002 sp. sauce (oz.)    0.01       400 09/30/87
     15  0003 lettuce leaf       0.01        90 10/03/87
     12  0004 cheese slice       0.02       255 10/09/87
     16  0005 pickle slice       0.03       900 09/15/87
     11  0006 ch. onion (oz.)    0.06       876 10/10/87
     18  0007 sesame seed bun    0.12       400 10/08/87
     17  0008 regular bun        0.10       200 10/03/87
     10  0009 catsup (oz.)       0.04       386 10/10/87
     14  0010 fren. fry (oz.)    0.01       999 10/12/87

. find 0013
. display
Record#  RMID DESC              COST INVENTORY LAST_ORDER
      5  0013 8 oz. cup          0.02       600 10/06/87

. find 0030
No find.
.
```

Command Line |<B:>|RAW_MATL |Rec: EOF/19 | |

Enter a dBASE III PLUS command.

FIGURE 6-7 Illustration of **INDEX** and **FIND** Commands
Note: Items entered by the user are in **boldface**.

Locating Records

The **LOCATE FOR** and **CONTINUE** commands are used to locate records in which {**condition**} is true. The general form of the commands is

> **locate for** {**condition**}
>> *other dBASE commands*
> **continue**

LOCATE starts at the first record and searches forward from that record. When the record for which the logical {**condition**} is true is found, the message "Record = *n*" is displayed (*n* is the number of the record which matches the {**condition**}).

The located record may be processed (*other dBASE commands*). Then the next record for which {**condition**} is true may be found with the **CONTINUE** command. **CONTINUE** means *perform the last* **LOCATE** *command, starting with the record after the current record.*

LOCATE works faster in a file used without an index, but may be used whether or not the file is indexed.

You may be wondering when you would ever use the **LOCATE** command. One instance would be when you wish to find a record that meets a specific criterion, but that criterion is not suitable as an index key. Also, **LOCATE . . . CONTINUE** is necessary if you wish to find more than the first occurrence of the criterion.

For instance, you may wish to locate all people who live in cities with *Bay* in the address (Coos Bay, Whitefish Bay, Bay City, Bayview). If you indexed the file on CITY (assuming that you have a field named CITY in the data file), you would be able to find only the first *Bay* (Bay City). If you were to use the command **LOCATE FOR ('Bay'$city)**, the first occurrence of *Bay* in a CITY field would be located, and dBASE would respond "Record = *n*." You could then do whatever you wanted with that record (perhaps edit it), then give the **CONTINUE** command to find the next *Bay*.

If you wish to search only a portion of your data file, **LOCATE** may be limited to a certain scope by specifying the range of records to be searched. For example

locate next 5 for ('Bay'$city)

starts with the current record, not the beginning of the file.

From the ASSIST Menu. **LOCATE** and **CONTINUE** are part of the ■ *Position* ■ menu. The command is initiated by the sequence

■ *Position* ■ *Locate* ■ *Build a search condition* ■

followed by the specification of a field, a comparison operator, an expression, more conditions if desired, a scope if desired, and finally command execution. The entire sequence to locate the first record in RAW__MATL for which the COST is 0.10, is

■ *Position* ■ *Locate* ■ *Build a search condition* ■ *COST* ■ = *Equal To* ■ *0.10* ■
No more conditions ■ *Execute the command* ■

To find the next record for which the COST is 0.10, the sequence is

■ *Position* ■ *Continue* ■

Illustration of LOCATE and CONTINUE

Use of the **LOCATE** command is illustrated in Figure 6-8. In this case, we wish to find all the cups in our inventory list. Since the word *cup* is not the first word in the description field, we are not able to use the **FIND** command. Another reason for using the **LOCATE** command is that **FIND** will find only one occurrence, and we must locate all occurrences of the word.

The first command opens the file, without an index. The **DISPLAY NEXT 10** command shows the first ten records, but leaves the record pointer at record number 1.

```
. use raw_matl
. go top
. display next 10
Record#  RMID DESC              COST INVENTORY LAST_ORDER
       1  0014 12 oz. cup       0.03       300 10/04/87
       2  0015 16 oz. cup       0.05       400 09/28/87
       3  0018 4 oz. fry pack   0.02       332 10/19/87
       4  0019 6 oz. fry pack   0.03       500 10/15/87
       5  0013 8 oz. cup        0.02       600 10/06/87
       6  0011 Coca Cola (oz.)  0.05       800 10/13/87
       7  0012 Sprite (oz.)     0.05       700 10/12/87
       8  0001 all-beef patty   0.10       100 10/01/87
       9  0016 apple pie        0.16       346 08/15/87
      10  0009 catsup (oz.)     0.04       386 10/10/87

. locate for 'cup'$desc
Record =        1
. display
Record#  RMID DESC              COST INVENTORY LAST_ORDER
       1  0014 12 oz. cup       0.03       300 10/04/87

. continue
Record =        2
. display
Record#  RMID DESC              COST INVENTORY LAST_ORDER
       2  0015 16 oz. cup       0.05       400 09/28/87

. continue
Record =        5
. display
Record#  RMID DESC              COST INVENTORY LAST_ORDER
       5  0013 8 oz. cup        0.02       600 10/06/87

. continue
End of LOCATE scope
.
```

Command Line |<B:>|RAW_MATL |Rec: EOF/19 | |

Enter a dBASE III PLUS command.

FIGURE 6-8 Illustration of **LOCATE** and **CONTINUE** Commands
Note: Items entered by the user are in **boldface**.

LOCATE FOR 'cup'$DESC yields the response `Record =        1`, telling us that dBASE has found a match. The record is displayed, then the **CONTINUE** command is used to find succeeding matches. The response `End of LOCATE scope` after the last **CONTINUE** tells us that we have found all that are in the data file.

GUIDED ACTIVITY

This activity requires you to duplicate the illustrations used in this unit.

1. Follow the startup procedure for your version of dBASE as outlined in Unit 2.

2. Duplicate the instructions in **boldface** type in Figure 6-7. Your screen should look like that figure as you progress through the exercise. You may also give these commands from the **ASSIST** menu.

3. Duplicate the instructions in **boldface** type in Figure 6-8. Your screen should look like that figure as you progress through the exercise. You may also give these commands from the **ASSIST** menu.

4. Now give the command **USE RAW_MATL INDEX RAW_MATL**

5. Give the command **LOCATE FOR 'cup'$DESC**

✔ **CHECKPOINT**
Which record is found first? Why?

_____

6. Use the **CONTINUE** command to find the other two records with *cup* in the DESC field.

7. Experiment further with **FIND** and **LOCATE**; for instance, you may wish to locate all raw materials that are *buns*.

8. *For Additional Practice*: If you would like additional practice using the commands discussed in this unit, do the following.

   a. From the dot prompt, give the command **USE TOURNEY** to save your current file and open TOURNEY.

   b. You may have noticed that the dates of the games are not in order. Use the **INDEX** command to create an index which puts the games in proper order.

   c. As with most tournaments, the last game is the championship. Determine who's *Number 1*.

   d. Determine the first game played by Moscow. Determine the last game played by Moscow. Remember that a team can be either home or visitor as you do these searches.

9. When you are finished, use the **QUIT** command to exit dBASE. Remember to backup your work and return all materials to the Lab Supervisor.

REVIEW QUESTIONS

1. What is the difference between indexing and sorting? Which creates another .DBF file? Which creates an .NDX file?

2. Indexing provides two benefits. What are they?

*3. What command would you use to index the file RAW_MATL on the field RMID, creating the file RAW_MATL.NDX?

4. Define each of the following terms:

  a. Current record

  *b. Physical record order

  *c. Logical record order

  d. Record pointer

5. Assume that you have indexed RAW_MATL as suggested in question 3.

  *a. What command will take you directly to the record with RMID field of 0010?

  b. Refer to Table 1-1 in Unit 1. What command will take you to the apple pie record?

6. How you you know if

  *a. a **FIND** has been successful?

  *b. a **FIND** has not been successful?

  *c. a **LOCATE** has been successful?

  *d. a **LOCATE** has not been successful?

7. What commands would you use to determine the most expensive item on the Chez Jacques menu (finished goods file)?

8. Jacques wants you to change his menu, replacing the English word *Pie* with the French word *Tarte* in all relevant records. What commands will you use to locate the first occurrence of *Pie* in the DESC field, edit the record, then proceed to the next occurrence.

*9. Both the **LOCATE** ... **CONTINUE** and **LIST FOR** ... commands can be used to discover all records in a data file that match a certain logical condition. When would you need to use **LOCATE**, and when would **LIST** be sufficient?

DOCUMENTATION RESEARCH

Using the reference manual, determine the answers to the following questions which deal with the commands discussed in this unit. I recommend you also write the reference manual page number by the discussion of the command in this unit.

1. SORT TO {file} ON {field} — how can multiple fields be included in the sort key?

2. INDEX ON {expression} TO {index filename} — how can numeric and date fields be combined with character fields into the key {expression}?

3. INDEX ON {expression} TO {index filename} — what is the maximum length of the key {expression}?

4. REINDEX — which index file or files are rebuilt by this command?

5. GO TOP — what effect does an index in use have on this command?

6. GO BOTTOM — what effect does an index in use have on this command?

7. FIND {char string} — what must you do if the search key {char string} includes leading blanks?

8. LOCATE FOR {condition} — how do you force this command to start the search at the current record?

9. CONTINUE — if the **LOCATE** command is limited with a {scope}, how does this command use the original {scope}?

APPLICATION

B CHEZ JACQUES (II)

This application exercise requires you to use the data ordering and file searching commands in a data file.

1. Follow the startup procedure for your version of dBASE as outlined in Unit 2.

2. Put the disk containing files RAW_MATL.DBF, MIX.DBF, and FIN_GOOD.DBF in Drive B (or the only drive in a fixed-disk PC).

3. Index the file FIN_GOOD using FGID as the key and creating the file FIN_GOOD.NDX. (Note: the file must be used before it can be indexed.)

4. Next, index the file RAW_MATL using RMID as the key and creating RAW_MATL.NDX

5. Finally, index the file MIX, using FGID as the key and creating the file MIX.NDX

6. Open FIN_GOOD with its index.

7. **FIND** the record that has FGID of 1011. Use the **DISPLAY** command to show you what item that is. Do the same for item 1001. Do a screen print to capture this moment forever. (If you use the **ASSIST** menu, you must do several screen prints.)

8. Determine the most expensive item on the Chez Jacques menu. Do a screen print to show the commands you used. (There are four items that tie for this honor; finding any one of them is sufficient.)

9. Change the Chez Jacques menu, replacing the English word *Pie* with the French word *Tarte* in all relevant records. The **LOCATE . . . CONTINUE** commands may help.

10. When you have completed all of the above, give the command **QUIT** to exit dBASE. If everything is proper, turn off the computer and return the dBASE software to the Lab Supervisor.

UNIT

7

DATA FILE CHANGES

This unit deals with changing data files. There are four types of changes that may be made to a data file: adding records, changing data in existing records, deleting records, and changing the data file structure.

LEARNING OBJECTIVES

1. At the completion of this unit, you should know

   a. the differences among **EDIT**, **CHANGE** and **REPLACE** commands,

   b. the various stages of the record deletion process.

2. At the completion of this unit, you should be able to

   a. combine two data files,

   b. change selected fields of selected records,

   c. replace field contents on a selective basis,

   d. delete, recall, and purge records,

   e. modify the structure of a data file.

IMPORTANT COMMANDS

APPEND FROM {filename}
REPLACE {scope} {field} WITH {expression} FOR {condition}
CHANGE FIELDS {field list} FOR {condition}
BROWSE

        DELETE {scope} FOR {condition}
        SET DELETED ON/OFF
        RECALL {scope} FOR {condition}
        PACK
        ZAP
        DISPLAY STRUCTURE
        MODIFY STRUCTURE

ADDING DATA FROM ANOTHER DATA FILE

The **APPEND FROM** command may be used to bring data from another data base (.DBF) file into the file currently open. All records from the **FROM** file will be included unless you use a {condition}. If the two data files have different structures, only fields that have the same structure (name and type) will be copied. This command may be used to combine the work of two or more people. For instance, if two persons had worked together to build the RAW_MATL file, with Person A calling his version RAW_MATL.DBF and Person B calling her version RAW_MAT2.DBF (to be on the same disk, the filenames must be different[1]), then the following commands would combine the two files into one, complete, RAW_MATL.DBF:

        use raw_matl
        append from raw_mat2

The records from the second file are added after (in physical order) the records in the file in use. **APPEND FROM** is not available on the **ASSIST** menu.

CHANGING DATA IN EXISTING RECORDS

There are two main reasons for changing data in existing records. The first, to correct errors of input, is best done with the **EDIT** command that allows you to selectively change the data in a specific record. (The use of the **EDIT** command was discussed in Unit 3.)

    The second reason for changing data in existing records is to reflect changes that have taken place since the data were initially entered. For instance, salaries may have changed as a result of the yearly budget process. Or, all employees at Boca Raton may have been transferred to Montvale. Or, someone may have gotten married and changed his name. Except where the changes affect only one record (the last instance), it is usually better to use **CHANGE, BROWSE,** or **REPLACE** commands to effect this type of change. **REPLACE** is best when the changes are systematic (i.e., where there is a global replacement [change all *Boca Raton* to *Montvale*] or a consistent relationship [all salaries up 10 per cent]). **CHANGE** and **BROWSE** are necessary when the changes are unsystematic (i.e., where there is no direct relationship between old value and new value).

---

[1]   Normally, both persons will use the same filename on different disks. Before entering dBASE, Person B's file must be copied to Person A's disk, with the DOS command **COPY A:RAW_MATL.DBF B:RAW_MAT2.DBF.** Notice that this command changes the name as it copies the file.

Systematic Changes

The quickest way to make systematic changes is with the **REPLACE** command. Use this command when there is a consistent relationship between old and new values of one or more numeric fields, or when any type of field is to be changed based on the contents of itself or another field. The general form of the command is

replace {scope} {field} with {expression} for {condition}

which will replace the contents of **{field}** with the value of **{expression}**. Both **{scope}** and **FOR {condition}** are optional; **REPLACE** will change only the current record if neither is specified. The **{scope}** is usually **ALL**, which will change all records, or all records for which the **FOR {condition}** clause is true.

Examples:

replace all salary *1.05   *Everybody gets a 5% increase.*

replace salary with salary*1.1 for state='AK'   *Alaska employees get a 10% increase.*

replace city with 'Montvale' for city='Boca Raton' *Everybody in Boca Raton moves to Montvale.*

The use of the **REPLACE** command is illustrated in Figure 7-1 (this is part of the Guided Activity for this unit). The file RAWX is opened, then all costs are increased by 20 per cent. The **LIST** command shows the result in the first five records.

From the ASSIST Menu. **REPLACE** is found on the ■ *Update* ■ menu. The sequence to accomplish the replacement illustrated in Figure 7-1 would be

■ *Update* ■ *Replace* ■ **COST** ■ **COST*1.2** ■ <LEFT ARROW> ■ *Specify scope* ■ *ALL* ■ *Execute the command* ■

Unsystematic Changes

There are times when the change is not systematic but the fields or records to be changed can be specified. For instance, the salary review system may yield differential pay increases based on individual performance. In this case, you must change each salary field individually, but you need to change only the salary field, not the other fields.

The **CHANGE** command allows you to change specific fields in a specified group of records.[2] The general form of the command is

change fields {field list} for {condition}

---

[2] In dBASE III Plus, the **CHANGE** and **EDIT** commands are identical. In earlier versions of dBASE, they were different, with **CHANGE** offering greater flexibility as to fields and conditions.

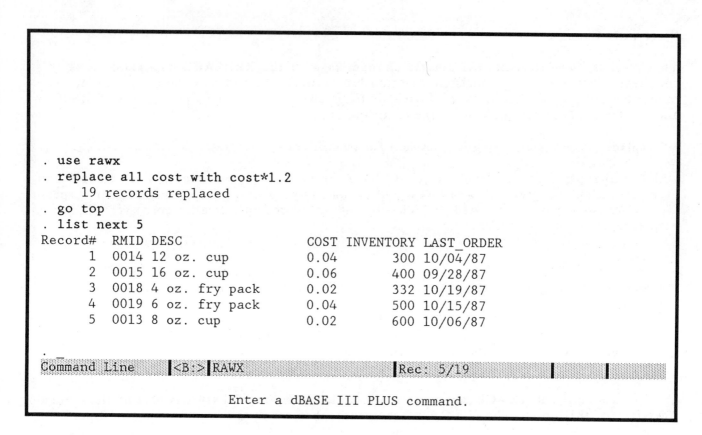

```
. use rawx
. replace all cost with cost*1.2
    19 records replaced
. go top
. list next 5
Record#  RMID DESC               COST INVENTORY LAST_ORDER
      1  0014 12 oz. cup         0.04       300 10/04/87
      2  0015 16 oz. cup         0.06       400 09/28/87
      3  0018 4 oz. fry pack     0.02       332 10/19/87
      4  0019 6 oz. fry pack     0.04       500 10/15/87
      5  0013 8 oz. cup          0.02       600 10/06/87
.
```

Command Line   ◼<B:>◼RAWX   ◼Rec: 5/19   ◼   ◼

Enter a dBASE III PLUS command.

FIGURE 7-1 Illustration of the **REPLACE** Command
Note: Items entered by the user are in **boldface**.

All records, or all that meet the {**condition**}, will be presented for editing. Only the fields listed will be displayed. Neither the list of fields nor the condition is required; **CHANGE** by itself will take you through all fields of all records.

Examples:

> **change fields salary,name**
> *To make individual salary adjustments; the NAME field is included so you will know whose salary is being changed.*

> **change for city='Mobile'**
> *To edit records of all Mobile employees.*

> **change fields salary,name for city='Mobile'**
> *To Combine the effect of the first two examples.*

The **BROWSE** command is one of the most amazing commands of dBASE. **BROWSE** displays up to twenty records on the screen at one time, and you use Full Screen mode to move about your data file and make changes. Those who are used to spreadsheet programs will find similarities in **BROWSE**. It is a great way to make multiple changes, as well as a great way to make *big* mistakes. **BROWSE** only after you have made a backup copy of your file. The **BROWSE** command is illustrated in Figure 7-2.

```
┌──────────────────┬──────────────────┬─────────────────┬──────────────────────┐
│ CURSOR   <-- -->  │        UP  DOWN   │     DELETE      │ Insert Mode:  Ins    │
│  Char:     ←   →  │ Field:   ↑    ↓   │  Char:   Del    │ Exit:        ^End    │
│  Field: Home End  │ Page:  PgUp PgDn  │  Field:  ^Y     │ Abort:        Esc    │
│  Pan:     ^← ^→   │ Help:    F1       │  Record: ^U     │ Set Options: ^Home   │
└──────────────────┴──────────────────┴─────────────────┴──────────────────────┘
```

```
RMID DESC---------- COST---- INVENTORY LAST_ORDER
0001 all-beef patty    0.10       100 10/01/87
0002 sp. sauce (oz.)   0.01       400 09/30/87
0003 lettuce leaf      0.01        90 10/03/87
0004 cheese slice      0.02       255 10/09/87
0005 pickle slice      0.03       900 09/15/87
0006 ch. onion (oz.)   0.06       876 10/10/87
0007 sesame seed bun   0.12       400 10/08/87
0008 regular bun       0.10       200 10/03/87
0009 catsup (oz.)      0.04       386 10/10/87
0010 fren. fry (oz.)   0.01       999 10/12/87
0011 Coca Cola (oz.)   0.05       800 10/13/87
```

```
BROWSE           |<B:>|RAW_MATL              |Rec: 8/19        |         |
```

View and edit fields.

FIGURE 7-2   The **BROWSE** Command

From the ASSIST Menu. **BROWSE** is found on the ■ *Update* ■ menu. Enter

■ *Update* ■ *Browse* ■

yielding the display in Figure 7-2. Although **CHANGE** is not on any menu, the ■ *Update* ■ *Edit* ■ selection is the equivalent of **CHANGE** with no {condition} or {field list}.

DELETING ENTIRE RECORDS

Deleted records in dBASE are not really *gone*; they remain in the data file. Deletion may be used for two purposes:

» To make certain records temporarily *invisible* to data base inquiries without eliminating those records permanently.

» As a preliminary to physical removal from the data file.

The commands necessary to accomplish these two types of deletion are discussed in this section.

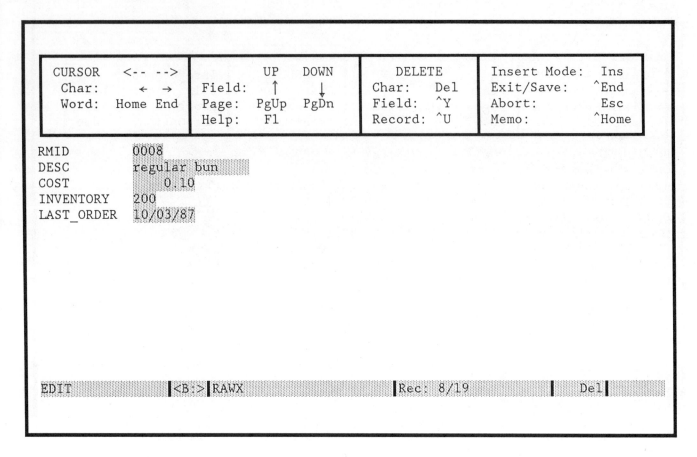

FIGURE 7-3 Editing a Deleted Record

Each record in a data file has a *flag character* that tells dBASE whether or not the record is deleted. (The flag character is why the total record length is one byte greater than the sum of the field widths.) *Marking a record as deleted* with the **DELETE** command means the flag is set to indicate that the record is deleted, but the record is still in the data file. The condition of the flag can be reversed, to normal or nondeleted status, by the **RECALL** command. Normally, dBASE will treat deleted records just like other records: it will count them in sums, replaces, and so on. dBASE can be instructed to ignore those records, however, with the **SET DELETED ON/OFF** command. The data file may also be purged of deleted records with the **PACK** command.

To select just records marked for deletion use **DELETED( )**, the *deleted-record function.* **DELETED( )** is a logical function that is true if the current record is marked for deletion, and false otherwise. Example:

display for deleted( )

When listed or displayed, an ***** (asterisk) appears next to the record number of each record that has been marked for deletion (illustrated in Figure 7-4). When a deleted record is edited, `Del` appears on the right side of the status bar (illustrated in Figure 7-3).

```
. use rawx
. delete for inventory>=100
     17 records deleted
. list
Record#   RMID DESC              COST INVENTORY LAST_ORDER
       1 *0001 all-beef patty    0.10      100 10/01/87
       2 *0002 sp. sauce (oz.)   0.01      400 09/30/87
       3  0003 lettuce leaf      0.01       90 10/03/87
       4 *0004 cheese slice      0.02      255 10/09/87
       5 *0005 pickle slice      0.03      900 09/15/87
       6 *0006 ch. onion (oz.)   0.06      876 10/10/87
       7 *0007 sesame seed bun   0.12      400 10/08/87
       8 *0008 regular bun       0.10      200 10/03/87
       9 *0009 catsup (oz.)      0.04      386 10/10/87
      10 *0010 fren. fry (oz.)   0.01      999 10/12/87
      11 *0011 Coca Cola (oz.)   0.05      800 10/13/87
      12 *0012 Sprite (oz.)      0.05      700 10/12/87
      13  0013 8 oz. cup         0.02       91 10/06/87
      14 *0014 12 oz. cup        0.03      300 10/04/87
      15 *0015 16 oz. cup        0.05      400 09/28/87
      16 *0016 apple pie         0.16      346 08/15/87
      17 *0017 cherry pie        0.14      200 09/19/87
      18 *0018 4 oz. fry pack    0.02      332 10/19/87
      19 *0019 6 oz. fry pack    0.03      500 10/15/87

. set deleted on
. list
Record#   RMID DESC              COST INVENTORY LAST_ORDER
       3  0003 lettuce leaf      0.01       90 10/03/87
      13  0013 8 oz. cup         0.02       91 10/06/87

. recall all
No records recalled
. set deleted off
. recall all
     17 records recalled
.
```

```
Command Line   |<B:>|RAWX                    |Rec: EOF/19       |        |
```

Enter a dBASE III PLUS command.

FIGURE 7-4 Illustration of the Deleted-Record Commands
Note: Items entered by the user are in **boldface**.

Marking Records as Deleted

The **DELETE** command is used to mark records as deleted. The general form of the command is

> **delete {scope} for {condition}**

The command can be used to delete a specific record (e.g., **DELETE RECORD 5**), or to delete all records that meet a condition (e.g., **DELETE FOR (SALARY > 30000).AND.(SALARY < 60000)**). (If you specify a record number, as in the first example, dBASE will delete the fifth *physical record*, even if the file is opened with an index.) If neither **{scope}** nor **{condition}** are specified, **DELETE** deletes the current record.

Records also may be deleted during an **EDIT**, **CHANGE**, or **BROWSE** operation. Pressing ^U (Ctrl-U) will toggle the deleted-record mark on and off for the record being edited.

From the ASSIST Menu. DELETE is found on the ■ *Update* ■ menu. Initiate with

> ■ *Update* ■ *Delete* ■

then specify scope, build a search condition, and build a scope condition, as necessary, before executing the command.

Including and Ignoring Deleted Records

The **SET DELETED ON/OFF** command is used to inform dBASE whether or not to include deleted records in other commands. **SET DELETED** is normally off, which means that information in records marked as deleted is included in all commands. When turned on, deleted records are ignored by all commands except **INDEX** and **REINDEX**.

Removing the Deleted-Record Mark

The **RECALL** command changes the mark from deleted to not deleted. This command would be used to reverse the effect of a *temporary* deletion. The general form of the command is

> **recall {scope} for {condition}**

Give the command **SET DELETED OFF** before using this command. You can use the command to recall a specific record (e.g., **RECALL RECORD 5**), to recall all records that meet a condition (e.g., **RECALL FOR (SALARY > 30000).AND.(SALARY < 60000)**), or to recall all records (i.e., **RECALL ALL**). If neither **{scope}** nor **{condition}** are specified, **RECALL** affects only the current record.

As mentioned earlier, pressing ^U during an **EDIT**, **CHANGE**, or **BROWSE** operation will toggle the deleted-record mark.

From the ASSIST Menu. RECALL is found on the ■ *Update* ■ menu. Initiate with

> ■ *Update* ■ *Recall* ■

then specify scope, build a search condition, and build a scope condition, as necessary, before executing the command.

Purging Deleted Records

The **PACK** command purges all records marked for deletion. Before **PACK**, deleted records are present in the file. After **PACK**, deleted records are gone forever. It is wise to make a backup copy of your file before packing.

From the ASSIST Menu. **PACK** is found on the ■ *Update* ■ menu. Execute with

■ *Update* ■ *Pack* ■

Once you select **PACK**, the command executes without further intervention.

Emptying a Data File

The **ZAP** command removes all records from the active data file. It is the equivalent of **DELETE ALL** followed by **PACK**, but much faster. Some care is recommended. This command is not available on the **ASSIST** menu.

Examples

Two examples may clarify the use of record deletion commands. The first example uses temporary deletion, the second example uses permanent deletion.

Temporary Deletion. I keep my student grade book in a dBASE file. At the beginning of the semester, all names are entered into the file. As the semester progresses, some students will withdraw from the course. These students are assigned a 'W' in the GRADE field. I want to keep the student names and scores in the data file for future reference, but not include their scores when computing class averages. The following series of commands is used:

```
delete for grade='W'
set deleted on
average testscore
set deleted off
recall all
```

Permanent Deletion. Organizations that maintain mailing lists want to periodically purge those lists of inactive addressees. For instance, a mail-order firm may remove names of people who have not ordered in the last two years. This would be a permanent removal. Assume that the field LAST_ORDER contains the date of the last order, and that the system date is set to today's date. The following two commands would purge the file of all people who have not ordered in the last two years:

```
delete for ((date( )-last_order)>730)
pack
```

Illustration

Chez Jacques wants a list of raw materials for which the inventory quantity has fallen below one hundred items. Although a **LIST** command would suffice, we will use the deleted-record capabilities of dBASE. (This illustration may be found in Figure 7-4.)

The first step is to open the file RAWX. Then we use **DELETE FOR INVENTORY<=100** to mark as deleted all records with more than 100 units in inventory. dBASE responds with a message indicating how many records were deleted.

The **LIST** command shows us which records are deleted and which are not by placing asterisks before the first field of records that are marked as deleted. To obtain a list of only records that are not marked for deletion, we **SET DELETED ON** and **LIST** again. This time, only two records are listed.

In the next command, we attempt to **RECALL ALL**, but no records are recalled because dBASE is ignoring all records marked as deleted. We must first **SET DELETED OFF**, and then we may **RECALL ALL**.

MODIFYING THE STRUCTURE OF A DATA FILE

One of the virtues of dBASE is that you may change your mind about the relevant data file fields and reconfigure your data file after data have been entered. It is possible to keep previously entered data, but it is also possible to erase many hours of work if you are careless. Read this section carefully.

Before the structure of a file can be modified, the file must be opened (**USE** command).

The general method of modifying the structure of a data file:

1. Copy the contents of the file to a temporary file.

2. Modify the structure of the file.

3. Append the data from the temporary file into the modified file.

dBASE III will perform steps 1 and 3 automatically, but you should know that they are occurring in case a problem arises during the modification process.

First, use the **DISPLAY STRUCTURE** command (F5 key) to display the structure as it exists. From the **APPEND** menu, use the sequence ■ *Tools* ■ *List Structure* ■. You may decide to leave things alone.

Changes may be necessary, however. You may not have made a field wide enough, or you may need more decimal places, or you may need to change the type of field. If so, give the command **MODIFY STRUCTURE**. (From the **ASSIST** menu: ■ *Modify* ■ *Database file* ■.) dBASE will rename the old file with the original {filename} and a .BAK extension, and copy the current structure of the file into a new file with the original filename and .DBF extension. You will be shown a full-screen version of the file structure which you can modify using many of the full-screen editing commands. (This is similar to the screen you completed in the

CREATE command.) It is possible to add fields, delete fields, and change the size of fields by simply changing the specification that appears before you.

To *insert a field*, type ^N (Ctrl-N); to *delete a field*, type ^U (Ctrl-U). Other structure changes are made by editing the structure displayed. For instance, to change a field name, simply type over the old name.

To *change field type* you have to be very careful. If you change field type, exit **MODIFY STRUCTURE** and restart before making any other changes. This is because dBASE will copy the data into the file from the .BAK version based on position in the file (i.e., based on which items are in which columns). If you change data type, especially from Character to Numeric, then you must copy this data *before* making any field-width changes.

Do not change both field name and field length (width) at the same time. If field names are changed, then dBASE will reenter the data based on its position in the file. If field widths are changed, then dBASE will reenter the data based on field names. Changing both will cause dBASE to use names, causing the loss of data in any field whose name was changed. Change names, exit **MODIFY STRUCTURE**, then reenter **MODIFY STRUCTURE** to change the widths.

When the structure is the way you want it to be, exit from **MODIFY STRUCTURE** by typing ^End (Ctrl-End). dBASE III will automatically retrieve the data that existed in the data file before the modification. Check the results with the **DISPLAY STRUCTURE** command. If the effect is not what you want, you may repeat the process. After modifying the structure of a file, recreate the indexes associated with that file using either **INDEX** or **REINDEX** commands.

If, for some reason, the process does not work, you may still save your data. The .BAK file is a valid database file containing your original data and structure. You may use either the DOS or the dBASE **RENAME** commands (discussed in Unit 8) to change the extension of the file from .BAK to .DBF and try the process again.

GUIDED ACTIVITY

This activity requires you to use the data file modification commands.

1. Start or reset the computer as necessary. Before entering dBASE, put a data disk which has the file RAW_MATL.DBF in Drive B. Then give the command

   copy b:raw_matl.dbf b:rawx.dbf

   This will create a duplicate copy of the database file for use in this Guided Activity. When the copying is complete, follow the startup procedure for your version of dBASE as outlined in Unit 2.

2. **USE RAWX**

3. Using the **REPLACE** command, increase all costs by 20 per cent. This operation is illustrated in Figure 7-1.

✔ **CHECKPOINT**
What command do you use to increase all costs by 20%?

_____

4. Using the **CHANGE** command, change the following quantities:

Stock Number	Quantity on Hand
0014	200
0015	229
0013	91

If you are quite clever, you will be able to structure the **CHANGE** command so that it presents only those three records.

✔ **CHECKPOINT**
What command would you use to change only those three records?

_____

5. **DELETE** all records that have one hundred or more units on hand, then **LIST** the data base. Are all nineteen records displayed? **SET DELETED ON** and **LIST** again. You should have only two records this time. Give the command that will remove the deleted flags. This operation is illustrated in Figure 7-4.

✔ **CHECKPOINT**
What command will perform the deletion?

_____

✔ **CHECKPOINT**
What commands do you use to remove the deleted flags?

_____

6. **MODIFY STRUCTURE** to change the width of the COST field to five columns.

7. _For Additional Practice_: If you would like additional practice using the datafile-change commands, do the following:

   a. **USE TOURNEY**

   b. Modify the structure of the file to add the following three fields:

Field	Field name	Type	Width	Dec
6	YEAR	Numeric	4	
7	MONTH	Numeric	2	
8	DAY	Numeric	2	

c. Next, replace the YEAR field in all records with the year portion of the DATE field. You must use the YEAR( ) function.

d. Do the same for the MONTH and DAY fields.

e. **LIST** your file to see the results. We made these changes because we want to be able to copy this data into a file for use in a spreadsheet program, which we will accomplish in Unit 8.

8. When you have completed this Activity, give the command **QUIT** to exit dBASE. Remember to backup your work. If everything is proper, turn off the computer and return the dBASE software to the Lab Supervisor.

REVIEW QUESTIONS

1. What are the four types of changes that can be made to a data file? Give a reason for performing each.

2. Which command or commands would you use in each of the following situations? (Use any appropriate field name.)

   *a. Increase everybody's age by one year.

   *b. Review and change as necessary the phone numbers of all persons in the Marketing department.

   *c. Change Robert Smith's last name to Smith-Jones.

3. What is the difference between the following commands?

   a. **SET DELETED ON** and **DELETE**

   b. **DELETE** and **PACK**

   c. **PACK** and **ZAP**

   d. **SET DELETED OFF** and **RECALL**

DOCUMENTATION RESEARCH

Using the reference manual, determine the answers to the following questions which deal with the commands discussed in this unit. I recommend you also write the reference manual page number by the discussion of the command in this unit.

1. APPEND FROM {filename} — what will happen if the field width of a field in the file in **USE** (the target file) is less than the field width of a field with the same name in the **FROM** (source) file?

2. REPLACE {scope} {field} WITH {expression} FOR {condition} — what happens to the index if the replacement affects a field that is part of the index key?

3. CHANGE FIELDS {field list} FOR {condition} — how do you edit a memo field?

4. BROWSE — what parameters may be specified with this command?

5. BROWSE — what is the *menu bar* and what options does it provide?

6. DELETE {scope} FOR {condition} — if neither {scope} nor {condition} are specified, how many records will be marked for deletion?

7. RECALL {scope} FOR {condition} — what effect does this command have on records that have been removed by **PACK** or **ZAP** commands?

8. PACK — what effect does this command have on open index files?

9. ZAP — what effect does **SET SAFETY ON** have on this command?

UNIT

8 OPERATING PARAMETERS AND DISK FILES

This unit is devoted to a discussion of commands that deal with disk file storage and the operating environment of dBASE. As you become a more advanced dBASE user, you will learn how to use these commands to make your work easier.

LEARNING OBJECTIVES

1. At the completion of this unit, you should know

   a. how to identify the purpose a file serves by the file extension,

   b. the purpose of the various operating parameters and how to alter those parameters.

2. At the completion of this unit, you should be able to

   a. obtain a directory of data files on a disk,

   b. obtain a directory of all files on a disk,

   c. obtain a directory of all files of a certain type,

   d. copy all or a portion of a data file to another data file,

   e. copy all or a portion of a data file to a file suitable for importation into a spreadsheet or word processing program,

   f. display the current settings of function keys,

   g. change the current settings of function keys.

IMPORTANT COMMANDS

DISPLAY STATUS
SET DEFAULT TO {drive}
SET PRINT ON/OFF
SET FUNCTION {number} TO {character string}
COPY TO {filename}
COPY FILE {source} TO {target}
TYPE
DIR
ERASE {filename}
RENAME {filename}
APPEND FROM {filename}
IMPORT FROM {filename} TYPE PFS
EXPORT FROM {filename} TYPE PFS

OPERATING PARAMETERS

It is possible to change many of the operating parameters of dBASE, such as screen appearance and the commands issued by the function keys. This section is concerned with a version of the **DISPLAY** command that shows you what the parameters are, and with the **SET** commands that allow you to change those parameters.

Displaying Parameters

The **DISPLAY STATUS** command is used to provide a summary of the current operating status. The command will list any open databases and their indexes as well as the current settings of most **SET** commands. This command is illustrated in Figure 8-1.

You may use **DISPLAY STATUS TO PRINT** to obtain a printed copy. **LIST STATUS** will also display operating status, but does not pause after filling the screen with information. The **DISPLAY STATUS** command may be given by pressing the F6 key.

Changing Parameters

The **SET** command allows many operating parameters to be changed. There are over thirty versions of the **SET** command. Rather than write a book on the various options, we will discuss a few of the most useful here and refer to others in later units as appropriate. Table 8-1 contains a list of all **SET** commands for your future reference.

A few of the most common **SET** commands may be given through the **ASSIST** menu. The best method for issuing **SET** commands, however, is to type **SET** at the dot prompt. You will be presented with a full-screen menu, as illustrated in Figure 8-2. In that illustration, I have used the <ARROW> keys to select ■ *Keys* ■ *F4* ■. Press <CR> to select the highlighted key to change, enter the desired text, press <CR> when finished. (See the discussion of **SET FUNCTION** for a more thorough discussion of the command.)

```
. use raw_matl index raw_matl
. display status

Currently Selected Database:
Select area:  1, Database in Use: B:raw_matl.dbf    Alias: RAW_MATL
     Master index file:  B:raw_matl.ndx  Key: rmid

File search path:
Default disk drive: B:
Print destination:  PRN:
Margin =       0
Current work area =      1

Press any key to continue...

ALTERNATE  - OFF   DELETED    - OFF   FIXED      - OFF   SAFETY     - ON
BELL       - ON    DELIMITERS - OFF   HEADING    - ON    SCOREBOARD - ON
CARRY      - OFF   DEVICE     - SCRN  HELP       - ON    STATUS     - ON
CATALOG    - OFF   DOHISTORY  - OFF   HISTORY    - ON    STEP       - OFF
CENTURY    - OFF   ECHO       - OFF   INTENSITY  - ON    TALK       - ON
CONFIRM    - OFF   ESCAPE     - ON    MENU       - ON    TITLE      - ON
CONSOLE    - ON    EXACT      - OFF   PRINT      - OFF   UNIQUE     - OFF
DEBUG      - OFF   FIELDS     - OFF

Programmable function keys:
F2  - assist;
F3  - list;
F4  - dir;
F5  - display structure;
F6  - display status;
F7  - display memory;
F8  - display;
F9  - append;
F10 - edit;

.
Command Line     |<B:>|RAW_MATL              |Rec: 8/19        |        |
                 Enter a dBASE III PLUS COMMAND.
```

FIGURE 8-1 Illustration of the **DISPLAY STATUS** Command
Note: Commands entered by the user are in **boldface.**

TABLE 8-1 SET Commands

SET . . .	Function
ALTERNATE ON/**OFF**	Records all keyboard entries and screen displays in an output file for later reference.
ALTERNATE TO . . .	Names the output file.
BELL **ON**/OFF	Sounds bell when input data fills field.
CARRY ON/**OFF**	Copies data from previous record to new record during APPEND.
CATALOG ON/**OFF**[1]	Controls updating of an open catalog.
CATALOG TO . . .[1]	Names the catalog file.
CENTURY ON/**OFF**[1]	Allows input of dates other than 20th century.
COLOR TO . . .	Changes colors or screen attributes.
CONFIRM ON/**OFF**	Controls whether or not input skips to next field when current field is full during APPEND and EDIT.
CONSOLE **ON**/OFF	Turns video display on and off from within programs files.
DATE . . .[1]	Changes the format of date display.
DEBUG ON/**OFF**	Used to locate errors in programs.
DECIMALS TO . . .	Controls number of decimal places displayed for some calculations.
DEFAULT TO . . .	Changes default drive for file operations.
DELETED ON/**OFF**	Determines whether records marked for deletion are considered by other commands.
DELIMITERS ON/**OFF**	Sets method of marking field widths for APPEND and EDIT.
DELIMITERS TO . . .	Defines character(s) for delimiting.
DEVICE TO . . .	Routes @ command output to screen or printer.
DOHISTORY ON/**OFF**[1]	Captures command file commands in memory.
ECHO ON/**OFF**	Controls whether or not command lines from programs are displayed on the screen.
ESCAPE **ON**/OFF	Determines whether or not an Esc will abort commands.
EXACT ON/**OFF**	Affects character string equivalence in {conditions}.
FIELDS ON/**OFF**[1]	Works with command below to limit the fields available.
FIELDS TO . . .[1]	Defines a list of fields that may be accessed.
FILTER TO . . .	Allows only records that meet a condition to be available.
FIXED ON/**OFF**	Displays specific number of decimal places for all numeric output.
FORMAT TO . . .	Selects customized format.
FUNCTION . . .	Reprograms function keys.
HEADING **ON**/OFF	Controls display of column titles with DISPLAY, LIST, SUM, and AVERAGE.
HELP **ON**/OFF	Turns help query on and off.
HISTORY **ON**/OFF[1]	Allows prior commands to be recalled, edited, and executed.
HISTORY TO . . .[1]	Specifies number of commands to be stored (default is 20).
INDEX TO . . .	Opens index files, alternative to USE . . . INDEX command.
INTENSITY **ON**/OFF	Determines display of fields for APPEND and EDIT.
MARGIN TO . . .	Sets left margin for printed output.
MEMOWIDTH TO . . .[1]	Adjusts the width of memo field output (default is 50).
MENU **ON**/OFF	Displays a cursor key menu when appropriate.

[1] dBASE III Plus only

Note: default settings are in **boldface**.

TABLE 8-1 SET Commands (continued)

SET . . .	Function
MESSAGE TO . . .[1]	Displays a user-defined text string at bottom of screen.
ORDER TO . . .[1]	Establishes any index file as the master.
PATH TO . . .	Sets path to be searched for files (PC-DOS 2.0 and later).
PRINT ON/**OFF**	Directs output to printer as well as screen.
PRINTER TO . . .[1]	Changes default printer output device.
PROCEDURE TO . . .	Opens a procedure file (similar to a set of subroutines).
RELATION TO . . .	Links two files (see Part 3 of this manual).
SAFETY **ON**/OFF	Provides protection against inadvertent erasing of files.
SCOREBOARD **ON**/OFF[1]	Displays messages on status bar or top of screen.
STATUS **ON**/OFF[1]	Display status bar.
STEP ON/**OFF**	Used to cause program to execute a step at a time.
TALK **ON**/OFF	Causes response to commands to be displayed.
TITLE **ON**/OFF[1]	Turns catalog file title on and off.
TYPEAHEAD TO . . .[1]	Controls how many characters dBASE will hold (default is 20).
UNIQUE ON/**OFF**	Used with INDEX to eliminate records with duplicate keys.
VIEW TO . . .[1]	Opens a view file.

[1] dBASE III Plus only
Note: default settings are in **boldface**.

Default Disk Drive. The default disk drive is where dBASE will store a file you create and look for a file you open. The **SET DEFAULT** command tells dBASE which drive to use. The person responsible for the software should have created a file named CONFIG.DB on the System disk (i.e., the disk in Drive A or the hard disk) that accomplishes this automatically. If the file does not exist, you must remember to type **SET DEFAULT TO B:** (or **A:**, or whatever your desired default drive is) each time you start dBASE.

From the ASSIST Menu. **SET DEFAULT** is part of the ■ *Tools* ■ menu. The sequence is

   ■ *Tools* ■ *Set drive* ■ *B:* ■

Printer Toggle. Most versions of dBASE allow you to toggle the printer on and off with the **SET PRINT** command. After **SET PRINT ON**, almost all screen output will be sent to the printer as well as to the screen. Use **SET PRINT OFF** to stop the effect. Also, **SET PRINT ON** before sending special control codes to the printer. If you want to shift a printer to compressed type, use the following sequence:

   set print on
   ? chr(15)
   set print off

CHR(15) is the equivalent of ^O (Ctrl-O), a fairly standard code for shifting printers to compressed type face.

TABLE 8-2 Function Key Assignments

F1	Help;	F2	Assist;
F3	List;	F4	Dir;
F5	Display Structure;	F6	Display Status;
F7	Display Memory;	F8	Display;
F9	Append;	F10	Edit;

Function Keys. The ten function keys have been assigned useful commands, which appear in Table 8-2. If you wish to change the default setting, use the **SET FUNCTION** command:

   set function {number} to {character string}

where **{number}** is the number of the key to be reassigned and **{character string}** is the command that pressing the key should produce. The **{character string}** may include up to thirty characters, including spaces. The **{character string}** should include a ; (semicolon) wherever the <CR> key should be pressed. More than one command may be assigned to a function key, within the thirty character limit. Function key F1 cannot be reassigned.

Examples:

   set function 4 to 'use raw_matl;'
   set function 7 to 'set print on;list;'
   set function 8 to 'eject;set print off;'

   See Figure 8-2 for an illustration of changing the function key assignment using the full-screen **SET** menu.

   The default function key assignments may be changed in the CONFIG.DB file. Again, this is the task of the person responsible for the software, not the individual user.

DISK FILES

This section deals with the storage of files on disks. Most PC-DOS application programs, including dBASE, use the file extension to designate the purpose the file serves (i.e., the file type). If you are not familiar with the general rules for file names and extensions, refer to the appendix to this manual.

   Some of the commands already discussed deal with disk files. For instance, **CREATE** and **INDEX** create files on the disk. **APPEND** adds data to a data file. **USE** opens a disk file for reading or writing. The commands discussed in this unit complement commands already presented.

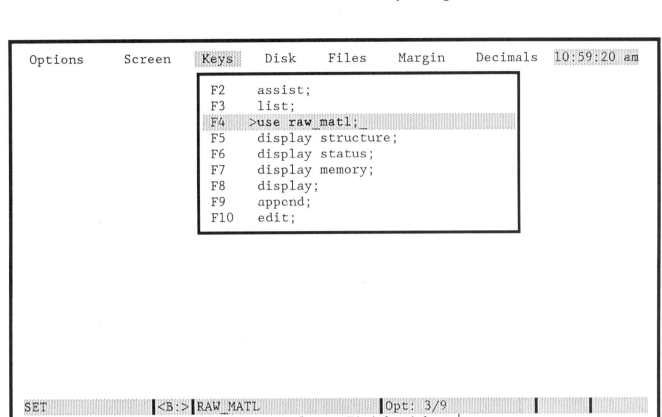

FIGURE 8-2 Using the Full-Screen **SET** Menu to Change a Function Key
Note: Command entered by the user is in **boldface**.

TABLE 8-3 dBASE File Types

Type of File	Extension	
Catalog	.CAT	(dBASE III Plus only)
Database	.DBF	
Database memo	.DBT	
Index	.NDX	
Command or procedure	.PRG	
Format	.FMT	
Label	.LBL	
Memory	.MEM	
Query	.QRY	(dBASE III Plus only)
Screen	.SCR	(dBASE III Plus only)
View	.VUE	(dBASE III Plus only)
Report form	.FRM	
Text output	.TXT	

File Type

dBASE creates several types of files, each with a unique file extension (see Table 8-3). In most cases, you can specify a different extension for the file, but it is best to let dBASE assign its default extensions to simplify operations. These file types are discussed as necessary throughout this manual.

Copying Files

Database to Database Copies. The **COPY** command duplicates all or part of the open file in another file. The general form is

    copy to {filename}

where {filename} is any legal filename. A .DBF extension is added automatically. The copy operation may be limited to a certain {field list} or to records that meet a logical {condition}:

    copy to {filename} fields {field list}
    copy to {filename} for {condition}
    copy to {filename} fields {field list} for {condition}

Examples:

    copy to backup
    copy to ages fields name, age
    copy to vip for salary > 100000
    copy to prospect fields name, address for income > 50000

Database to Text File Copies. COPY can also be used to copy all or a portion of the open file to a text file for inclusion into a word processor, spreadsheet, or other database manager. (See the section entitled "Output to Other Applications Software" later in this unit).

Copy of Any File. The **COPY FILE** command creates a copy of any disk file. The format is

    copy file {source filename.ext} to {target filename.ext}

This command performs the same function as the DOS **COPY** command.

Directory of Files

The **DIR** command provides a list of database files (.DBF extension) on the default disk. The output (see Figure 8-3 for an example) includes the size of the file, number of records, and date of last update, except that information on currently open files may not reflect changes since the file was opened.

The **DIR** command may be given by pressing the F4 key.

```
. dir
Database Files       # Records      Last Update      Size
DATEBOOK.DBF              4          12/29/86         318
FIN_GOOD.DBF             17          11/13/84        1024
RAW_MATL.DBF             19          06/26/85        1024
MIX.DBF                  82          10/13/84        1536

   3902 bytes in      4 files.
 289792 bytes remaining on drive.

. _

Command Line     |<B:>|RAW_MATL                    |Rec: 8/19        |         |
```
                    Enter a dBASE III PLUS command.

FIGURE 8-3 Illustration of the **DIR** Command
Note: Item entered by the user is in **boldface**.

        You may specify a specific file name, and you may also use the ? and * wildcard characters to look for specific types of files. Examples:

   dir *.txt
   dir c:*.ndx

From the ASSIST Menu. DIR is found on the ■ *Tools* ■ menu. The command lists only the names and extensions of a specified type of file, and does not include information such as number of records, last update, and size. The menu sequence is

   ■ *Tools* ■ *Directory* ■ *B:* ■ *.dbf Database Files* ■

The dot-prompt version provides more information about database files, but the **ASSIST** menu version is quicker for getting information about other types of files.

Erasing Files

The **ERASE** command in dBASE III deletes a file on the disk. Do not erase from within dBASE unless you need the space on disk or you have a well-developed and debugged program. It is much better to erase files at the PC-DOS level. Example:

   erase temp.ndx

From the ASSIST Menu. ERASE is found on the ■ *Tools* ■ menu, where the sequence is

   ■ *Tools* ■ *Erase* ■

followed by your choice of drive and then a file on that drive.

Renaming Files

The **RENAME** command does what it says. Follow the same cautions as **ERASE**. Example:

rename temp.ndx to old.ndx

From the ASSIST Menu. **RENAME** is also found on the ■ *Tools* ■ menu. The command begins

■ *Tools* ■ *Rename* ■

and is completed by selection of drive, selection of file to be renamed, and input of new filename.

OUTPUT TO OTHER APPLICATIONS SOFTWARE

The **COPY** command may be used to extract data from the data file that will be used by a word processing program (such as WordStar MailMerge) in form letters and other applications. This command can also extract data for further analysis by a spreadsheet program such as VisiCalc, Multiplan, or Lotus 1-2-3, or for input to a programming language such as BASIC. The output file may be constrained using a {**field list**} or {**condition**}. This use of the **COPY** command is not available through the **ASSIST** menu.

To make the data available to other software, the output of the command must be either a file in *ASCII text* or a file with special information recognized by the specific program. First, we will discuss the creation of ASCII text files for word processors and computer languages (such as BASIC), then we will discuss the creation of specially-coded spreadsheet files.

ASCII Text Output

ASCII (American Standard Code for Information Interchange) text might also be called plain text; it is not coded in any special way by dBASE. Most applications software can read ASCII text, so it is a good way (if not an especially efficient method) to move data among programs. The dBASE III command **TYPE** {**filename.ext**} may be used to display the contents of an ASCII file on screen or printer.

Notice, in Figure 8-4, that two variations of the **COPY** command produce ASCII files. **DELIMITED** output is almost always preferred, but you may use **SDF** (*Structured Data Format*) output if your applications program is written in FORTRAN or COBOL and requires a structured format.

Finally, notice how dBASE III converts date-type fields for ASCII output. Your application program may or may not be able to make use of such a format.

COPY TO {**filename**} **SDF** creates a file in ASCII text of the entire database (or, a portion of the database if you use a {**field list**} or a {**condition**}). Fields are aligned similar to the output of the **LIST** command. This is useful when you want to include a table of data into a text document being edited by a word processor.

```
. copy to sdf_ex for cost>.10 sdf
      3 records copied
. type sdf_ex.txt
0007sesame seed bun     0.1240019851008
0016apple pie           0.1634619850815
0017cherry pie          0.1420019850919

. copy to delim_ex for cost>.10 delimited
      3 records copied
. type delim_ex.txt
"0007","sesame seed bun",0.12,400,19851008
"0016","apple pie",0.16,346,19850815
"0017","cherry pie",0.14,200,19850919

.
Command Line     |<B:>|RAW_MATL                 |Rec: EOF/19         |          |
```

Enter a dBASE III PLUS command.

FIGURE 8-4 Variations of the **COPY** Command
Note: Items entered by the user are in **boldface**.

COPY TO {filename} DELIMITED creates a file in ASCII text of the entire database (or, a portion of the database if you use a **{field list}** or a **{condition}**). Character-type fields are enclosed in quotation marks and all fields are separated by commas.

A default extension of .TXT will be assigned unless you specify otherwise.

WordStar MailMerge Users: Use the **DELIMITED** form: **COPY TO OUTPUT DELIMITED**. You will be able to use the file as a MailMerge data file without editing.

BASIC Language Programmers: Use the **DELIMITED** form: **COPY TO OUTPUT DELIMITED**. You will be able to read the file as a sequential file with **INPUT #** statements without editing.

Spreadsheet File Output

dBASE III Plus (but not the original dBASE III[2]) allows you to output a file which can be directly read by three of the most popular spreadsheet programs: VisiCalc, Multiplan, and Lotus 1-2-3. Records are placed in rows, with fields in columns. The basic forms of the command are as follows:

copy to {filename} type dif   *Creates a file in VisiCalc format.*

---

[2] *Lotus 1-2-3 Users*: With the original dBASE III, you must use the **DELIMITED** form and specify a .PRN extension: **COPY TO OUTPUT.PRN DELIMITED**. You will be able to /FileImport without editing.

```
A2: [W4] '0014                                                          READY


      A          B          C       D      E      F        G        H
1   RMIDDESC              COST    INVLAST_ORDER
2   001412 oz. cup          0   ***19871004
3   001516 oz. cup          0   ***19870928
4   00184 oz. fry pack      0   ***19871019
5   00196 oz. fry pack      0   ***19871015
6   00138 oz. cup           0   ***19871006
7   0011Coca Cola (oz.)     0   ***19871013
8   0012Sprite (oz.)        0   ***19871012
9   0001all-beef patty      0   ***19871001
10  0016apple pie           0   ***19870815
11  0009catsup (oz.)        0   ***19871010
12  0006ch. onion (oz.)     0   ***19871010
13  0004cheese slice        0   ***19871009
14  0017cherry pie          0   ***19870919
15  0010fren. fry (oz.)     0   ***19871012
16  0003lettuce leaf        0    90 19871003
17  0005pickle slice        0   ***19870915
18  0008regular bun         0   ***19871003
19  0007sesame seed bun     0   ***19871008
20  0002sp. sauce (oz.)     0   ***19870930
25-Mar-87   08:55 AM
```

FIGURE 8-5 A Lotus 1-2-3 Worksheet Created by the **COPY . . . TYPE WKS** Command

copy to {filename} type sylk   *Creates a file in Multiplan format.*

copy to {filename} type wks   *Creates a file in Lotus 1-2-3 format.*

Example for Lotus 1-2-3. To test this feature, I opened the file RAW_MATL and then issued the command

   copy to raw_matl type wks

A file named RAW_MATL.WKS was created on my default disk. Then, I **QUIT** dBASE III and entered Lotus 1-2-3. I used the Lotus /**FileRetrieve** command to load the worksheet file. The result appears in Figure 8-5.

Note that the Lotus column widths are set to the dBASE field widths, resulting in a line of ******* across the INVENTORY field column and the hiding of part of the field name. This can be easily corrected by setting the column width to a larger number (in Lotus, or in dBASE before making the copy). The numeric format of the COST field also needs to be changed. No information is lost: but some information is hidden because of the differing uses of column widths and numeric formats by the two programs.

Finally, the dates are copied as a label (character string), which may be converted by a Lotus 1-2-3 Release 2 function. For instance, to convert the date in E2 to a Lotus-style date, you could use the following function in cell F2 (all three lines are one cell entry).

@DATE(@INT(((@VALUE(E2)-19000000)/10000),
    @INT(@MOD((@VALUE(E2)-19000000),10000)/100),
    @MOD(@INT(@MOD((@VALUE(E2)-19000000),10000)),100))

It would be less cumbersome, however, to add three fields to the database before it is copied: one for year, one for month, and one for day. (The **MODIFY STRUCTURE** command, which is used to change database structure, is discussed in Unit 7.) Then, use the **REPLACE** command (also discussed in Unit 7) as follows (this is one command, do not separate it with <CR> into two lines).

**replace all year with year(last_order), month with month(last_order), day with
    day(last_order)**

After this, the dBASE **COPY** command will create a Lotus column for each of year, month, and day, and the Lotus function @DATE(F2-1900,G2,H2), placed in I2 and copied down column I, should work nicely.

INPUT FROM OTHER APPLICATIONS SOFTWARE

The transfer of data from other applications software, such as a word processor or spreadsheet, is essentially the reverse of the process to output data to those programs. The **APPEND FROM** command is used, with the basic forms:

append from {filename} delimited	*For data in delimited format.*
append from {filename} sdf	*For data in structured format.*
append from {filename} type dif	*For data in a VisiCalc spreadsheet.*
append from {filename} type sylk	*For data in a Multiplan spreadsheet.*
append from {filename} type wks	*For data in a Lotus 1-2-3 worksheet.*

where {**filename**} is an ASCII text file, or a file in the appropriate spreadsheet format. dBASE assumes a .TXT file extension for ASCII text files (or, you may specify a different extension), and the appropriate extension for each of the spreadsheet types. Examples:

append from ws_file delimited	*For data separated by commas, with character strings enclosed by " (quotation) marks.*
append from lot_file.prn sdf	*For structured data created by a Lotus /PrintFile command.*
append from lot_file type wks	*For data from a Lotus 1-2-3 Release 1A worksheet.*

append from lot_file.wk1 type wks   *For data from a Lotus 1-2-3 Release 2 worksheet; because Lotus has changed the default worksheet file extension (to .WK1), it must be specified.*

Before appending from an another file, you must **CREATE** a data file to hold the incoming data. The structure you create must match the type and width of the data being imported. The receiving data file is then opened with the **USE** command, and the appropriate version of **APPEND FROM** is given.

Word Processor Users: You may create the file with commas separating data elements and use **DELIMITED** form, or you may carefully align the data in columns and use **SDF** form.

BASIC Programmers: Use the **WRITE #** statement, which creates delimited output, then import with the **DELIMITED** qualifier.

Spreadsheet Users: Make sure that the type of data is the same in each column (i.e., all character or all numeric). Before leaving the spreadsheet program, make careful notes of width, data type, and number of decimal places in each column. Also, remove column headings and anything else which is not part of the data to be imported by dBASE. (You may want to work with an extra copy of the file.)

You now have two choices:

» From within the spreadsheet program, you may use the command that creates an ASCII output file (e.g., /PrintFile in Lotus 1-2-3) to put the data on a disk file. When you are in dBASE, create a file structure that matches the spreadsheet columns and use the **SDF** option on input. (Because some spreadsheet programs automatically assign extensions to ASCII output files, you may have to specify the extension as part of the command: **APPEND FROM LOT_FILE.PRN SDF.**)

» Exit the spreadsheet and enter dBASE. Create a file structure which matches the spreadsheet columns, and then use the appropriate **APPEND FROM . . . TYPE . . .** command. (If you are using the original dBASE III, this choice is not available, and you must use the SDF option above.)

INTERCHANGING DATA WITH PFS:FILE

dBASE III Plus (but not the original dBASE III) has the ability to input and output data directly to the PFS:FILE program. The commands are **IMPORT** (PFS to dBASE) and **EXPORT** (dBASE to PFS). The commands transfer the data file and an associated format file.

Examples:

import from pfs_data type pfs
export to pfs_file. type pfs

From the ASSIST Menu. IMPORT and **EXPORT** are found on the ■ *Tools* ■ menu. You are prompted for file names as necessary.

GUIDED ACTIVITY

This activity requires you to use the commands discussed in this unit.

1. Follow the startup procedure for your version of dBASE as outlined in Unit 2.

2. Put the disk containing RAW_MATL.DBF, MIX.DBF, and FIN_GOOD.DBF in Drive B (or the only drive on a fixed-disk PC).

3. Open the file RAW_MATL with its index.

4. Use the **DISPLAY STATUS** command to see the initial system status, which will look similar to Figure 8-1. Use <SHIFT>PrtSc twice to print a copy.

5. Change the meaning of function key F10 to **DIR *.*;**

✔ **CHECKPOINT**
What command do you use to change this function key definition?

_____

6. **SET PRINT ON**

7. **DISPLAY STATUS** again. Did the output go to the printer? What has changed?

8. Use the **COPY** command to make a second copy of RAW_MATL.DBF with the name RAW2.DBF. You will see a "records copied" message similar to the one in Figure 8-4.

✔ **CHECKPOINT**
What command will you use to make this copy?

_____

9. Output a file listing all raw materials and their unit costs suitable for input into a text-merge program. This file should contain *only* the fields DESC and COST.

✔ **CHECKPOINT**
What command do you use to output a file named MERGE.TXT?

_____

10. Output a file listing all raw materials and their unit costs suitable for input into a spreadsheet program. This file should contain the fields DESC, COST, and INVENTORY, and be limited to those items with an inventory of greater than 100. (The exact command depends on the spreadsheet program, if any, that is used in your organization.)

✔ **CHECKPOINT**
What command do you use to output a file named INVENTRY.WKS?

_____

11. *For Additional Practice*: If you would like more practice using the commands discussed in this unit, do the following:

    a. From the dot prompt, give the command **USE TOURNEY** to save your work and open the file TOURNEY.

    b. Make a copy of TOURNEY suitable for your favorite spreadsheet program. Before using the **COPY** command, you should have modified the structure to include YEAR, MONTH, and DAY fields, and entered (replaced) the relevant data, as discussed in Unit 7.

    c. **QUIT** dBASE, then enter your spreadsheet and load the copy of TOURNEY. Do whatever formatting is necessary to provide a readable spreadsheet. (If you are using Lotus 1-2-3, you must subtract 1900 from YEAR when using it in the @DATE( ) function.)

12. If everything is proper, turn off the computer and return all software to the Lab Supervisor.

REVIEW QUESTIONS

1. What kind of data is contained in files with the following extensions?

    a. .DBF

    b. .TXT

    c. .NDX

2. What command will list all database files on a disk?

*3. What command will tell you what the current function key settings are?

4. What command would you use to change the meaning of function key F10 to be **DIR *.*;**

5. Look at Figure 8-4. What are the characteristics of Structured Data Format and Delimited Format. What are the differences?

*6. What commands would you use to output a file listing all raw materials and their unit costs suitable for input into a text-merge or spreadsheet program?

DOCUMENTATION RESEARCH

Using the reference manual, determine the answers to the following questions which deal with the commands discussed in this unit. I recommend you also write the reference manual page number by the discussion of the command in this unit.

1. DISPLAY STATUS — what information is provided for each open database file?

2. SET DEFAULT TO {drive} — how does this command differ from **SET PATH TO . . .?**

3. SET PRINT ON/OFF — how do you route full-screen displays to the printer?

4. COPY TO {filename} — what happens to records marked for deletion?

5. COPY FILE {source} TO {target} — if this command is used to copy a database file with memo-type fields, what else must be done?

6. DIR — under what circumstances might this command yield incorrect information about a database file?

7. ERASE {filename} — under what circumstances will this command not erase the file?

8. RENAME {filename} — what must be specified if the file to be renamed is not on the default disk drive?

9. APPEND FROM {filename} — if the **DELIMITED** option is used, how is the end of a field indicated?

10. IMPORT FROM {filename} TYPE PFS — what does this command accomplish in addition to creating a database file?

11. EXPORT FROM {filename} TYPE PFS — how does this command differ from **COPY**?

APPLICATION

C

MILWAUKEE BANKS

In this application exercise, you will conduct inquiry and data file modification operations.

1. Start by signing out the dBASE manual and software, as well as the Exercises Disk.

2. Insert the Exercises Disk in Drive A. Insert a formatted disk in Drive B. This disk will hold the files that you create and edit.[1]

3. Reset or turn on the machine, as appropriate. Remember to enter the date and time as prompted.

4. Once the system is loaded and the date and time set you should see the DOS command prompt (A>_). Give the command

   copy mil_bank.dbf b:

   which will copy a database file from the Exercises Disk to your disk.

5. Once the copying is finished, remove the Exercises Disk and follow the startup procedure for your version of dBASE as outlined in Unit 2.

6. For the remainder of this exercise, you will make extensive use of the data file MIL_BANK,[2] which you have copied onto your data disk. **USE** the file, and display its structure. Assets, Deposits, Loans, Operating Income, and Operating Expenses fields are in units of 1000 (i.e., multiply assets by 1000 to get actual assets). Where a field = 0, the data were not available. Banks that were not ranked in the top 25 in 1983 are given a RANK_83 of 26.

---

[1] If you are using a fixed disk PC, your instructor will tell you how to do steps 2-4.
[2] The data in this file are excerpted from a list published by *The Business Journal Serving Greater Milwaukee* in 1984.

```
. display all
Record#   RANK_84 NAME                                            ADDRESS
                     TELEPHONE CEO              ASSETS DEPOSITS   LOANS OP_INC
OME OP_EXPENSE RET_ON_ASS HOLDING_CO                  HO_CO_TKR DIVIDEND
 RANK_83
      1         1 First Wisconsin National Bank of Milwaukee 777 E. Wisconsin Ave
., Milwaukee         765-4321  Hal Kuehl         3422805 2365040 2428042     296
811     291040       0.320 First Wisconsin Corp.          FWC         1.0875
      1
      2         2 M&I Marshall & Ilsley Bank                  770 N. Water St., Mi
lwaukee              765-7700  J. A. Puelicher  1576133   834640  788418     142
131     129094       0.860 Marshall & Ilsley Corp.          MNI         1.9600
      2
      3         3 Marine Bank, N.A.                           111 E. Wisconsin Ave
., Milwaukee         765-3000  George Slater    1446316  1036087  972377     114
461     108410       0.630 Marine Corp.                     MAR         1.1600
      3
Press any key to continue..._
Command Line      |<B:>|MIL_BANK                 |Rec: 1/25              |       |
```

                    Enter a dBASE III PLUS command.

FIGURE C-1 Display of All Fields
Note: Command entered by the user is in **boldface**.

7. **DISPLAY ALL.** You will notice that the records are too wide to fit on one line of the screen (see Figure C-1). With this data file, you will have to use the form **DISPLAY ALL {list}** to display just the fields you are interested in.

   For instance, to display the names of the banks, give the command

   display all name

   (See Figure C-2.)

8. Following are several questions that you must answer using the MIL__BANK data file. There are many ways to answer these questions: you can list the relevant field or fields and count the occurrences or compute the ratio asked for; better, you can list the relevant field or fields for only records that meet the condition; or, best, when data from individual records are not requested, you can use the summary statistics and not list anything. In some cases, you will have to create a temporary index.

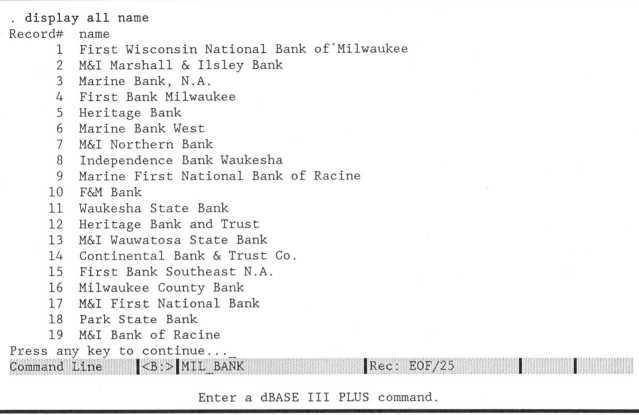

```
. display all name
Record#   name
      1   First Wisconsin National Bank of Milwaukee
      2   M&I Marshall & Ilsley Bank
      3   Marine Bank, N.A.
      4   First Bank Milwaukee
      5   Heritage Bank
      6   Marine Bank West
      7   M&I Northern Bank
      8   Independence Bank Waukesha
      9   Marine First National Bank of Racine
     10   F&M Bank
     11   Waukesha State Bank
     12   Heritage Bank and Trust
     13   M&I Wauwatosa State Bank
     14   Continental Bank & Trust Co.
     15   First Bank Southeast N.A.
     16   Milwaukee County Bank
     17   M&I First National Bank
     18   Park State Bank
     19   M&I Bank of Racine
Press any key to continue...
Command Line      <B:> MIL_BANK              Rec: EOF/25
```

Enter a dBASE III PLUS command.

FIGURE C-2 Display of a Single Field
Note: Command entered by the user is in **boldface**.

As you determine the answers to the questions, make screen prints (i.e., <SHIFT>PrtSc) and circle the answer. Also, identify the screen print by writing the question number (e.g., 8a.) on it.

a. How many banks are affiliated with the Holding Company of Marshall & Ilsley Corp.?

To answer this question, you need to know how to identify banks that are affiliated with a particular holding company, then how to identify those that are affiliated with this particular holding company.

We do another **DISPLAY STRUCTURE** and notice that there is a field named HOLDING_CO. We give the command

display all name,holding_co

and note that there are several banks that list *Marshall & Ilsley Corp.* as the holding company. We could simply count them on our fingers, but we decide to be more elegant.

The next step is to display only banks with the holding company of Marshall & Ilsley Corp. The command that will do this is

display name,holding_co for holding_co='Marshall & Ilsley'

We do not have to specify the entire match string ('Marshall & Ilsley Corp.'), but what we do specify will be checked starting in byte 1 of the field and extending as far as the length of the match string. This command will give us a list of only the banks we are interested in, but we still must use our fingers to count them.

Remembering that dBASE has a **COUNT** command, we next give the command

count for holding_co='Marshall & Ilsley'

which yields the answer directly.

b. How many banks are in Milwaukee?

Our first inclination is to give the command **COUNT FOR CITY='Milwaukee'**, but that will not work because there is no field named CITY. With a bit of thought, we find a field named ADDRESS, but soon discover that the city is not the first item in ADDRESS. We must therefore write a conditional expression that is true when the string *Milwaukee* appears in the field ADDRESS. Recalling the substring comparison operator ($), we use the command

count for 'Milwaukee'$address

which will work reasonably well. For intellectual exercise, try to think of a situation where this command would yield an answer that is greater than the number of banks that are in the city of Milwaukee.

c. How many banks are ranked higher in 1984 than in 1983? A lower number indicates a *higher rank*; thus a bank with a 1984 ranking of 8 and a 1983 ranking of 9 would rank higher in 1984 than in 1983.

This is another count operation, but this time the conditional expression must be true only when one field is greater than the other. I leave it to you to determine the condition.

d. Which bank or banks had operating expenses higher than operating income?

This is not a count operation. Here you must display the name of all banks for which the condition **OP_EXPENSE > OP_INCOME** is true.

e. If the banks were ranked by loans instead of assets, which would be ninth largest?

To answer this question, you must create a temporary index based on the field containing loans. Then you must figure out how to determine which bank is ninth largest. I recommend the following commands:

index on -1*loans to temp
display next 9 name

The first command builds the index in descending order of loans; the second command lists the top nine, the last in the list being the answer sought.

f. What is the ratio of assets:deposits for Milwaukee County Bank?

There are three things you must determine here. First, What is meant by ratio of assets:deposits?; second, How do we get dBASE to calculate that ratio?; third, How do we get dBASE to calculate the ratio for a specific bank?

A ratio is the quotient of two numbers. The result is usually expressed as *something to 1*, as in 2:1 when the first number is twice the amount of the second. Therefore, the asset:deposit ratio will be the result of dividing the assets by the deposits.

dBASE will calculate and display mathematical results as a part of the **DISPLAY** command. To print the name and asset:deposit ratio of all records, simply give the command

display all name,assets/deposits

We can scan the list for Milwaukee County Bank, or we could further modify the command to be

display name,assets/deposits for name='Milwaukee County Bank'

g. Which bank has the highest ratio of assets to deposits?

You should be able to do this one by yourself.

9. Copy the file to a new file called NEW_BANK.

10. **USE NEW_BANK**

11. Use the **REPLACE** command to change the dividend to 1.46 for all banks affiliated with the Holding Company of *Marine Corp.*

12. Use the **DELETE** command to delete all banks with the Holding Company of *none*. List all bank names on the printer.

13. **SET DELETED ON**, then list all bank names on the printer again.

14. When you are finished with all of the above, **QUIT** to exit dBASE. Remember to backup your work, turn off the computer, and return the dBASE software and Exercises Disk to the Lab Supervisor.

UNIT

9 REPORT GENERATION

This unit deals with the creation and production of reports. The exact procedure differs between dBASE III Plus and the original dBASE III, but the general considerations are the same. This unit will discuss those general considerations and will then provide specific instructions for preparing reports in dBASE III Plus.

LEARNING OBJECTIVES

1. At the completion of this unit, you should know the terminology of reports.

2. At the completion of this unit, you should be able to create and produce a report.

IMPORTANT COMMANDS

CREATE REPORT {form file}
MODIFY REPORT {form file}
REPORT FORM {form file}

GENERAL CONSIDERATIONS

A *report* is a method of displaying the data in a data file. There are three parts to a report: the heading, the body, and totals and subtotals. Not all reports will be composed of all three parts. The *report heading* contains identifying information, such as page number, date, and title. The *report body* includes column headings and can include data from individual records, or it may contain only summary data. The report may also contain *totals* and *subtotals* of numeric data, and may be *grouped* according to some *key*. The data included in the body of the report may be arranged in a specific order, and may be all the data in a file or a subset of a data file.

```
Page No.      1
10/20/87
                     Raw Materials Inventory Report

                     prepared by Steven C. Ross

 ID   Description        Cost  Quantity    Material Last      Inventory
                          per  on Hand        Value Order          Age
                         Unit                       Date        (days)


0014 12 oz. cup          0.03       300       9.00 10/04/87        16
0015 16 oz. cup          0.05       400      20.00 09/28/87        22
0018 4 oz. fry pack      0.02       332       6.64 10/19/87         1
0019 6 oz. fry pack      0.03       500      15.00 10/15/87         5
0013 8 oz. cup           0.02       600      12.00 10/06/87        14
0011 Coca Cola (oz.)     0.05       800      40.00 10/13/87         7
0012 Sprite (oz.)        0.05       700      35.00 10/12/87         8
0001 all-beef patty      0.10       100      10.00 10/01/87        19
0016 apple pie           0.16       346      55.36 08/15/87        66
0009 catsup (oz.)        0.04       386      15.44 10/10/87        10
0006 ch. onion (oz.)     0.06       876      52.56 10/10/87        10
0004 cheese slice        0.02       255       5.10 10/09/87        11
0017 cherry pie          0.14       200      28.00 09/19/87        31
0010 fren. fry (oz.)     0.01       999       9.99 10/12/87         8
0003 lettuce leaf        0.01        90       0.90 10/03/87        17
0005 pickle slice        0.03       900      27.00 09/15/87        35
0008 regular bun         0.10       200      20.00 10/03/87        17
0007 sesame seed bun     0.12       400      48.00 10/08/87        12
0002 sp. sauce (oz.)     0.01       400       4.00 09/30/87        20
*** Total ***
                                            413.99
```

FIGURE 9-1 Sample dBASE III Report

The general operation of a report generator is that it first prints the heading and column headings, then scans each record of the report in physical or logical order (the latter if the file is opened with an index). If the record is to be included in the report, the contents of the record are formatted according to the report format and printed on screen or paper. Totals and subtotals are accumulated and printed as appropriate.

The body of the report is defined by the report format. This includes information on column contents, column width, decimal places for numeric data, whether or not numeric data in the column is to be totaled (and subtotaled), and the column heading. In dBASE, the term *report field* (or field) is used to mean *report column*. It may be useful to think of the report format as a template for the output of the data.

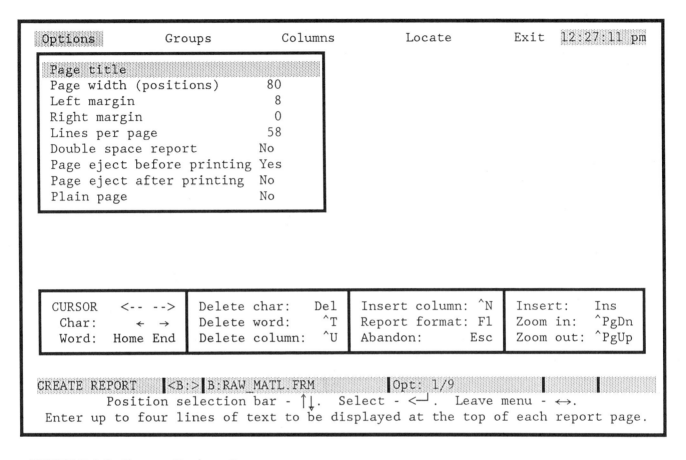

FIGURE 9-2 Report Options Screen

A sample report is contained in Figure 9-1. The heading area contains page number, date, and title information. The body of the report contains information drawn from the RAW_MATL data file, including some calculated fields (columns). Notice that one field is totaled, with the result at the end of the report.

The remainder of this unit is devoted to a discussion of the creation and preparation of the sample report.

CREATING THE REPORT FORMAT

The report format is created or edited with one command and executed with another. The format is stored in a disk file with an .FRM extension. In this section we discuss how to create and modify a report format.

There are two commands to create and modify report format files:

create report {form file}
modify report {form file}

```
Options          Groups        Columns          Locate        Exit  12:50:25 pm

 Page title                    >
 Page width (positions)       80          ┌────────────────────────────────┐
 Left margin                   8          │ Raw Materials Inventory Report  │
 Right margin                  0          │                                 │
 Lines per page               58          │ prepared by Steven C. Ross      │
 Double space report          No          │                                 │
 Page eject before printing  Yes          └────────────────────────────────┘
 Page eject after printing    No
 Plain page                   No

 ┌──────────────────────┬─────────────────────┬──────────────────────┬────────────────────┐
 │ CURSOR    <-- -->     │ Delete char:   Del  │ Insert column:  ^N   │ Insert:     Ins    │
 │ Char:      ← →        │ Delete word:   ^T   │ Report format:  F1   │ Zoom in:   ^PgDn   │
 │ Word:    Home End     │ Delete column: ^U   │ Abandon:       Esc   │ Zoom out:  ^PgUp   │
 └──────────────────────┴─────────────────────┴──────────────────────┴────────────────────┘

CREATE REPORT    |<B:>|B:RAW_MATL.FRM          |Opt: 1/9
                Enter report title.  Exit - Ctrl-End.
Enter up to four lines of text to be displayed at the top of each report page.
```

FIGURE 9-3 Completed Report Heading
Note: Items entered by the user are in **boldface**.

Use either command to create or modify a *report format file* for use with the report command. Example:

modify report raw_matl

You will be led through a series of screens as the form file is created or modified. The form file will have the extension .FRM. Before starting the report creation process, **USE** the file from which the data will be reported.

From the ASSIST Menu. CREATE REPORT is found on the ■ *Create* ■ menu, and **MODIFY REPORT** is found on the ■ *Modify* ■ menu. Although ■ *Create* ■ *Report* ■ can be used to modify an existing report (by entering that report's filename), it is most efficient to use ■ *Create* ■ for original creation and ■ *Modify* ■ for later changes. Once you identify the report filename to dBASE, the remainder of the process is the same whether you initiate it from the dot prompt or from the **ASSIST** menu.

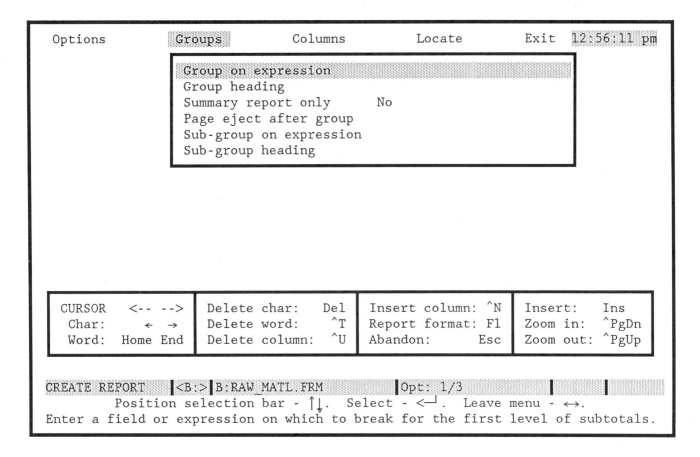

FIGURE 9-4 Group/Subtotal Menu

To make a change to any entry in the report, you must position the selection bar with <UP> and <DOWN>, then press <CR> to inform dBASE that you wish to change that entry. You will be told, at the bottom of the screen, to press Ctrl-End or <CR> when you have finished with the entry. To move to a different menu, press <LEFT> or <RIGHT>.

The first menu, *Options*, allows you to enter a *title* of up to four lines and to specify parameters such as page width, left and right margins, number of lines per page, and the spacing of the report. Whatever is entered in the heading section will be centered on the page when the report is printed.

When the **CREATE REPORT** command is first given, the screen clears and the first menu of the report format appears, as illustrated in Figure 9-2. Figure 9-3 illustrates the first page with a heading entered. Although none of the format parameters were changed in this example, you can change page width, margins, and so on, by making appropriate entries.

The second menu, *Groups*, allows you to specify a key field upon which *group subtotals* will be computed. If your file is sorted or indexed on a field, and you want a *subtotal* for each different value of the field, then make appropriate entries here. If you do not want group subtotals, skip this menu. The group/subtotal menu is illustrated in Figure 9-4. Groups are discussed later in this unit.

```
 Options           Groups           Columns           Locate           Exit   01:04:09 pm
                          ┌─────────────────────────────────────────────────────┐
                          │ Contents                    >                        │
                          │ Heading                                              │
                          │ Width                       0                        │
                          │ Decimal places                                       │
                          │ Total this column                                    │
                          └─────────────────────────────────────────────────────┘




   ┌─Report Format──────────────────────────────────────────────────────────────┐
   │>>>>>>>>---------------------------------------------------------------------│
   │                                                                             │
   │                                                                             │
   │                                                                             │
   ├─────────────────────────────────────────────────────────────────────────────┤
   │                                                                             │
   └─────────────────────────────────────────────────────────────────────────────┘

  CREATE REPORT     |<B:>|B:RAW_MATL.FRM              |Column: 1         |        |
              Enter an expression.  F10 for a field menu.  Finish with <─┘ .
          Enter a field or expression to display in the indicated report column.
```

FIGURE 9-5 Field Definition Screen

If you use a subtotals field, the file should be indexed or sorted on that field. The report will start a new subtotal each time the subtotals field changes, and an unindexed/unsorted file will not produce the report you intended.

The third menu, *Columns*, allows you to define each column (*field*) of the report. A blank field definition screen appears as Figure 9-5. First, the contents are specified. The *field contents* may be a database field, a memory variable, a character string, or a computed result.

To help you specify field contents, you may press the F10 key which will display the structure of the file in use (see Figure 9-6). Once the contents of the field is defined, you may specify a field (i.e., column) heading of up to four lines. Finally, the field width is specified. The width will default to the wider of the heading or the field, but you may enter a different width if you wish. If the field contents is a numeric value, then you will be allowed to specify the number of decimal places and whether or not you wish to total that field. (dBASE assumes that you wish to total numeric fields, so the default is *Yes*.) The format of a totaled field is shown with # (pound) signs in the *Report Format* section of the screen. Nontotaled numeric fields are shown with 9s. You can see the difference in Figure 9-8.

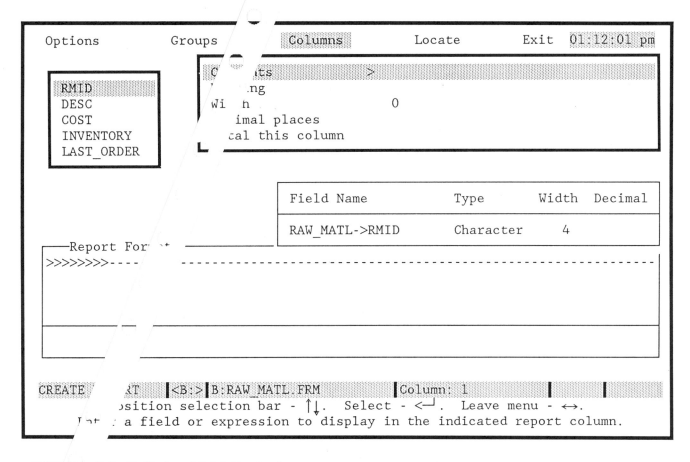

FIGURE 9-6 Defining Field Contents

Completed field definition screens are illustrated in Figures 9-7, 9-8, and 9-9. The field in Figure 9-7 is fairly simple. It is based on one data file field (RMID), and is a character-type field, so no decimal places or totals need be specified. The field in Figure 9-8 is more complex. It is the numeric product of two fields (COST and INVENTORY), it will be totaled, and will display two decimal places. Notice the ; (semicolon) in the Column Heading: this indicates that the heading will be printed on two lines, and was automatically inserted by dBASE.

dBASE functions may also be included in field definitions. For example, the last field in this report (Inventory Age) is computed by subtracting the date of the last order from the system date: **DATE( )-LAST_ORDER**.

As you create or modify your report, the screen will display an illustration of the headings and field formats, as well as an indication of the number of columns remaining.

You may move among the screens with the PgUp and PgDn keys. To move quickly, use the *Locate* menu, which will list the contents of each field for your selection.

When finished, type ^End (Ctrl-End) to exit.

```
   Options           Groups           Columns             Locate          Exit   01:14:33 pm
                          ┌──────────────────────────────────────────────────┐
                          │  Contents            RMID                         │
                          │  Heading             ID                           │
                          │  Width                    4                       │
                          │  Decimal places                                   │
                          │  Total this column                                │
                          └──────────────────────────────────────────────────┘




   ┌─Report Format──────────────────────────────────────────────────────────────┐
   │>>>>>>>>ID      - - - - - - - - - - - - - - - - - - - - - - - - - - - - - - - -│
   │                                                                              │
   │                                                                              │
   │                                                                              │
   ├──────────────────────────────────────────────────────────────────────────────
   │        XXXX                                                                  │
   │                                                                              │
   └──────────────────────────────────────────────────────────────────────────────
  CREATE REPORT     │<B:>│B:RAW_MATL.FRM            │Column: 1        │        │
     Position selection bar - ↑↓.   Select - ←┘.   Prev/Next column - PgUp/PgDn.
                 Enter the number of characters for the column width.
```

FIGURE 9-7 Completed Field Definition Screen
Note: Items entered by the user are in **boldface**.

To make changes later, give the **MODIFY REPORT** command, and you may move through the menus and columns making changes as desired.

PRODUCING THE REPORT

Once the report format is created or modified, the **REPORT FORM** command is used to produce the report. The general form of the command is

report form {form file}

which will produce the report on the screen. dBASE assumes that the **{form file}** has an .FRM extension.

dBASE will output the report in either logical or physical order, depending on whether or not the file was opened with an index (or indexed subsequent to opening and prior to reporting). If you want a special order, or if you are using groups and subtotals, sort or index the file before giving the **REPORT FORM** command.

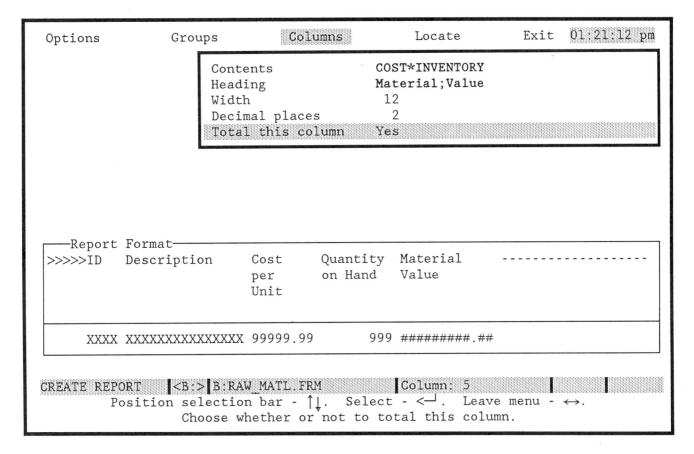

FIGURE 9-8 Field Definition Screen
Note: Items entered by the user are in **boldface**.

Alternate versions of the command may be used:

report form {form file} to print
report form {form file} to print noeject
report form {form file} for {condition}
report form {form file} to file {filename}

The effect of the first of these is to send the report to the printer. dBASE gives a page eject before it starts printing the report, unless you specify **NOEJECT** (second example). The default (*eject*) ensures that the report always starts on a new page, while the alternate (*no eject*) may save paper. (Eject options may also be set on the *Options* menu when defining the report format.) To produce the report that appears as Figure 9-1, you will give the command

report form raw_matl to print

Unless you specify a **FOR {condition}**, dBASE will include all data file records in the report. Logical conditions in report commands work just as they do everywhere else in dBASE.

```
   Options          Groups          Columns          Locate        Exit   01:26:13 pm
                       ┌──────────────────────────────────────────────────┐
                       │ Contents            DATE()-LAST_ORDER             │
                       │ Heading             Inventory;Age;(days)          │
                       │ Width               9                            │
                       │ Decimal places      0                            │
                       │ Total this column   No                           │
                       └──────────────────────────────────────────────────┘



 ┌─Report Format──────────────────────────────────────────────────────────┐
 │ Cost      Quantity   Material      Last      Inventory                  │
 │ per       on Hand    Value         Order     Age                        │
 │ Unit                               Date      (days)                     │
 ├──────────────────────────────────────────────────────────────────────── │
 │ XXX 99999.99       999 #########.## mm/dd/yy 999999999                  │
 └──────────────────────────────────────────────────────────────────────── ┘

 CREATE REPORT    |<B:>|B:RAW_MATL.FRM          |Column: 7      |         |
            Position selection bar - ↑↓.  Select - <┘.  Leave menu - ↔.
                  Choose whether or not to total this column.
```

FIGURE 9-9 Field Definition Screen
Note: Items entered by the user are in **boldface**.

Finally, the report may be sent to a file for inclusion in other documents by a word processor, or perhaps for importation into a spreadsheet. For instance, the report that appears as Figure 9-1 was produced with the command

report form raw_matl to file raw_matl

which created a file named RAW_MATL.TXT that was read into the text for this unit.

From the ASSIST Menu. REPORT FORM is found on the ■ *Retrieve* ■ menu. As with other options on this menu, you may specify a scope, build a search condition, or build a scope condition before executing the command.

GROUPS AND SUBTOTALS

If you want your report to be arranged in groups, with subtotals computed for each group, then you must do two things:

» Use the *Groups* menu to define the expression on which the groups will be divided.

» Index or sort the data file so all records with the same value of the expression are together. Normally, you will index on the same expression as you divide the groups.

Example. To group Chez Jacques inventory according to month of last order, we select the *Group* menu. The menu is completed as follows:

```
Group on expression       month(last_order)
Group heading             Month:
Summary report only       No
Page eject after group    No
Sub-group on expression
Sub-group heading
```

Before producing the report, we index the file on the LAST_ORDER field. The resulting report is illustrated in Figure 9-10.

GUIDED ACTIVITY

This activity requires you to use the report generation commands.

1. Follow the startup procedure for your version of dBASE as outlined in Unit 2.

2. **USE RAW_MATL**

3. Following the examples provided in this unit, create a report form file named RAW_MATL.

4. If you are using dBASE III Plus, the screen should look like Figure 9-9 after you have defined the last field. Use the <RIGHT> arrow to move to *Exit* then choose *Save*. Use the command **REPORT FORM RAW_MATL** to produce the report on the screen.

5. If the report on the screen is not correct, give the command **MODIFY REPORT RAW_MATL** and correct as necessary. Repeat steps 3 to 5 until your report looks like Figure 9-1 (except that the numbers in the last column will differ because the system date you enter will be different than the date in the example).

6. If the report is correct on the screen, give the command **REPORT FORM RAW_MATL TO PRINT** to print a copy.

7. Print the report in RMID order. (Hint: you will need an index file.)

✔ CHECKPOINT
What commands do you use to print this report?

Page No.   1
10/20/87
                         Raw Materials Inventory Report

                         prepared by Steven C. Ross

ID	Description	Cost per Unit	Quantity on Hand	Material Value	Last Order Date	Inventory Age (days)
** Month: 8						
0016	apple pie	0.16	346	55.36	08/15/87	66
** Subtotal **						
				55.36		
** Month: 9						
0005	pickle slice	0.03	900	27.00	09/15/87	35
0017	cherry pie	0.14	200	28.00	09/19/87	31
0015	16 oz. cup	0.05	400	20.00	09/28/87	22
0002	sp. sauce (oz.)	0.01	400	4.00	09/30/87	20
** Subtotal **						
				79.00		
** Month: 10						
0001	all-beef patty	0.10	100	10.00	10/01/87	19
0003	lettuce leaf	0.01	90	0.90	10/03/87	17
0008	regular bun	0.10	200	20.00	10/03/87	17
0014	12 oz. cup	0.03	300	9.00	10/04/87	16
0013	8 oz. cup	0.02	600	12.00	10/06/87	14
0007	sesame seed bun	0.12	400	48.00	10/08/87	12
0004	cheese slice	0.02	255	5.10	10/09/87	11
0009	catsup (oz.)	0.04	386	15.44	10/10/87	10
0006	ch. onion (oz.)	0.06	876	52.56	10/10/87	10
0012	Sprite (oz.)	0.05	700	35.00	10/12/87	8
0010	fren. fry (oz.)	0.01	999	9.99	10/12/87	8
0011	Coca Cola (oz.)	0.05	800	40.00	10/13/87	7
0019	6 oz. fry pack	0.03	500	15.00	10/15/87	5
0018	4 oz. fry pack	0.02	332	6.64	10/19/87	1
** Subtotal **						
				279.63		
*** Total ***						
				413.99		

FIGURE 9-10 Report with Groups and Subtotals

8. Print the report again, including only items which have more than $10 material value.

✔ **CHECKPOINT**
What commands do you use to print this report?

_____

9. Modify the report format to group the data by month of last order. Print the report again.

10. *For Additional Practice*: If you would like additional practice using the report commands, do the following.

   a. Open the TOURNEY file. Create a report which contains all of the fields in the file. Total the home- and visiting-team scores.

   b. Print your report in date-order.

   c. Change the report format to group on the DATE field; then print the report again.

11. When you have completed this Activity, exit dBASE. Remember to backup your work. If everything is proper, turn off the computer and return the dBASE software to the Lab Supervisor.

REVIEW QUESTIONS

1. Define the following terms:

   a. Report

   b. Report heading

   c. Report body

   d. Totals

   e. Report field

*2. Assume that you have created RAW_MATL.FRM. What sequence of commands would you give to print the report in RMID order?

DOCUMENTATION RESEARCH

Using the reference manual, determine the answers to the following questions which deal with the commands discussed in this unit. I recommend you also write the reference manual page number by the discussion of the command in this unit.

1. MODIFY REPORT {form file} — what is the options menu, and how is it accessed?

2. REPORT FORM {form file} — what is the effect of the **PLAIN** and **HEADING** options?

UNIT

10

LABEL GENERATION

This unit deals with the creation and production of labels. The illustrations in this unit deal with the creation of labels for Chez Jacques's inventory, an activity that you will perform at the end of the unit. The process of label creation is similar in both versions of dBASE III, although the screen displays of the original dBASE III are different from what you will see in this unit.

LEARNING OBJECTIVE

At the completion of this unit, you should be able to create labels.

IMPORTANT COMMANDS

CREATE LABEL {form file}
MODIFY LABEL {form file}
LABEL FORM {form file}

GENERAL CONSIDERATIONS

Labels are very much like reports, in that they are a method of displaying the data in a data file. The label commands are provided so you may create output in a form suitable for use as mailing or package labels. See Figure 10-1 for sample labels.

Data displayed in labels may be data file fields, character strings, or memory variables. As with the report commands, label creation is a two-step process. First, a label format file is created. Then, the labels are printed based on some or all of the data file data.

Before creating the label, you should acquire the medium on which the labels will be printed. This is usually a special computer form consisting of self-adhesive labels on a perforated backing sheet with pin feed holes along the edge. Depending on the size of the printer, this form may vary in width up to 15 inches, with one to four labels across.

```
Chez Jacques Inventory          Chez Jacques Inventory
RMID: 0014                      RMID: 0015
12 oz. cup                      16 oz. cup
Cost:       0.03                Cost:       0.05
Last Ordered: 10/04/87          Last Ordered: 09/28/87


Chez Jacques Inventory          Chez Jacques Inventory
RMID: 0018                      RMID: 0019
4 oz. fry pack                  6 oz. fry pack
Cost:       0.02                Cost:       0.03
Last Ordered: 10/19/87          Last Ordered: 10/15/87


Chez Jacques Inventory
RMID: 0002
sp. sauce (oz.)
Cost:       0.01
Last Ordered: 09/30/87
```

FIGURE 10-1 Sample Labels
Note: This is a partial set; not all labels are displayed.

Measure the individual label. A typical size is 3 7/16 inches wide by 15/16 inch high. The typical printer prints 10 characters per inch (wide) and 6 lines per inch (high), which means that five 34-character lines will fit on this label. Fortunately, that is the default label size for dBASE III. If your label or printer are different, you may have to change the default values on the label dimensions screen.

For practice and testing, you may use regular computer paper. The most common paper is 8 1/2 inches wide and 11 inches long, which will support 22 labels (2 wide by 11 deep).

The ranges of label specifications are as follows:

Width of label	1 - 120 characters
Height of label	1 - 16 lines
Left margin	0 - 250
Lines between labels	0 - 16 (vertical)
Spaces between labels	0 - 120 (horizontal)
Number of labels across	1 - 15
Width of all labels on line	1 - 250 characters

CREATING THE LABEL FORMAT

The label format is stored in a file with an .LBL extension. Two commands are provided to create or modify the label format file:

create label {form file}
modify label {form file}

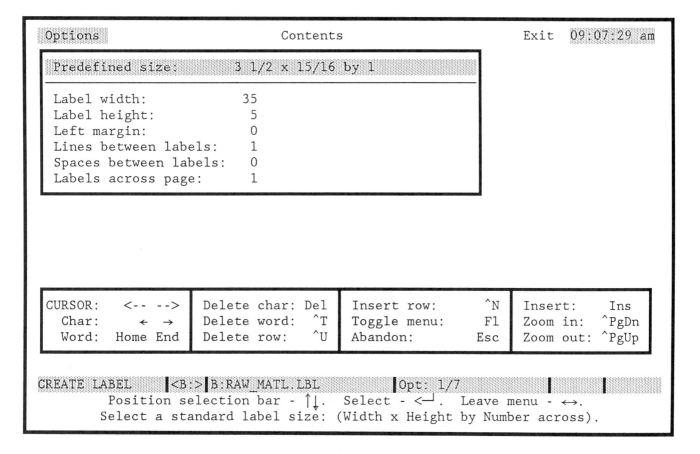

```
 Options                      Contents                    Exit  09:07:29 am

 Predefined size:        3 1/2 x 15/16 by 1

 Label width:            35
 Label height:           5
 Left margin:            0
 Lines between labels:   1
 Spaces between labels:  0
 Labels across page:     1




 CURSOR:    <-- -->  | Delete char: Del | Insert row:   ^N | Insert:    Ins
   Char:     ←   →   | Delete word: ^T  | Toggle menu:  F1 | Zoom in:  ^PgDn
   Word:  Home End   | Delete row:  ^U  | Abandon:     Esc | Zoom out: ^PgUp

 CREATE LABEL    |<B:>|B:RAW_MATL.LBL        |Opt: 1/7
        Position selection bar - ↑↓.  Select - <┘.  Leave menu - ↔.
        Select a standard label size: (Width x Height by Number across).
```

FIGURE 10-2 Initial Label Options Screen

Use either command to create or modify a *label format file* for use with the **LABEL** command. Example:

modify label raw_matl

Before issuing the command, open (**USE**) the data file from which the labels will be produced.

From the ASSIST Menu. CREATE LABEL is found on the ■ *Create* ■ menu, and **MODIFY LABEL** is found on the ■ *Modify* ■ menu. Although ■ *Create* ■ *Label* ■ can be used to modify an existing label format (by entering that label format's filename), it is most efficient to use ■ *Create* ■ for original creation and ■ *Modify* ■ for later changes. Once you identify the filename to dBASE, the remainder of the process is the same whether you initiate it from the dot prompt or from the **ASSIST** menu.

There are two screens for the creation or modification of the label format. The first screen (Figures 10-2 and 10-3) is provided for dimensional information; the second screen (Figures 10-4 and 10-5) is provided for label contents.

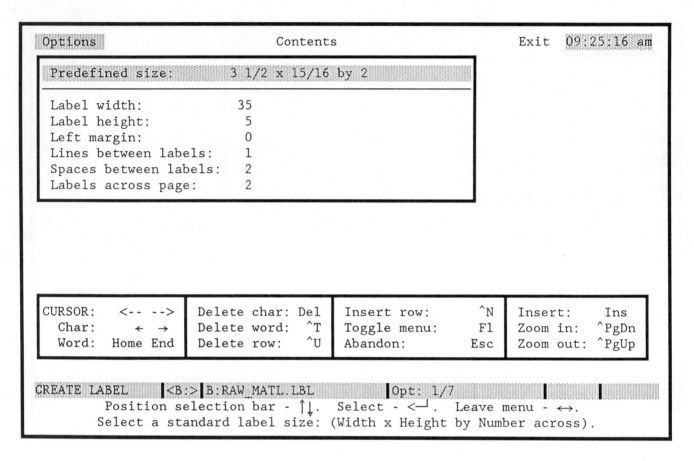

| Options | Contents | Exit | 09:25:16 am |

| Predefined size: | 3 1/2 x 15/16 by 2 |

Label width:	35
Label height:	5
Left margin:	0
Lines between labels:	1
Spaces between labels:	2
Labels across page:	2

CURSOR:	<-- -->	Delete char: Del	Insert row:	^N	Insert:	Ins
Char:	← →	Delete word: ^T	Toggle menu:	F1	Zoom in:	^PgDn
Word:	Home End	Delete row: ^U	Abandon:	Esc	Zoom out:	^PgUp

CREATE LABEL |<B:>|B:RAW_MATL.LBL |Opt: 1/7
Position selection bar - ↑↓. Select - <┘. Leave menu - ↔.
Select a standard label size: (Width x Height by Number across).

FIGURE 10-3 Completed Label Options Screen

Completing the dimensional screen is usually quite easy. In the example case, we wished to change the default predefined size to two labels across. We press <CR> and notice that one of the predefined sizes is *3 1/2 x 15/16 by 2*: exactly what we need. If dBASE had not given us what we wanted in one of the five predefined sizes, we could <ARROW> down and change the entries for width, height, and so on. Since we chose a predefined size, the entries below changed automatically (compare the *Labels across page:* entry in Figures 10-2 and 10-3).

The label contents screen is more of a challenge. We will discuss each line of the label contents; refer to Figure 10-1 for the finished product and to Figure 10-5 for the label structure. To enter or change the contents of a line, position the highlight on that line using <UP> and <DOWN>. Press <CR> to initiate editing of that line. You may enter the contents directly, or press F10 for a list of fields.

The first line of the label is composed of the text **'Chez Jacques Inventory'**. This is a character string that will be constant on each label. Note that such character strings are enclosed in quotation marks (single or double quotation marks, or brackets may be used).

The second line of the label is a combination of the character string **'RMID: '** and the field RMID, joined by the + (string concatenation) operator.

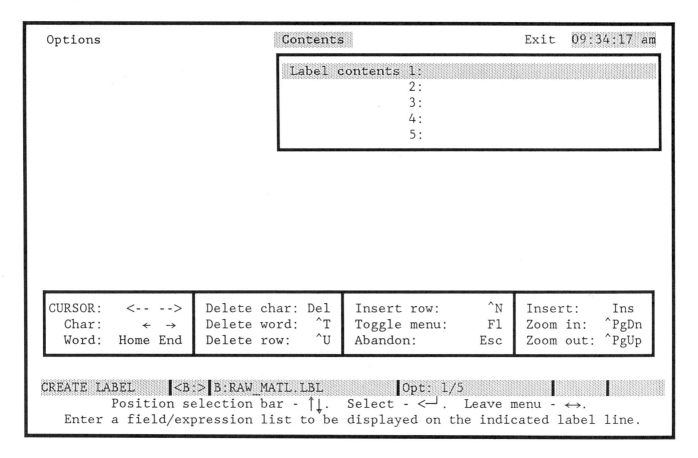

FIGURE 10-4 Blank Label Contents Screen

The third line consists of the field DESC.

The fourth line is the combination of the string 'Cost: ' and the expression **STR(COST,8,2)**. Recall from Unit 4 that the **STR(numeric expression,length,decimals)** (string function) evaluates a numeric expression and yields a character string. In this instance, the numeric expression is the COST field, and the length and decimals were set to be the same as the field (8 and 2). It is necessary to change the COST field to a string because it is combined with character-type data in this label line. If COST were used alone on this label line, then it would not have to be converted.[1]

The fifth line consists of the string '**Last Ordered: **' and the character equivalent of the LAST_ORDER field: **DTOC(LAST_ORDER)**. The **DTOC(date expression)** (date to character function) is used to convert the date-type field to character-type data for the expression on this label line. As with line 4, this conversion is necessary only when the date is combined with a character string on the same line.[1] Note, in Figure 10-5, that only part of the expression is visible: dBASE scrolls left and right as necessary to keep the cursor within the label contents box on the screen.

---

[1] In the original dBASE III, labels may not contain numeric- or date-type data, so information from fields of those types must be converted to character-type data in all cases.

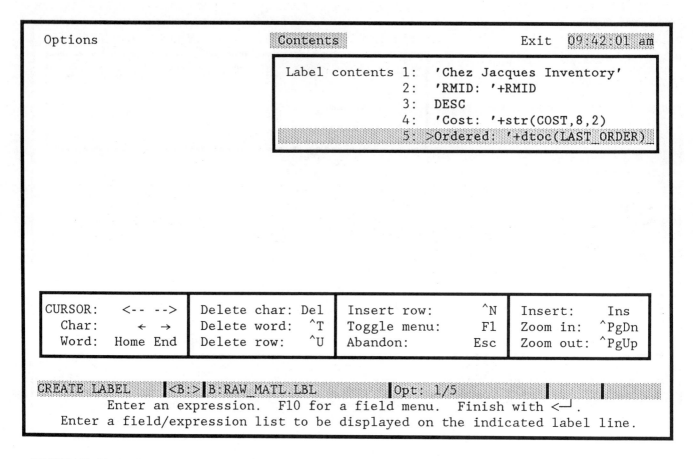

FIGURE 10-5 Completed Label Contents Screen
Note: Items entered by the user are in **boldface**.

Typical Mailing Labels

The labels for the Chez Jacques inventory represent a comprehensive example of what the **LABEL** command can accomplish. For many applications, however, simple mailing labels are all that is required. (The database for this label is discussed in Application D, which follows this unit.)

```
Season's Greetings from
    Ed and Bruce, to
Joyce Miller
1724 S 89 St
Prineville OR 97701
```

In this case, all data is character-type, and the main problems are printing the standard message ("Seasons Greetings . . . ") and removing excess blanks from fields such as the first name, last name, and city. The standard message is easy: just include it in quotation marks as we did for the inventory labels.

dBASE makes the removal of excess blanks on the right side of a field easy. When two fields are separated by a , (comma) in the label contents definition, dBASE will remove all blanks from the right side of the first field; then display the two fields with one space between them. Consider the following label contents, and compare it to the resulting label.

```
Label contents 1:   "Season's Greetings from"
               2:   "     Ed and Bruce, to "
               3:   first_name, last_name
               4:   street
               5:   city, state, zip
```

You will create labels such as this in Application D, which follows this unit.

PRODUCING THE LABELS

Once the label format is created or modified, the **LABEL FORM** command is used to produce the labels. The general form of the command is

label form {form file}

which will produce the labels on the screen. dBASE assumes that the {**form file**} has an .LBL extension.

dBASE will output the labels in either logical or physical order, depending on whether or not the file was opened with an index (or indexed subsequent to opening and prior to producing the labels). If you want a special order, sort or index the file before giving the **LABEL FORM** command.

Alternate versions of the command may be used:

label form {form file} sample to print
label form {form file} to print
label form {form file} for {condition}
label form {form file} to file {filename}

The effect of the first of these is to print test labels to assure proper alignment of the forms in the printer. The *test labels* will be a series of * (asterisks) covering the printed area defined in the first label screen.

The second version will send the labels to the printer. To produce the labels that appears as Figure 10-1, you will give the command

label form raw_matl to print

Unless you specify a **FOR {condition}**, dBASE will include all records in the data file in the labels. Conditional expressions in label commands work just as they do everywhere else in dBASE.

Finally, the labels may be sent to a file for inclusion in other documents with a word processor, or perhaps for importation into a spreadsheet. For instance, the labels that appear as Figure 10-1 were produced with the command

label form raw_matl to file raw_labl

which created a file named RAW_LABL.TXT that was read into the text for this unit.

From the ASSIST Menu. **LABEL FORM** is found on the ■ *Retrieve* ■ menu. As with other options on this menu, you may specify a scope, build a search condition, or build a scope condition before executing the command.

GUIDED ACTIVITY

This activity requires you to use the label generation commands.

1. Follow the startup procedure for your version of dBASE as outlined in Unit 2.

2. **USE RAW_MATL**

3. Following the examples provided in this unit, **CREATE LABEL RAW_MATL**

4. The screen should look like Figure 10-5 after you have defined the contents. Type Ctrl-End, or select ■ *Exit* ■ *Save* ■ to exit the creation process. Type **LABEL FORM RAW_MATL** to produce the labels on the screen.

5. If the labels on the screen are not correct, give the command **MODIFY LABEL RAW_MATL** and correct as necessary. Repeat steps 3 and 4 until your labels look like Figure 10-1 (except that you will have more labels than shown in that figure).

6. If the labels are correct on the screen, give the command **LABEL FORM RAW_MATL TO PRINT** to print a copy.

7. Print the labels in RMID order. (Hint: you will need an index file.)

✔ **CHECKPOINT**
What commands do you use to print the labels in RMID order?

_____

8. Print the labels for all items whose last-order date is 10/02/87 or later.

✔ **CHECKPOINT**
What command do you use?

_____

9. When you have completed this Activity, give the command **QUIT** to exit dBASE. Remember to backup your work. If everything is proper, turn off the computer and return the dBASE software to the Lab Supervisor.

DOCUMENTATION RESEARCH

Using the reference manual, determine the answers to the following questions which deal with the commands discussed in this unit. I recommend you also write the reference manual page number by the discussion of the command in this unit.

1. MODIFY LABEL {form file} — how do you select among the standard label types?

2. MODIFY LABEL {form file} — how can you remove excess blanks from a label line?

3. LABEL FORM {form file} — how does the **SAMPLE** option function?

APPLICATION

D   ED AND BRUCE SPECIALTIES (I)

This application exercise requires you to use the reporting and label commands in a data file.

1. Start by signing out the dBASE manual and software, as well as the Exercises Disk.

2. Insert the Exercises Disk in Drive A, and your data disk in Drive B.[1]

3. Reset or turn on the machine, as appropriate. Remember to enter the date and time as prompted.

4. Once the system is loaded and the date and time are set, give the command

   copy mailing.dbf b:

   which will copy a database file from the Exercises Disk to your disk.

5. Once the copying is finished, remove the Exercises Disk and follow the startup procedure for your version of dBASE as outlined in Unit 2.

6. Ed and Bruce Specialties (E&BS) is a small mail-order company that specializes in clothes, gadgets, and specialty foods. One of the data files kept by E&BS is a list of customer names, addresses, and whether or not that customer has ordered each of the three types of merchandise. This is the MAILING.DBF file.

---

[1] If you are using a fixed-disk PC, your instructor will tell you how to accomplish steps 2 through 4.

177

The structure of the file is

Field	Field name	Type	Width	Dec
1	LAST_NAME	Character	15	
2	FIRST_NAME	Character	10	
3	STREET	Character	26	
4	CITY	Character	14	
5	STATE	Character	2	
6	ZIP	Character	5	
7	CLOTHES	Logical	1	
8	GADGETS	Logical	1	
9	SP_FOOD	Logical	1	

Fields 1 through 6 are self-explanatory. Fields 7 through 9 are True if the customer has ordered that particular type of merchandise within the last three years, and False otherwise. If, for instance, you wished to obtain a list of all people who had ordered clothes, the command would be **LIST FOR CLOTHES**. These may be combined with the logical operators (e.g., **LIST FOR .NOT.CLOTHES** produces a list of those who have not ordered clothes). Other examples follow.

7. You have been asked to query the file and provide certain outputs:

   a. A list containing the names and cities of those who have purchased items in all of the three categories.

   b. A set of mailing labels for those who have ordered tools, but have not ordered clothes.

   c. A report showing names and states of those who have not ordered from any of the categories.

   Each of these outputs requires that you develop a logical condition. For the labels and report, you must also create format files. Name the format files EBS.FRM and EBS.LBL. (Remember that dBASE will automatically add the extensions .FRM and .LBL.) The following commands may give you some hints (but they are not the exact commands necessary to accomplish the necessary output).

   ```
   list off city,state,zip for clothes .and. gadgets
   label form ebs for sp_food .and. (.not. gadgets)
   report form ebs for .not. clothes
   ```

8. When you are finished with this Application, **QUIT** to exit dBASE. Remember to backup your work, turn off the computer, and return the dBASE software and Exercises Disk to the Lab Supervisor.

PART

3

ADVANCED
DATA BASE
OPERATIONS

In this part we will discuss advanced data base operations. These include the use of command files to automate data base operations as well as the use of multiple data files at once.

The first four units in this part address the creation and use of memory variables and command files. Command files are an extremely important part of the dBASE system because they allow you to save and repeat a series of often-used or lengthy commands. Through the use of command files, it is possible to automate much of what is done in dBASE, and to establish a system for use by those with less dBASE facility than yourself. Command files are written in dBASE's own *command language* using the commands discussed previously, as well as some others.

The purpose of these units is to provide familiarity with the essentials of dBASE programming. Those who have never written programs will probably need additional instruction before writing complex dBASE programs. These units are designed to provide a basis for the writing of simple but useful programs.

The remainder of the units discuss the use of more than one file at a time, establishing a link between two files, updating one file based on the information contained in another, creating a new file based on information contained in two others, and creating a file of subtotals.

The tools discussed in this part allow for the creation of very sophisticated applications. For instance, we will discuss how to link two files together to minimize the duplication of information, and how to use one file to update another. The treatment of these topics will be necessarily brief, but sufficient to expose you to the advanced capabilities of dBASE.

UNIT

11 MEMORY VARIABLES

This unit deals with the creation and use of memory variables. Although dBASE is a field-and record-oriented system, there are occasions when it is expedient or necessary to use memory variables for storage of intermediate results. These variables are usually discarded at the end of a program, but they may be written to a disk file for later recovery and use.

Memory variables can be used in the Direct mode of operation (i.e., from the dot prompt) or within command files (see the remainder of Part 3).

LEARNING OBJECTIVES

1. At the completion of this unit, you should know

    a. the difference between a variable and a field,

    b. the types of memory variables,

    c. how to create and name memory variables.

2. At the completion of this unit, you should be able to

    a. create memory variables,

    b. use memory variables in expressions,

    c. determine currently active memory variables,

    d. store memory variables in a disk file,

    e. retrieve memory variables from a disk file,

    f. remove memory variables from memory.

IMPORTANT COMMANDS

    STORE {expression} TO {memory variable}
    {memory variable} = {expression}
    AVERAGE {expression list} TO {memory variable list}
    COUNT TO {memory variable}
    SUM {expression list} TO {memory variable list}
    SAVE TO {filename}
    RESTORE FROM {filename}
    DISPLAY MEMORY
    RELEASE

CREATING MEMORY VARIABLES

Most of us who have programmed in a language such as FORTRAN or BASIC have used memory variables as a matter of course. The BASIC statement **LET A=5** creates a *memory variable* called A; the statement **LET C=A+B** adds the value of variables A and B and stores the result in C. We have become familiar with the idea that a *memory variable name* represents an address at which something (a number or text string) is stored. A given memory variable name represents one piece of data. Thus, we can answer the question "What is the value of A?" (a variable) with "The value of A is 5."

In dBASE, we have been using *fields* as the point of data storage. But a *field name* is not sufficient to locate a piece of data; we must also know the *record number*. For instance, referring to the RAW_MATL data file, we cannot answer the question "What is the value of COST?" (a field) until we have the answer to the question "What item are we discussing?" (a record). If asked "What is the cost of an all-beef patty?" then we may answer "The cost of an all-beef patty is ten cents."

This field and record approach is very useful when we want to store similar information about a number of items. It is less useful when we want to store a unique piece of information, such as the average of the item costs. For such instances, dBASE provides us with memory variables that are used very much like memory variables in BASIC.

Memory variables are created as a result of dBASE commands. Before creating variables, it is useful to understand what the various types of memory variables are and how they may be named.

Types of Memory Variables

Memory variable data types parallel the types of fields. There are four available types: Character, Date, Numeric, and Logical.

The type of a memory variable is determined by the method by which it is created, and a subsequent operation may change the type of the variable.. If character or text data is stored in the variable, then it will be a character-type variable, and so forth with numeric and logical data.

Date variables are created when date data are stored in the variable. The result of a date plus or minus a date will be a numeric variable, but a date plus or minus a number is another date. This makes sense:

07/24/87 - 07/14/87 = 10
01/14/86 + 5 = 01/19/86

(These equations are not valid dBASE commands; they are intended to illustrate the relationship between numeric- and date-type data.)

Memory Variable Names

Memory variable names follow the same rules as field names. The name must start with a letter, and can be up to ten characters long. Acceptable characters are letters (A through Z), numerals (0 through 9), and _ (the underscore). There is no difference between upper- and lowercase.

Each memory variable will have a unique name. Unlike variables in BASIC and some other languages, variable names in dBASE do not denote data type. You may give memory variables the same names as fields, but that practice can lead to confusion.

I start memory variable names with **M_** to differentiate them from data file fields (e.g., **M_NAME** is a memory variable that corresponds to the field NAME in my data file). If you do create a memory variable with the same name as a field, then you may later refer to that variable by preceding the name with **M->** (e.g., M->NAME). The *arrow* is entered as the minus sign followed by the greater-than sign.

The following are legitimate memory variable names:

**sum
count2
r2d2
dbase_iii**

The name of a given memory variable is assigned when the variable is created with one of the commands discussed in the following sections.

Commands that Create Memory Variables

Memory variables are created by the following commands: **STORE, AVERAGE, COUNT, SUM, INPUT, ACCEPT, WAIT,** and **PARAMETERS.** Memory variables must be created from the dot prompt; it is not possible to create them from the **ASSIST** menu.

The STORE Command is the fundamental variable-creating command. It is the equivalent of a **LET** statement in BASIC. The general form is

store {expression} to {memory variable}

which computes the value of {expression} if necessary, and stores the result in {memory variable}. The variable will be created by this command if it did not already exist.

Examples:

> store 'West Virginia' to state
> store 200000 to income
> store income*.85 to taxes
> store income-taxes to net_inc

You may use the alternate version:

> {memory variable} = {expression}

for example, **STATE='West Virginia'**

The AVERAGE, COUNT, and SUM Commands were introduced in Part 2. The results of the commands may be stored in memory variables using the form

> average {expression list} to {memory variable list}
> count to {memory variable}
> sum {expression list} to {memory variable list}

See the earlier discussion for more detail about these commands. You must provide a memory variable name for each sum or average requested. Examples (using RAW_MATL data file):

> average cost,inventory,cost*inventory to avgcost,avginven,avgvalue
> count for cost*inventory>10 to highvalue
> sum cost,inventory,cost*inventory to sumcost,suminven,sumvalue

The ACCEPT, INPUT, and WAIT Commands will be discussed in a later unit.

The PARAMETERS Command is used in advanced programming that is beyond the scope of this book.

MANAGING MEMORY VARIABLES

Memory variables usually are created for temporary use by dBASE, but may be saved in a disk file for later reference. This section discusses housekeeping: knowing what variables are in use, keeping the computer free of extraneous variables, and moving variables to and from disk storage.

In Memory

Memory variables normally reside in the memory of the computer. Because there are limits to how many variables can be used and how much room is available, the programmer must be aware of what variables are currently in use and of how to remove those that are no longer needed.

```
. use raw_matl index raw_matl
. display
Record#  RMID DESC              COST INVENTORY LAST_ORDER
      8  0001 all-beef patty    0.10       100 10/01/87

. ? cost
   0.10
. cost=cost*2
      0.20
. ? cost
   0.10
. ? m->cost
       0.20
. display memory
COST        pub  N         0.20 (        0.20000000)
   1 variables defined,      9 bytes used
 255 variables available,  5991 bytes available

. display
Record#  RMID DESC              COST INVENTORY LAST_ORDER
      8  0001 all-beef patty    0.10       100 10/01/87

. m_cost=cost*2
      0.20
. ? cost
   0.10
. ? m->cost
       0.20
. ? m_cost
       0.20
. display memory
COST        pub  N         0.20 (        0.20000000)
M_COST      pub  N         0.20 (        0.20000000)
   2 variables defined,     18 bytes used
 254 variables available,  5982 bytes available

.
```

```
Command Line    |<B:>|RAW_MATL              |Rec: 8/19         |         |
```

Enter a dBASE III PLUS command.

FIGURE 11-1 Memory Variable Illustration
Note: Commands entered by the user are in **boldface**.

The **DISPLAY MEMORY** command displays name, type, and contents of all currently active memory variables, as well as bytes of memory used by the variables. This command is useful in debugging. This command is among those illustrated in Figure 11-1. The **DISPLAY MEMORY** command may be given by pressing the F7 key.

The **RELEASE** command is used to delete all (**RELEASE ALL**) or selected (**RELEASE {list}**) memory variables so that the space may be reused for other memory variables. This command is seldom needed in dBASE III, but is available for instances when you wish to clear all or many memory variables.

On Disks

On occasion, you may wish to save the current values of memory variables to a disk file for later use. The command

save to {filename}

saves all currently defined memory variables to **{filename}.MEM** (the extension is added automatically by dBASE). You may direct the command to save only a portion of the variables.

To retrieve the variables, use one of the following commands:

restore from {filename}
restore from {filename} additive

These commands will restore saved memory variables from **{filename}.MEM**. The first version will erase all currently active memory variables; the second version will add the restored variables to those already present, as capacity permits.

Examples:

save to memfile
restore from memfile
restore from memfile additive

USING MEMORY VARIABLES IN CALCULATIONS

Typically, you create memory variables as you work, to hold intermediate results. Often you will use these results in later calculations. Refer to the example in Figure 11-1. We will discuss the entries in **boldface**, which I typed. First, I used the raw material file with its index. The first item in index (logical) order is *all-beef patty*, which is evident after the **DISPLAY** command. **? COST** tells us that the COST field is 0.10 (recall that the ? is the *what-is* command).

Next, the memory variable COST is created with the command **COST=COST*2**. The result is 0.20, but when I asked dBASE **? COST**, the answer was 0.10, the value of the field COST. To learn the value of the variable COST, I had to use the command **? M->COST**.

The **DISPLAY MEMORY** command also tells me the value of COST, as well as how many variables are defined and available, and how many bytes are used and available. The **DISPLAY** command assures me that no changes have been made to the original record.

```
. sum cost*inventory to value
     19 records summed
    cost*inventory
         413.99
. display memory
COST        pub    N         0.20  (          0.20000000)
M_COST      pub    N         0.20  (          0.20000000)
VALUE       pub    N       413.99  (        413.99000000)
    3 variables defined,         27 bytes used
  253 variables available,     5973 bytes available

. ? value
       413.99
. sum inventory to k
     19 records summed
    inventory
         8784
. ? value/k
         0.05
. unit_val=value/k
         0.05
. display memory
COST        pub    N         0.20  (          0.20000000)
M_COST      pub    N         0.20  (          0.20000000)
VALUE       pub    N       413.99  (        413.99000000)
K           pub    N        8784   (       8784.00000000)
UNIT_VAL    pub    N         0.05  (          0.04713001)
    5 variables defined,         45 bytes used
  251 variables available,     5955 bytes available

.
```

Command Line |<B:>|RAW_MATL |Rec: EOF/19 | |

Enter a dBASE III PLUS command.

FIGURE 11-2 Using Memory Variables in Data Analysis
Note: Commands entered by the user are in **boldface**.

Typing -> to display memory variables is confusing and awkward, so I decide to use a different variable name. I give the command **M_COST=COST*2**, which creates a variable M_COST. Note the results of the three commands **? COST**, **? M->COST**, and **? M_COST**. A final **DISPLAY MEMORY** tells me that I now have two memory variables.

The example presented in Figure 11-1 is rather simple. A more complex example, determining the total value and average value per unit of Chez Jacques's inventory, is illustrated in Figure 11-2. First we use the command **SUM COST*INVENTORY TO VALUE** to create a variable named VALUE with the numeric result contained therein. To see the contents of VALUE, we could either **DISPLAY MEMORY** or **? VALUE**. In the example, both are used.

Next, we compute the average inventory value per unit of raw material. We give two commands, **SUM INVENTORY TO K** and **? VALUE/K**, to yield the answer. As usual, dBASE displays only two decimal places. To achieve a more precise result, the result was stored in a memory variable (**UNIT_VAL=VALUE/K**) and the contents of memory were displayed again.

USING MEMORY VARIABLES IN COMMANDS: THE MACRO FUNCTION

Character-type memory variables may be included in commands through the use of the *macro function*:

    &   *Macro function*, substitutes the contents of a character-type memory variable into an expression. This function is used primarily in command files.

For instance, if the memory variable FIELD contained the string 'first_name,last_name', then the command **LIST &FIELD** would be the equivalent of **LIST FIRST_NAME,LAST_NAME**.

Using the macro function with memory variables allows you to effectively rewrite command files as they execute. A portion of a command can be input by the user, or assigned through program logic, then the macro command is used to interject that portion of the command into the program. This capability will be demonstrated in Application E.

THE IMMEDIATE-IF FUNCTION

dBASE III Plus (but not the original dBASE) provides a very useful function called the *immediate-if function*:

    IIF(condition,expression1,expression2) *Immediate-if function*, returns expression1 if the condition is true, otherwise returns expression2.

This function can be used to set the value of a memory variable, an {expression} in a list, or a report or label field, based on a certain logical condition. When creating or changing a memory variable, the function is used as the {expression} as follows:

    store iif(condition,expression1,expression2) to {memory variable}
    {memory variable} = iif(condition,expression1,expression2)

Both expression1 and expression2 must be the same data-type (Character, Numeric, Date, or Logical), and the result of the function will be of that type. Consider the following examples:

    highcost = iif(cost>.10,.T.,.F.)   *HIGHCOST is a logical-type memory variable which is true if the cost of the item exceeds .10, false otherwise.*

    highnote = iif(cost>.10,'high','low')   *HIGHNOTE is a character-type memory variable which has the value* high *if the cost of the item exceeds .10,* low *otherwise.*

reord_date = iif(date( )-last_order > 30, date( ), last_order+30)   *REORD_DATE is a date-type variable which has the value of today's date if it has been more than 30 days since the last order, otherwise it has the value 30 days past the last-order.*

reord_days = iif(date( )-last_order > 30, 0, last_order+30-date( ))   *REORD_DAYS is a numeric-type variable which has the value of 0 (zero) if it has been more than 30 days since the last order, otherwise it is the number of days from today to the date which is 30 days past the last-order date.*

list desc, iif(date( )-last_order > 30, 0, last_order+30-date( ))   *This command will list all descriptions and reorder dates.*

Each of the preceding IIF functions could be used as the contents of a report field or as part of a label line.

GUIDED ACTIVITY

This activity requires you to use the memory variable commands.

1. Follow the startup procedure for your version of dBASE as outlined in Unit 2.

2. Duplicate the example illustrated in Figure 11-1.

3. Compute the total raw material value (cost times the quantity on hand for all items) and store the result in a variable called VALUE.

✔ **CHECKPOINT**
What command do you use to compute this sum?

_____

4. Compute the total number of items on hand and store the result in a variable called K.

✔ **CHECKPOINT**
What command do you use to compute this sum?

_____

5. Compute and print on the screen the average value per unit (i.e., VALUE/K). Do not create another memory variable.

✔ **CHECKPOINT**
What command do you use to compute and print this average?

_____

6. Use a memory variable to determine a more precise result.

7. *For Additional Practice*: If you would like more practice working with memory variables, do the following.

   a. Open the file TOURNEY with the index you built based on the DATE field. (If you do not remember the name of the index, you can give the **INDEX** command again.)

   b. Move the cell pointer to the first game.

   c. Store the name of the winner (i.e., the team with the highest score) in a memory variable called WINNER. Store the winning score in WINSCORE. Do the same for the loser (LOSER) and their score (LOSESCORE). Use the IIF( ) function.

   d. Display the memory to see the result.

   e. Move the cell pointer to the championship (last) game. Repeat Step c. Remember that you can repeat the last twenty commands by pressing <UP> (and <DOWN>) to display each of those commands, editing as necessary, then pressing <CR>.

   f. Display the memory again. The original WINNER, LOSER, and so on should have been replaced by the new values.

   g. Note that the memory variables were assigned values based on the current record. We can use this feature to great advantage in a report. Modify the report you created at the end of Unit 9 as follows:

      » Instead of printing the home team name in column 1, print the winner's name using the IIF( ) function you used to create the memory variable WINNER.

      » Print the winner's score in the second column.

      » Print the loser's name in the third column.

      » Print the loser's score in the fourth column.

      » Change column headings as necessary.

   h. Print your revised report.

8. When you have completed this activity, give the command **QUIT** to exit dBASE. Remember to backup your work. If everything is proper, turn off the computer and return the dBASE software to the Lab Supervisor.

REVIEW QUESTIONS

*1. What is the difference between a variable and a field?

2. What are the types of memory variables?

3. How would you create and name the following memory variables?

   *a. A variable called NAME that contains the string 'Genghis Khan'

   *b. A variable called AGE that contains the number 16

4. What expression would you write to accomplish the following?

   *a. Add the string 'the Magnificent' to NAME

   *b. Double AGE, with the result in OLDER

5. What command would you use to determine currently active memory variables?

*6. What command would you use to store all memory variables in a disk file with the filename MEMORY?

*7. What command would you use to retrieve memory variables from the disk file MEMORY, without destroying the currently active variables?

8. What command would you use to remove all memory variables from memory?

DOCUMENTATION RESEARCH

Using the reference manual, determine the answers to the following questions which deal with the commands discussed in this unit. I recommend you also write the reference manual page number by the discussion of the command in this unit.

1. STORE {expression} TO {memory variable} — how can you store the same expression to several memory variables?

2. {memory variable} = {expression} — if the memory variable already existed, what happens with a subsequent **STORE** operation?

3. SAVE TO {filename} — how do you save only some of the memory variables?

4. RESTORE FROM {filename} — what is the effect of the **ADDITIVE** option?

5. DISPLAY MEMORY — numeric variables are displayed in two ways. What are they?

6. RELEASE — what are the functions of the **LIKE** and **EXCEPT** options?

Using the reference manual, answer the following questions:

7. How many memory variables can be active at one time?

8. What is the maximum amount of memory available for memory variables?

9. What is the maximum or default length of each type of memory variable?

10. How is the & (macro function) used?

UNIT

12

COMMAND FILE CREATION AND PROGRAM FLOW

The ability to program a series of steps so they can be repeated, even by people unfamiliar with dBASE commands, is a major feature of dBASE. You can, for instance, write a program to automate the production of various reports and mailing labels, or to handle the various inquiries that have been the subject of earlier units. Command files must be created and executed from the dot prompt, and are not available on the **ASSIST** menu.

This unit deals with the creation of dBASE command files (programs and procedures), and the commands that control program flow. Unit 13 discusses commands for input and output, which are essential to most program operations.

LEARNING OBJECTIVES

1. At the completion of this unit, you should know

   a. how command files differ from immediate mode,

   b. what a program is,

   c. what a loop is.

2. At the completion of this unit, you should be able to

   a. create a command file,

   b. create a program that processes all records in a file,

   c. create a program that uses conditional logic,

   d. execute a command file.

IMPORTANT COMMANDS

MODIFY COMMAND {filename}
DO {filename}
CLEAR ALL
NOTE or *
DO WHILE {condition} . . . ENDDO
SKIP
EXIT
LOOP
DO CASE . . . CASE {condition} . . . OTHERWISE . . . ENDCASE
IF {condition} . . . ELSE . . . ENDIF
RETURN
CANCEL

COMMAND FILES VERSUS IMMEDIATE MODE

To this point, we have used dBASE in the *immediate mode*: commands are executed as soon as we press <CR>. With *command files*, the commands are stored in a disk file until we direct dBASE to execute them. Because the commands are in a disk file, we can reissue the commands several times, and we can edit the command file if necessary to correct errors or change what it does.

Following are some guidelines for when to use command files. I recommend that you build a command file whenever:

» You will use a series of several commands.

» You will use the same command a number of times.

» You are using a complicated command, one that you may have to revise several times before it does what you wish it would.

On the other hand, you would probably not use a command file if you were going to use a single, simple command once. These guidelines are not strict, however. dBASE will allow you to issue a lengthy series of commands in the immediate mode, or to put a simple command into a command file.

A VERY SHORT LESSON IN PROGRAMMING

Although this book is not intended to be a book on programming, a few notes on program development are in order before we discuss the various commands and functions used in dBASE programming. These should be helpful to those of you who have little or no experience writing computer programs, as well as useful to those of you who are experienced programmers.

There is one fundamental principle that will guide almost all of your programming with dBASE:

Think of a database as a box full of cards, each card having the information about a different object. Describe what you want to accomplish, and how to accomplish it, as if you were telling another person how to accomplish the task using the box of cards.

If you can describe the task in these terms, then you should have no problem converting the description to a dBASE program.

Steps in Writing a Program

The following is an outline of steps that I follow when developing a program.

First, Make Some Notes:

    a. Objective of the Program

    b. Input

        » What is needed

        » Where it comes from (disk file, keyboard)

    c. What the Program Must Accomplish

        » Calculations

        » Decisions

    d. Output

        » What is to be output

        » To where (device, disk file)

        » In what format

Then, List the Sequence of Steps:

    1. What happens first

    2. What happens second

    3. . . .

    4. . . .

    5. . . .

> Make special note of steps which are
>
>   » Repeated
>
>   » Executed only under some conditions

99. How does the program know to stop?

Once you have outlined the sequence of the program, you may put appropriate dBASE commands by each of the steps. Some steps will require multiple commands; and sometimes you may combine several steps into one command. The important lesson is this: *Figure out what you are attempting to accomplish, and how to accomplish it in general terms, before attempting to create a dBASE program.*

A Sample Problem

> *Chez Jacques is concerned about the age of some of the items in his inventory. He wants a program that will scan through his raw material data file and display on the screen any raw material item for which the last order date is more than ten days prior to the current date. Although a list would suffice, Jacques eventually will want to be able to enter a new order for some of the items displayed; therefore, a command file will be necessary.*

Steps in Writing a Program, Annotated

First, Make Some Notes:

a. Objective of the Program   *to display all raw materials more than 10 days old*

b. Input

>> What is needed   *today's date, date of last order, other information such as description*

>> Where it comes from (disk file, keyboard)   *today's date from DATE( ) function, remainder from RAW_MATL.DBF*

c. What the Program Must Accomplish

>> Calculations   *subtract last order date from today's date*

>> Decisions   *if difference is greater than 10, display information*

d. Output

>> What is to be output   *item description, last order date, cost, amount in inventory*

>> To where (device, disk file)   *screen*

>> In what format   *not specified*

Then, List the Sequence of Steps:

1. *open RAW_MATL file*

2. *check first record for over 10 days old*

3. *if over 10 days old, display*

4. *go to next record*

5. *repeat from step 2.*

99. How does the program know to stop? *when the end of the RAW_MATL file is reached*

Make special note of steps which are

Repeated *steps 2-4*

Executed only under some conditions *step 3*

INPUT, OUTPUT, RECORD, AND ENVIRONMENT FUNCTIONS

This is a broad class of functions which are used primarily in command (program) files. We will introduce them as needed throughout Part 3.

BOF( ) *Beginning of file function*, this is a logical function that is true if the beginning of the file has been reached. This function is used in conjunction with search operations. Note that even when you are at the first logical or physical record, you have not reached the beginning of the file. You only reach the beginning when you try to move up (back) from the first record. (See "Skipping Through a File" later in this unit for an example.)

EOF( ) *End of file function*, this is a logical function that is true if the end of file has been reached. This function is used in conjunction with search operations. Note that even when you are at the last logical or physical record, you have not reached the end of the file. You only reach the end when you try to move down (forward) from the last record. (See "Skipping Through a File" later in this unit for an example.)

FILE(string expression) *File function*, this is a logical function that is true if a file whose name matches the string expression exists and false otherwise. This function is used to determine whether or not a given file is on the disk, and is useful in some programming situations to determine whether or not the user has put the proper disk in a specific disk drive.

? file("RAW_MATL.DBF") *Will return* **.T.** *if the file is on the default disk;* **.F.** *otherwise. Note that the extension must be specified.*

? file("A:RAW_MATL.DBF")   *Will return* **.T.** *if the file is on the disk in Drive A;* **.F.** *otherwise.*

? file("RAW_MATL")   *Will return* **.F.**, *unless you have a file named RAW_MATL without any extension on your disk.*

CREATING COMMAND FILES

A command file is a series of dBASE commands that are stored on the data disk (usually in Drive B on a floppy-disk system, or the only drive on a hard-disk system). To create such a file from within dBASE, type the command

    modify command {filename}

Short command files (up to 4096 bytes in length) are easily written using this command. If you do not specify an extension, dBASE will add a .PRG extension to {filename}. For command files more than fifty lines in length, you are advised to use a word processor such as WordStar.

After you type **MODIFY COMMAND**, the screen will clear (see Figure 12-1). You enter the command file using full-screen editing keys (illustrated in the top portion of Figure 12-1); the process is very similar to creating a file in most word processors. Press <CR> at the end of each command line. If the line is too long, dBASE will wrap the line to the next line. You may also continue a long line by typing ;<CR> (a semicolon followed by <CR>) and entering the remainder of the command on the following line. Example:

    This is an example of how you would continue a very ;
       long command onto a second line.

When you are finished entering the commands, type either ^W or ^End (Ctrl-W or Ctrl-End) to exit and save. If you have made changes that you do not wish to keep, type either ^Q or Esc, and the previous version will remain the current version.

To make further changes to the file, simply issue the same **MODIFY COMMAND** {filename} from the dot prompt. See Figure 12-2 for an example of a short command file as it appears during the modification process.

COMMANDS TO CONTROL PROGRAM FLOW

Starting a Program

The **DO** command is used to invoke (execute) a command file:

    do {filename}

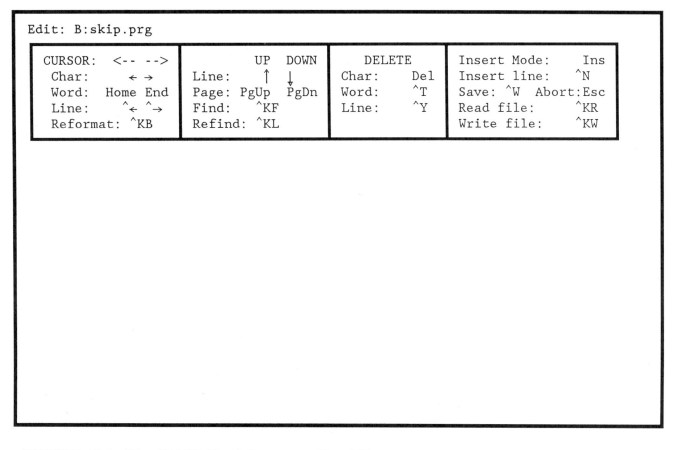

FIGURE 12-1 The dBASE Word Processor, New File

Unless you specify a file extension, dBASE assumes a .PRG extension. Think of all command files as subroutines; therefore, **DO {filename}** can either initiate a program from the dot prompt, or call a program or subprogram from within a command file. If the program terminates with a **RETURN** statement, then control returns to the statement following the **DO** command.

dBASE III also contains a provision for *procedure files*. A procedure file may contain several procedures that operate in the same manner as program files. (See the reference manual descriptions of **PROCEDURE** and **SET PROCEDURE** for more detail; these commands are not covered further in this manual.)

In dBASE III, memory variables created by subordinate programs or procedures are released when the program or procedure is exited, unless you make provisions for their retention. (See discussions of **PARAMETERS**, **PRIVATE**, and **PUBLIC** in the reference manual.)

Resetting dBASE. The **CLEAR ALL** command is used to reset dBASE. Any open data files are unused and closed, all memory variables are released, and work area 1 is selected. It is usually a good idea to start a main program with **CLEAR ALL**, to ensure that data or files from previous work do not contaminate your new activity.

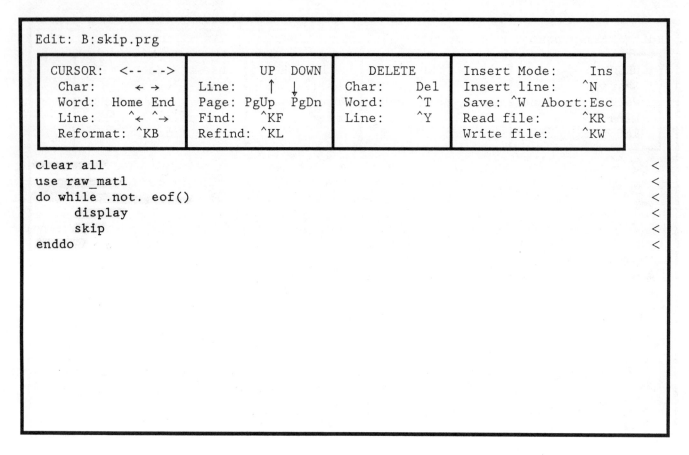

```
Edit: B:skip.prg

CURSOR:   <-- -->                 UP  DOWN        DELETE          Insert Mode:      Ins
  Char:        ← →        Line:    ↑    ↓         Char:    Del    Insert line:      ^N
  Word:   Home End        Page: PgUp  PgDn        Word:    ^T     Save: ^W  Abort:Esc
  Line:      ^← ^→        Find:    ^KF            Line:    ^Y     Read file:        ^KR
  Reformat: ^KB           Refind: ^KL                            Write file:       ^KW

clear all                                                                              <
use raw_matl                                                                           <
do while .not. eof()                                                                   <
    display                                                                            <
    skip                                                                               <
enddo                                                                                  <
```

FIGURE 12-2 The dBASE Word Processor with File
Note: Lines entered by the user are in **boldface**.

Comments. **NOTE** or * as the first nonspace character in a line allows *comments* to be placed in the command file. The comments are not normally displayed on the screen and thus are available only when the program is being edited. Comments may also be placed on the same line as commands, to the right of the command. Precede the comment with **&&**. Examples:

   * The following command displays the current record
   display   && This line displays the current record

The Loop

One of the fundamental aspects of almost every programming language is the *loop*. Loops allow the program to repeat the same instructions several times. One of the fundamental errors of programming is to create an *endless loop*, one that is not programmed to end. We use loops when we identify steps which are repeated in our analysis of the program; and we must remember to instruct dBASE when to stop executing the loop.

Starting the Loop. In dBASE, the loop is initiated by the **DO WHILE** command and terminated by the **ENDDO** command. Between these two commands are statements that are to be repeated. The fundamental structure of the loop is

> **do while {condition}**
>> *statements*
> **enddo**

The {**condition**} of a loop is a logical condition like the {**scope condition**} introduced in Unit 6. If {condition} is a logical true, then the *statements* following the **DO WHILE** are executed until **ENDDO** is encountered. The {**condition**} is reevaluated and control either jumps to the statement following **ENDDO** (if {**condition**} is false) or the *statements* are executed again.

Indentation. In the examples in this book, I indent statements within a loop. Although indentation is not necessary, it does make the program easier to read and is strongly recommended.

Exiting the Loop. There are four ways to exit a **DO WHILE** loop, and you must employ one or more of these to avoid endless loops:

» Change the value of {**condition**} within the loop so that is is no longer true. This may occur as a result of reading records (if a field is part of the {**condition**}), reaching the beginning or end of the file (if the BOF( ) or EOF( ) functions are in the {**condition**}), or a program statement which changes the value of a variable which is part of the {**condition**}.

» Use the **EXIT** command.

» Use the **RETURN** command.

» Use the **CANCEL** command.

The last two commands are discussed later in this unit.

The **EXIT** command is used within a **DO WHILE** loop to transfer control to the statement immediately following the **ENDDO** statement.

The **LOOP** command is used within the body of a **DO WHILE** loop to skip all commands up to the **ENDDO** command. This causes the initiating {**condition**} to be reevaluated, but does not necessarily lead to an exit from the loop.

Skipping through a File

A primary use of loops is to process (read, print, or change) every record in a data file. To move the record pointer to the next record and read the contents of all fields of that record, use the **SKIP** command. **SKIP** by itself will advance the pointer one record, **SKIP 5** will move forward five records, and **SKIP -18** will move back (toward the beginning) eighteen records.

Processing All Records in a File. To process all records in a file, we normally would wish to start with the first record and proceed one record at a time until the end of the file is reached. To accomplish this, we should remember a few things. First, a file that has just been opened is positioned at the first record. Second, **SKIP** moves forward (toward the end of the file) and reads one record at a time. Finally, the function **EOF( )** is true when we have attempted to read (i.e., **SKIP**) after the last record in the file.

The following program would open the file RAW_MATL, read and display each record, and terminate when the last record had been read. I suggest that you create the program and try it.

```
clear all
use raw_matl
do while .not. eof( )
    display
    skip
enddo
```

In some cases, you may wish to process records from the logical or physical end of the file, instead of from the beginning. This is often the case when you have indexed the data in order of dates, and you wish to display the data with the most recent record first. The following program would be used to display our raw materials from the most-recently-ordered material to the first-ordered material.

```
clear all
use raw_matl
index on last_order to temp
go bottom
do while .not. bof( )
    display
    skip -1
enddo
```

In addition to, or instead of, the **DISPLAY** command, the program could have several other commands that process each record in turn. The program might be written to ask you if you wish to reorder. Or, the program might be set up to allow the user to change costs. What is accomplished by the program is determined by the objectives for the program, and a clear statement of objectives is important at the beginning of the programming process.

Conditional Operations

Conditional operations allow the computer program to make some of our decisions for us. These operations are necessary when we have identified steps which must be executed only under certain conditions. Consider the teacher who must assign grades to her class. She may have a rule such as "90 and above are A, 80 to 89 are B . . . " She could write a computer program that would read the numeric score and assign a letter grade based on the score. The challenge is to write the program so that it makes the decision the way we want it to.

dBASE offers two sets of conditional commands. The first, based on the **IF** command, is best used when there are two choices, such as true or false, male or female. The second set, based on the **DO CASE** command, is used when there are multiple choices, such as when the teacher assigns grades.

The IF Command provides a means for selecting one of two choices. The general format of the command is

```
if {condition}
    statements
else
    statements
endif
```

If the {condition} is true, then the *statements* between the **IF** and the **ELSE** (or **ENDIF** if there is no **ELSE**) will be executed. If {condition} is false, then *statements* following the **ELSE** (if any) will be executed. **IF** commands may be nested up to any level, but improperly nested commands will lead to embarrassment worse than ring around the collar.

The following program would read all items in the RAW_MATL file and display only those that had been ordered more than ten days ago. (This command file solves Chez Jacques's "Sample Problem" discussed at the beginning of this unit.) In this case, the **ELSE** clause is not used.

```
clear all
use raw_matl
do while .not. eof( )
    if (date( )-last_order)>10
        display
    endif
    skip
enddo
```

Recall the IIF( ) function introduced in Unit 11. IIF( ) is faster than the **IF** command when storing values to variables, but cannot be used when the situation calls for conditional execution of a command, as in the previous example.

The DO CASE Command is more flexible than **IF** or IIF( ) because multiple choices are accommodated in one set of statements. The general form is

```
do case
    case {condition}
        statements
    case {condition}
        statements
    otherwise
        statements
endcase
```

DO CASE will evaluate each **CASE** {condition} until it finds one that is true, then execute the *statements* up to the next **CASE** {condition}, upon which it exits to **ENDCASE**. If no **CASE** {condition} is true, then the *statements* following **OTHERWISE** will be executed. Any number of **CASE** {condition} statements may be included, and the **OTHERWISE** statement is optional. This command is especially useful when constructing menus.

Recall the example of the teacher, who might write a program that included the following (assuming that SCORE and GRADE are fields in the file GRADEBK):

```
clear all
use gradebk
do while .not. eof( )
    do case
        case score >= 90
            replace grade with 'A'
        case score >= 80
            replace grade with 'B'
        case score >= 70
            replace grade with 'C'
        case score >= 60
            replace grade with 'D'
        otherwise
            replace grade with 'F'
    endcase
    skip
enddo
```

Once you can follow the logic of the preceding program, answer this question: What prevents the assignment of a D to a person whose score is 75, which is greater than 60?

Exiting the Program

Three commands may be used to exit from a program or procedure. The **RETURN** command is used to exit a command file or a procedure, and will either return to the line following the **DO {filename}** command that called the command file (as a subprogram to another command file) or return to the dot prompt if the command file was executed directly. Normally **RETURN** is the last line in a command file. **RETURN** also may be used in conjunction with **IF** or **DO CASE** logic. The physical end of a command file is equivalent to a **RETURN** statement (i.e., command files need not end with this statement).

The **CANCEL** command cancels the execution of all command files and returns control to the dot prompt. **RETURN** is generally preferred, but **CANCEL** may be used to abort a process if something dreadful is about to occur. There is no difference between **CANCEL** and **RETURN** except when you are using subprograms: **CANCEL** stops all programs; **RETURN** stops only the current program and returns to the program which called it.

QUIT also may be used in a command file to terminate the file, close all open files, and return to the operating system.

GUIDED ACTIVITY

This activity requires you to use the program creation and flow commands.

1. Follow the startup procedure for your version of dBASE as outlined in Unit 2.

2. Give the command **MODIFY COMMAND SKIP**, which will allow you to create a command file named SKIP.PRG. The screen should clear and look like Figure 12-1.

3. Enter the program shown in Figure 12-2.

4. When the program is correct, exit by typing ^W or ^End.

5. Execute the program by typing **DO SKIP**

6. The program should display each record of RAW_MATL on the screen, as illustrated in Figure 12-3. If it does not, you probably made a typing error; fix it.

7. Change the program so it reads as follows:

```
clear all
use raw_matl
do while .not. eof( )
    if (date( )-last_order)>10
        display
    endif
    skip
enddo
```

8. Test the program and correct it, if necessary, until it works.

9. When you have completed this Activity, give the command **QUIT** to exit dBASE. Remember to backup your work. If everything is proper, turn off the computer and return the dBASE software to the Lab Supervisor.

REVIEW QUESTIONS

1. How do command files differ from immediate mode?

*2. What is a program?

*3. What is a loop?

*4. What command do you give to create a command file?

5. What series of commands will process all records in a file?

*6. How do you execute a command file?

```
. do skip
Record#  RMID DESC                COST INVENTORY LAST_ORDER
      1  0014 12 oz. cup          0.03       300 10/04/87


Record No.       2
Record#  RMID DESC                COST INVENTORY LAST_ORDER
      2  0015 16 oz. cup          0.05       400 09/28/87


Record No.       3
Record#  RMID DESC                COST INVENTORY LAST_ORDER
      3  0018 4 oz. fry pack      0.02       332 10/19/87


Record No.       4
Record#  RMID DESC                COST INVENTORY LAST_ORDER
      4  0019 6 oz. fry pack      0.03       500 10/15/87


Record No.       5
Record#  RMID DESC                COST INVENTORY LAST_ORDER
      5  0013 8 oz. cup           0.02       600 10/06/87


Record No.       6
Command          ▌<B:>▌RAW_MATL              ▌Rec: 6/19      ▌         ▌

                 Enter a dBASE III PLUS command.
```

FIGURE 12-3 The **SKIP** Program in Progress
Note: Command entered by the user is in **boldface**.

DOCUMENTATION RESEARCH

Using the reference manual, determine the answers to the following questions which deal with the commands discussed in this unit. I recommend you also write the reference manual page number by the discussion of the command in this unit.

1. MODIFY COMMAND {filename} — how can you read another file into the file being edited?

2. DO {filename} — according to the manual, how many open files may you have at one time?

3. CLEAR ALL — what is the difference between this command and the **CLOSE** command?

4. NOTE or * — what happens if the note line ends with a semicolon?

5. DO WHILE {condition} . . . ENDDO — what is the effect of comments on the **ENDDO** line, following the **ENDDO** statement?

6. SKIP — if this command is issued when the record pointer is on the last record in a file, what is value of the functions **RECNO( )** and **EOF( )** ?

7. EXIT — does this command cause the {**condition**} in the **DO WHILE** statement to be reevaluated?

8. LOOP — does this command cause the {**condition**} in the **DO WHILE** statement to be reevaluated?

9. LOOP — this command must be part of what other statements to function as intended?

10. DO CASE . . . CASE {condition} . . . OTHERWISE . . . ENDCASE — under what conditions will two **CASE** statements be selected?

11. IF {condition} . . . ELSE . . . ENDIF — what may follow the **ENDIF** statement on the same line?

12. RETURN — what is the effect of the **TO MASTER** option?

13. CANCEL — what is the difference between this command and **RETURN**?

UNIT

13 INPUT, OUTPUT, AND POSITIONING

This unit deals with the commands that move to specific points within the data file, accept data into the program, print data out of the program, and add to the data file. These commands, in conjunction with those discussed in Unit 12, provide for most of dBASE's programming utility. These commands complement the full-screen input and output commands, which are discussed in Unit 14.

LEARNING OBJECTIVES

1. At the completion of this unit, you should know the differences among **INPUT**, **ACCEPT**, and **WAIT** commands.

2. At the completion of this unit, you should be able to

   a. position the record pointer to any record in the file,

   b. input string and numeric data, using prompt strings,

   c. output field and variable contents as well as short and long character strings,

   d. add a blank record to the data file,

   e. add or change information in a data file record.

IMPORTANT COMMANDS

    SKIP
    FIND
    SEEK
    LOCATE . . . CONTINUE
    GO

```
INPUT 'prompt' TO {memory variable}
ACCEPT 'prompt' TO {memory variable}
WAIT 'prompt' TO {memory variable}
? {expression}
?? {expression}
EJECT
CLEAR
TEXT . . . ENDTEXT
APPEND BLANK
REPLACE
SET ECHO ON/OFF
SET TALK ON/OFF
SET STEP ON/OFF
SET DEBUG ON/OFF
```

MOVING ABOUT IN A DATA FILE

Most of the commands that are used to move about in the data file were introduced in earlier units. You may wish to review the section entitled "Searching through a File" in Unit 6 to refresh your memory concerning the record pointer, and finding and locating records. In addition to BOF( ) and EOF( ), the RECNO( ) and FOUND( ) functions are used to determine where our movements have taken us.

Functions

On occasion, your program will need to determine which record is the current record. The *current-record function* does just that.

> RECNO( ) *Current-record function*, the value of this function is the integer corresponding to the current *record number*.

Note that this function always displays *physical* record numbers, even if the file is used with an index. Consider the following sequence of commands (remember, RAW_MATL is indexed on the RMID field).

use raw_matl index raw_matl	*Data file is opened with index.*
? recno( )	*Displays 8 because the first record in logical order is number 8 in physical order.*
go bottom	*Record pointer is moved to last record in logical order.*
? recno( )	*Displays 4 because the last record in logical order is number 4.*
use raw_matl	*Data file is opened without index.*
? recno( )	*Displays 1.*
go bottom	*Record pointer is moved to last record.*
? recno( )	*Displays 19.*

When we use the **FIND, SEEK,** and **LOCATE . . . CONTINUE** commands from the immediate mode, dBASE will inform us by way of a screen message (or absence of a message) whether or not the search has been successful. The *successful search function* is used to inform a dBASE program whether or not the search has been successful.

FOUND( ) *Successful search function*, this function returns **.T.** (true) if the last **FIND, SEEK, LOCATE,** or **CONTINUE** has been successful, and **.F.** (false) if no match has been found. This function is available only in dBASE III Plus. These two examples assume that you are using RAW_MATL with its index based on RMID.

find 0010	*Will return* **.T.** *because there is a record with*
? found( )	*RMID of 0010.*
find 0020	*Will return* **.F.** *because there is no record with that*
? found( )	*RMID.*

Move to Next Record

The **SKIP** command was first discussed in Unit 12. Use this command to move the record pointer forwards or backwards from its current position. This command is especially useful for processing the data file one record at a time.

Move Based on a Criterion

If you wish to move to a record that matches a certain criterion (e.g., where the contents of a field is a certain value), then you will use one of the following commands.

The **FIND** command was first discussed in Unit 6. **FIND** is used with files that are indexed to move the record pointer to the first instance of a record that matches the index key. If there is no match, the message "NO FIND" will be displayed on the screen, and the **FOUND( )** function will be false. In command files, use the value of **FOUND( )** to test for a successful find.[1]

Often, you will wish to move to a record based on the value of a memory variable. The memory variable name is used with the & (macro function) in the **FIND** command. If the memory variable is named **MEMVAR,** then the proper command is **FIND &MEMVAR.** In effect, this function replaces "&MEMVAR" in the command with the contents of MEMVAR. If "0012" is stored in MEMVAR, then the command **FIND &MEMVAR** will be interpreted by dBASE as **FIND 0012.**

A variation of the **FIND** command is the **SEEK** command, which allows you to use a memory variable as the search criterion, with the command **SEEK MEMVAR.** This command is also used when the criterion is date-type data (e.g., **SEEK CTOD('04/07/87')**).

---

[1] **FOUND( )** is not available in the original dBASE III. Instead, you must check the **EOF( )** function, which will be true if there is no match. In command files, use the value of **EOF( )** to test for a successful find.

The **LOCATE . . . CONTINUE** command set was also discussed in Unit 6. This set of commands is used to search through a file for specific values in a field or in a portion of a field. They are generally used when you wish to find multiple occurrences of a field value or when the search criterion is not suitable for an index key. When the record is found, the message "Record = n" is displayed, and **RECNO( )** equals that record. If there is no match, then "End of LOCATE scope" is the message, **FOUND( )** is false, and {condition} is false.

Move to a Specific Physical Record

The **GO** or **GOTO** command is used to position the record pointer to a specific record in the data file. To go to a specific record, say record 25, enter one of the following:

    goto 25
    go 25
    25

To go to the first record, use **GO TOP**; to the last record, **GO BOTTOM**.

COMMANDS FOR DATA INPUT

Three commands are provided for the input of data into memory variables. Which you use is dependent upon the type of memory variable you wish to create.

Input to a Numeric or Logical Variable

The **INPUT** command may be used for input to memory variables. The general form of the command is

    input "prompt" to {memory variable}

For example:

    input 'New price: ' to newprice

This command is used in command files to enter values into memory variables. "Prompt" is optional. The memory variable is created if it did not exist before. The type of the memory variable is determined by the type of data input. If the input is delimited with ' or " or [ ], then a character-type variable is created. If the input is numeric, then a numeric variable is created. If the input is .T., .Y., .F., or .N., then a logical variable is created. If the input is a function which yields a date, then a date-type variable is created. For example, if, in response to the **INPUT** command above:

The User Enters:	The Result is:
1.35	*The variable NEWPRICE is numeric-type, with a value of* 1.35.
"Edmonton"	*The variable NEWPRICE is character-type, with a value of* Edmonton.

.F.   *The variable NEWPRICE is logical-type, with a value of* false.

ctod('11/22/87')   *The variable NEWPRICE is date-type, with a value of* 11/22/87.

Even though the last three entries may not make sense to us, dBASE is able to interpret them as noted. Because character data must be enclosed with quotation marks, the **ACCEPT** command is recommended for the entry of character data.

Input to a Character Variable

The **ACCEPT** command is used for input to character-type memory variables. The general form of the command is

accept "prompt" to {memory variable}

For example:

accept "City: " to city

The memory variable will be character-type regardless of what is entered. Delimiting quotation marks are not required. The "prompt" is again optional. For example, if, in response to the **ACCEPT** command above:

The User Enters:	The Result is:
Calgary	*The variable CITY is character-type, with a value of* Calgary.
8.09	*The variable CITY is character-type, with a value of* 8.09.
.T.	*The variable CITY is character-type, with a value of* .T. .
10/01/87	*The variable CITY is character-type, with a value of* 10/01/87.

Even though the last three entries may not make sense to us, dBASE is able to interpret them as noted. The "date" entered in the last example can be readily converted to date-type data:

datevar = ctod(city)

Input of a One-Character Response

The **WAIT** command serves two useful functions. First, it may be used as a pause; to suspend program operations until the user presses any key. This is normally used to halt the program while the user reads whatever is displayed on the screen. Second, the **WAIT** command may be used to capture a one-character response, such as a response to a menu. The two forms of the command are

wait
wait "prompt" to {memory variable}

After the **WAIT** command, dBASE will cease all operations until a character is entered from the keyboard. In the first form, **WAIT** may be used as a pause, to allow the user to read what is on the screen before execution continues. In the second form, the character is stored in a memory variable. If any nonprinting or control character is input, then the value of the memory variable is a null (ASCII zero). This command is useful for capturing a response to a menu or to a "Do you want to do more (Y/N)?" question. For example:

wait "Do you want to do more (Y/N)?" to answer

The INKEY( ) Function. dBASE provides a function which is similar in operation to the **WAIT** command. Instead of stopping the processing of the program, however, this function intercepts any key pressed during the execution of the program and makes its numeric (ASCII) code available to the program.

> INKEY( ) *Keypress during program execution function*, the value of this function is the integer corresponding to the ASCII code of a key pressed by the user while the program is executing.

The program can determine which key (if any) the user has pressed (including <ARROW> keys) by assigning the value of **INKEY( )** to a numeric variable; then behave in accordance with the user's instructions. We will illustrate this capability in Application G.

COMMANDS FOR OUTPUT TO THE USER

The four commands discussed in this section provide output to the user. These complement the full-screen commands that are discussed in Unit 14.

Output of a Field or Variable

The *what-is* command was first discussed in Unit 4. Recall that the command consists of a question mark followed by an expression. The three forms of the command are

```
?
? {expression list}
?? {expression list}
```

This command is used to print something on the output device. If **SET PRINT ON** has been executed, then print will go to both screen and printer. The solitary ? issues a line feed and carriage return (thus printing a blank line). ? {expression list} issues a line feed and carriage return and then prints the value of {expression list}. ?? {expression list} prints the value of {expression list} without the preceding line feed and carriage return.[2]

---

[2] Note to hard-core programmers: dBASE issues the line feed and carriage return (LF-CR) sequence before it prints a line rather than after; the latter method being more normal in computer languages. This can cause a problem with some parallel-interface printers that will not print a line until they receive the LF-CR. To make sure everything is printed, I recommend that you issue a solitary ? immediately after **SET PRINT ON** and another solitary ? immediately before **SET PRINT OFF**. This problem also exists in output commands such as **LIST** and **DISPLAY**.

Example: Suppose you wanted to print the value of the memory variable (or data file field) **FIRSTSON** following an identifying legend. To do so, you would use the following:

? "The value of FIRSTSON is "
?? firstson

If the current contents of FIRSTSON is "Cain" then the result would be

```
The value of  FIRSTSON   is Cain
```

Output of a Block of Text

If you wish to output a block of text that does not contain any fields or variables, then the **TEXT** command may be used. The general form of the command is

text
    lines of text
endtext

All of the *lines of text* will be sent to the screen (and printer if set on). This command is useful for output of a set of instructions or other information to the user. *Note*: **ENDTEXT** is one word; there is no space between **END** and **TEXT**. The use of this feature is illustrated in Application E.

Output on a New Screen or Page

The **CLEAR** command will clear the screen and home the cursor. *Home the cursor* means to move the cursor to the upper left corner of the screen.

The **EJECT** command causes the printer to do a *form feed*, which will move the paper to the top of the next page if the printer is set up properly.

COMMANDS FOR OUTPUT TO THE DATA FILE

Command files generally serve one of two purposes:

» To extract information from data files.

» To add to or modify the information in a data file.

To serve the second purpose, two additional commands must be discussed.

If you are using a command file to add data to a data file, two steps must be performed. First, add a blank record to the end of the file; then replace the information in the new record with input data.

The **APPEND BLANK** command adds a record to the end of the data file in use. All of the fields are blank (or zero or false). When adding to a file in a command program, you will usually **APPEND BLANK** and then **REPLACE FIELD1 WITH MEMVAR1, FIELD2 WITH MEMVAR2** . . . and so on.

The **REPLACE** command was first discussed in Unit 7. This command changes the value of one or more fields in one or more records of the data file. Some examples were discussed in Unit 7. In command files, you will often **REPLACE** a field in the current record with the contents of a memory variable:

　replace name with m_name

If neither **{scope}** nor **{condition}** are included in the command, **REPLACE** will change only the current record.

Example

Recall the data file DATEBOOK that was created in Unit 3. (See Figure 3-3 on page 36 for the structure of that file.) To add one record to that file, we could use the following commands:

```
use datebook
accept "Name:      " to m_name
input  "Age:       " to m_age
accept "Phone:     " to m_phone
accept "Last Date: " to m_last
append blank
replace name with m_name, age with m_age, phone with m_phone, ;
    last_date with ctod(m_last)
```

Note the **CTOD( )** function in the **REPLACE** command. The variable M_LAST is character type, and must be converted to date type before the **REPLACE** command will work.

In practice, these commands would probably be inside a loop that would continue as long as the user wanted to add more records.

SET COMMANDS THAT AFFECT COMMAND FILE OUTPUT

Four **SET** commands affect the output of command files. These commands may be issued from the immediate (dot prompt) mode or from within command files.

SET TALK OFF will eliminate the responses that dBASE normally provides after most commands. These responses are often distracting during command file execution, and programmers use this command for a less cluttered screen display. The effect is reversed with the **SET TALK ON** command. I usually set talk off at the beginning of a command file, and set talk back on just before the **RETURN** statement or the end of the program. This minimizes distraction during program execution but still provides feedback during the immediate mode.

These commands are useful for *debugging* a program (i.e., locating and correcting errors):

set echo on   *To display command lines as they are executed.*

set talk on   *To display intermediate results of those commands.*

set step on   *To force the program to execute one line at a time.*

set debug on   *To route* **SET ECHO** *output to the printer instead of to the screen.*

These commands may be issued from the immediate (dot prompt) mode or from within command files.

TABLE 13-1 New Prices for Finished Goods

Description	New Selling Price	Description	New Selling Price
Apple Tarte	0.83	Large Sprite	0.85
Big Jac	1.42	Jac Meal /Co/Ap	2.35
Cheese Burger	0.72	Jac Meal /Co/Ch	2.35
Cherry Tarte	0.83	Jac Meal /Sp/Ap	2.35
Giant Coke	0.99	Jac Meal /Sp/Ch	2.35
Giant Sprite	0.99	Regular Coke	0.59
Hamburger	0.62	Regular Fries	0.47
Large Coke	0.85	Regular Sprite	0.59
Large Fries	0.70		

GUIDED ACTIVITY

This activity requires you to use the input and output commands.

1. Follow the startup procedure for your version of dBASE as outlined in Unit 2.

2. Write a command file using **MODIFY COMMAND REPRICE** that will allow you to process each record in FIN_GOOD. As each record is read, the description and selling price should be displayed on the screen, and the user inputs a new price to replace the old prices in the file with the new prices shown in Table 13-1.

   Before sitting down at the computer, outline the commands that will accomplish the following tasks.

✔ **CHECKPOINT**
Write the commands on the lines to the right of the tasks.

   a. Reset dBASE and open the file FIN_GOOD   _____
   (two commands).

                                                       _____

```
. do reprice
Record#   desc              sell_price
      1   Apple Pie              0.79

New Price .83
      1 record replaced
Record No.       2
Record#   desc              sell_price
      2   Big Jac                1.35

New Price 1.42
      1 record replaced
Record No.       3
Record#   desc              sell_price
      3   Cheese Burger          0.69

New Price _
Command           |<B:>|FIN_GOOD                |Rec: 3/17         |          |Num
```

Enter a dBASE III PLUS command.

FIGURE 13-1 The REPRICE Program in Progress
Note: Items entered by the user are in **boldface**.

b. Start a loop that will continue until end
   of file is reached.   _____

c. Display the DESC and SELL_PRICE fields.   _____

d. Input the new selling price into a memory
   variable called NEW_PRICE.   _____

e. Replace SELL_PRICE with NEW_PRICE.   _____

f. Move forward one record.   _____

g. Terminate the loop.   _____

3. When you have finished the program, exit from **MODIFY COMMAND** by typing ^W or
   ^End. Try the program by typing **DO REPRICE**. If the program has no errors, you will be
   able to input the new prices, as illustrated in Figure 13-1. If the program has errors, use
   MODIFY COMMAND REPRICE to edit, and try again.

4. After the program runs successfully, **LIST TO PRINT** to prove that you have made the changes.

5. **TYPE REPRICE.PRG TO PRINT** to make a printed copy of your command file.

6. Experiment with the four **SET** commands introduced in this unit, giving them from the dot prompt (but do not use **SET DEBUG ON** if you do not have a printer). Set all four on and execute the program, then set all four off and again execute the program.

7. *For Additional Practice*: If you would like additional practice using the commands discussed in this unit, do the following.

    a. From the dot prompt, create a file, named COMSTOCK, which has the following structure:

Field	Field name	Type	Width	Dec
1	NAME	Character	20	
2	DATE	Date	8	
3	CLOSE	Numeric	7	3

    b. Write a command file which will allow you to enter data into this file. For inspiration, see the discussion using the DATEBOOK file on page 215.

    c. Use your program to enter the following data into COMSTOCK:

NAME	DATE	CLOSE
Ashton-Tate	03/12/87	26.750
Compaq Computer	03/12/87	33.750
Digital Equipment	03/12/87	166.625
Hewlett-Packard	03/12/87	55.375
IBM	03/12/87	144.250
Lotus Development	03/12/87	20.875
Micropro	03/12/87	4.750

8. When you have completed this activity, give the command **QUIT** to exit dBASE. Remember to backup your work. If everything is proper, turn off the computer and return the dBASE software to the Lab Supervisor.

REVIEW QUESTIONS

1. What are the differences among the **INPUT**, **ACCEPT**, and **WAIT** commands?

2. What command would you use to position the record pointer to

   *a. Record 15

   *b. The next record

*c. The first record whose contents is 'New York', assuming that the file is indexed on the CITY field.

3. What command would you use to input the following, using prompts?

   *a. The person's name, to the variable M_NAME

   *b. The person's age, to the variable M_AGE

*4. What command would you use to output the two variables input in question 3?

*5. What command is used to add a blank record to the data file?

*6. What command is used to add or change information in a data file record?

DOCUMENTATION RESEARCH

Using the reference manual, determine the answers to the following questions which deal with the commands discussed in this unit. I recommend you also write the reference manual page number by the discussion of the command in this unit.

1. SKIP — how can a memory variable be used with this command?

2. FIND — how can a memory variable be used with this command?

3. SEEK — how can a memory variable be used with this command?

4. LOCATE . . . CONTINUE — where is the record pointer after a successful search? after an unsuccessful search?

5. GO — what is the alternate version of this command?

6. INPUT 'prompt' TO {memory variable} — what happens if a <CR> is entered in response to this command?

7. ACCEPT 'prompt' TO {memory variable} — what happens if a <CR> is entered in response to this command?

8. WAIT 'prompt' TO {memory variable} — what happens if a <CR> is entered in response to this command?

9. ? {expression} — find the definition of "<expression list>" in the reference manual. How may more than one {expression} be output with a single ? command?

10. ?? {expression} — how does this command differ from the previous command?

11. EJECT — what is the ASCII code for *form feed*?

12. CLEAR — is it possible to clear only a portion of the screen?

13. TEXT . . . ENDTEXT — what is the effect of this command on the & (macro) function?

14. APPEND BLANK — where is the record pointer after this command is executed?

15. REPLACE — what is the problem with making multiple replacements on an indexed field?

16. SET ECHO ON/OFF — what is the normal state of this command?

17. SET TALK ON/OFF — what is the normal state of this command?

18. SET STEP ON/OFF — when stepping is on, what key leads to the next step? What key will cancel the process?

19. SET DEBUG ON/OFF — what is the normal state of this command?

UNIT
14

CUSTOM INPUT AND OUTPUT FORMS

In this unit, we introduce the commands that are used to develop custom input and output forms. This set of commands will allow you to create professional looking forms for data entry and to precisely format output from your application.

LEARNING OBJECTIVES

1. At the completion of this unit, you should understand the concept of screen addressing.

2. At the completion of this unit, you should be able to

   a. output field or variable data anywhere on the screen,

   b. create a form for data input.

IMPORTANT COMMANDS

```
@ . . . SAY
SET DEVICE TO . . .
@ . . . GET
READ
@ . . . TO
SET STATUS ON/OFF
SET FORMAT TO . . .
CREATE SCREEN {screen filename}
MODIFY SCREEN {screen filename}
```

FULL-SCREEN ADDRESSING

The standard personal computer screen is eighty columns wide and twenty-five rows high. The columns are numbered 0 (zero) to 79, the rows 0 to 24. 0,0 is the upper left corner, 24,79 is the lower right. dBASE will allow you to position the output anywhere within those screen dimensions through the use of the @ . . . command. The @ . . . command can also be used to format output to be sent to the printer.

Full-Screen Output

The command for full-screen output is the @ . . . **SAY** command. The simple form of the command is

@ *x,y* **say** {expression}

which will write an expression (character string, memory variable, or field) at row *x*, column *y*. You may write more than one expression to the same row, and it is not necessary to write the expressions in row order if you are writing to the screen (for example, the first write may be to row 5, and a later write may be to row 2). If you are writing to the printer (see the section entitled "Output Device," later in this unit), the rows must be written in ascending order.

To illustrate the use of the @ . . . **SAY** command, I wrote a short command file:

```
clear
use raw_matl index raw_matl
find 0001
display
@ 6,0 say desc
@ 10,30 say 'Desc: '+desc
@ 13,60 say cost
@ 16,10 say 'Cost: '+str(cost,8,2)
@ 20,30 say 'Full-Screen Output Example'
```

The result of executing this file appears in Figure 14-1. This should be self-explanatory, except for the command that reads @ **16,10 SAY 'Cost: '+STR(COST,8,2)**. dBASE will allow only one type of data in a given @ . . . **SAY** command; therefore, it was necessary to use the **STR( )** function to convert the numeric field COST to a string. Where the field is used by itself, as in @ **13,60 SAY COST**, then no conversion is necessary.

More precisely formatted output is obtained with a **PICTURE** {format} specification. It is possible to embed commas and leading $ or * signs. The command then would take the following form:

@ *x,y* **say** {expression} **picture** {format}

```
Record#  RMID DESC              COST INVENTORY LAST_ORDER
      8  0001 all-beef patty    0.10       100 10/01/87



all-beef patty




                        Desc: all-beef patty


                                                              0.10



       Cost:     0.10




                       Full-Screen Output Example
```

Command Line   <B:> RAW_MATL   Rec: 8/19

Enter a dBASE III PLUS command.

FIGURE 14-1 Example of Full-Screen Output

The format characters used with **@ ... SAY** are as follows:

- **!** *Converts all alpha characters to uppercase.*
- **$** *Displays dollar signs in place of leading zeros.*
- ***** *Displays asterisks in place of leading zeros.*
- **.** *Indicates position of decimal point.*
- **,** *Indicates position of comma.*

PICTURE formats are discussed in the dBASE manual with the **@ ...** command. Example:

@ 5,5 say cost picture '$$,$$$,$$$.$$'   *Yields a display such as* $$$100,000.00.

Output Device

The output of **@ ... SAY** is normally directed to the screen. To send the output to the printer instead of to the screen, give the command **SET DEVICE TO PRINT**. To change back to screen output, give the command **SET DEVICE TO SCREEN**. When output is directed to the printer, the rows must be output in order. Whenever a row with a number lower than the previously printed row is encountered, the printer will do a page eject (form feed).

Full-Screen Input

The command for full-screen input is the @ . . . GET command. The simple form of the command is

    @ x,y get {expression}
        more @ . . . GET commands may be given
    read

The {expression} may be either a character-type memory variable or a data file field of any type. Before getting a memory variable, the variable size and type must have been specified using either STORE or RESTORE commands. The current value of the variable or field is displayed at row x, column y. The user may retain the old value by pressing <CR>, or enter a new value. If the new value does not fill the field, the user presses <CR> to complete the entry.

The @ . . . GET command is not active until a subsequent READ is encountered. Once the READ command is given, then the user moves from input field to input field, entering data, much as in the APPEND operation. Full-screen cursor control keys are usable here, which allow the user to move forward or backward from one @ . . . GET field to another, until the last @ . . . GET is entry is completed.

The mistake made most often by dBASE programmers (especially yours truly) is forgetting to put a READ statement after the @ . . . GET statements. If you do not put a READ statement in the program, it will not stop for you to input data.

It is possible to limit the input to numbers only, to convert input letters to uppercase, and also to embed specific characters at specific positions within the field with the PICTURE {format} specification. The format characters used with @ . . . GET are as follows:

9   *Allows only digits for character data, digits and signs for numeric data.*
Allows only digits, blanks, and signs.
A   *Allows only letters.*
L   *Allows only logical data.*
N   *Allows letters and digits.*
X   *Allows any character.*
!   *Converts all input alpha characters to uppercase.*

Other characters in the {format} are accepted as is. For instance, the command to input telephone numbers might be

    @ 5,4 get tel_numb picture '(999)999-9999'

which would allow only numbers, and would automatically place the parentheses and hyphen. PICTURE formats are discussed in the dBASE manual with the @ . . . command.

In dBASE III, @ . . . GET may also check the range of numeric input data. For example:

    @ 9,9 get grade range 0,4

Combining Output and Input

The **@ . . . SAY** and **@ . . . GET** commands may be combined for prompted input. For example:

> **@ 5,4 say 'Telephone ' get tel_numb picture '(999)999-9999'**

will write the word "Telephone" at row 5, column 4, and then display the picture format on the same line — in this case at row 5, column 15.

Erasing Part of the Screen

To erase part of the screen, use one of the following:

@ x,y clear	*To erase the screen below and to the right of row* x, *column* y.
@ x,y	*To erase row* x *from column* y *to right side.*

For example, **@ 5,5** will erase row 5 from column 5 to 79.

Lines and Boxes

The **@ . . . TO** command is used to draw lines and boxes, and to clear rectangular areas of the screen. (This feature is available in dBASE III Plus only.) The various forms of the command are as follows:

@ x1,y1 to x2,y2	*Draws a single-line box with corners at row* x1, *column* y1; *row* x1, *column* y2; *row* x2, *column* y1; *and, row* x2, *column* y2
@ x1,y1 to x2,y2 double	*Draws a double-line box with corners at row* x1, *column* y1; *row* x1, *column* y2; *row* x2, *column* y1; *and, row* x2, *column* y2
@ x1,y1 clear to x2,y2	*Clears the area bounded by row* x1, *column* y1; *row* x1, *column* y2; *row* x2, *column* y1; *and, row* x2, *column* y2

When *x1* and *x2* are equal, a single or double line is drawn horizontally. When *y1* and *y2* are equal, a single or double line is drawn vertically. You can also clear a single column or row.

Hiding the Status Bar

Although the status bar at the bottom of the screen provides useful information, there are times when its presence will clutter the screen or confuse the user. To remove the status bar from the screen, use the command **SET STATUS OFF**. When you want the status bar returned to the display, give the command **SET STATUS ON**. When the status bar is off, some information, such as the fact that the Ins, Caps Lock, or Num Lock keys have been pressed, is displayed at the top of the screen.

Functions for Full-Screen Input and Output

There are five functions which deal with full-screen input and output. The first four return the position of the screen cursor or printer after the last @ . . . SAY or @ . . . GET operation, and allow you to position the cursor on the screen or printer relative to that last position for the next input or output operation.

COL( ) *Current screen column position function*, the value of this function is a number which represents the current position of the cursor on the screen.

ROW( ) *Current screen row position function*, the value of this function is a number which represents the current position of the cursor on the screen.

PCOL( ) *Printer column position function*, the value of this function is a number which represents the current position of the printer.

PROW( ) *Printer row position function*, the value of this function is a number which represents the current position of the printer.

READKEY( ) *Full-screen exiting keypress function*, the value of this function is a number which represents the key pressed by the user to exit from a full-screen command (such as **APPEND, EDIT,** or **READ**). This function is the only means of determining if the user pressed an <ARROW> or other control key when entering data in full-screen mode. (dBASE III Plus only)

I use the ROW( ) and PROW( ) functions most often. For instance, I could list the contents of the Ed and Bruce MAILING database file, five names at a time, on the screen using the following command file. (The MAILING data file was introduced in Application D.)

```
clear all
set status off
set talk off
use mailing
m_wait = ' '
do while .not.eof( )
   if row( ) > 19
      @ row( )+2,5 say ;
"Press PgUp for previous screen, any other key to continue . . . " get m_wait
      read
      m_key=readkey( )
      if m_key=6
         skip -10
      endif
      clear
   endif
   @ row( )+2,5 say trim(first_name)+' '+last_name
   @ row( )+1,5 say street
   @ row( )+1,5 say trim(city)+', '+state+' '+zip
   skip
enddo
```

Program listing is continued on following page

```
@ row( )+2,5 say "Press any key to continue . . . " get m_wait
read
set talk on
set status on
```

Notice how the current row position (**ROW( )** function) is used in the seventh line of the program to test whether or not the cursor is near the bottom of the screen; and how the function is used in several program lines to position a line of output one or two rows below the previous line of output (e.g., **ROW( )+1**).

The value returned by **READKEY( )** in the eleventh line of the program indicates the key pressed by the user after entering a response to the "Press PgUp for previous screen, any other key to continue . . . " question. In this case, we are only interested in the value if it is the PgUp key — in which case **READKEY( )** will return the value 6 — and the twelfth line of the program checks to see if that particular key has been pressed. If the value is 6, then the program will skip back ten records, which is where the record pointer was at the beginning of the screen prior to the screen which the user will be viewing at the time. The values returned by the **READKEY( )** function for several common keys are listed in Table 14-1. For a complete list, see the reference manual.

TABLE 14-1 READKEY( ) Values

Key Pressed by User	Value of READKEY( )
<LEFT ARROW>	1
<RIGHT>	0
<UP>	4
<DOWN>	5
Home	2
End	3
PgUp	6
PgDn	7

CHANGING THE DEFAULT SCREEN FORMAT

By now you are familiar with the standard dBASE format for edit and append operations. It is possible to create a special file, with an .FMT extension, of @ . . . **SAY** and @ . . . **GET** commands that will be used by dBASE instead of the standard format for **EDIT** and **APPEND**. Once created, the default is changed with the following command:

set format to {format filename}

The format file is created using **MODIFY COMMAND** or other editors. With dBASE III Plus, you may create the format with the **CREATE SCREEN** command, and subsequently change the format with the **MODIFY SCREEN** command.

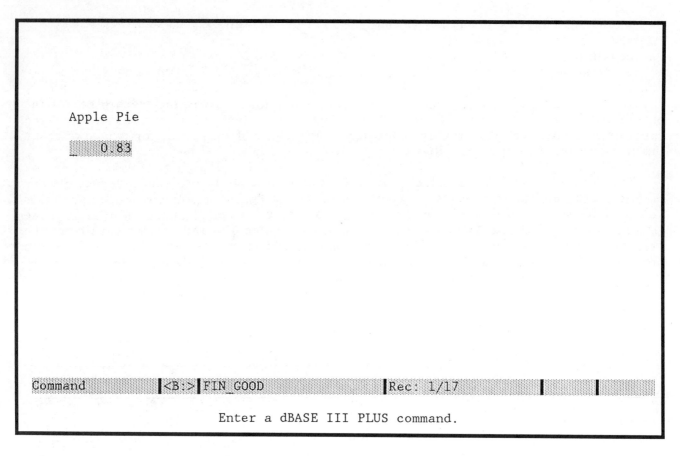

Apple Pie

0.83

Command |<B:>|FIN_GOOD |Rec: 1/17 | |

Enter a dBASE III PLUS command.

FIGURE 14-2 The Completed Screen Format

create screen {screen filename}
modify screen {screen filename}

These commands use a special type of file, with an .SCR extension, which must be translated into an .FMT file before it may be used by dBASE or edited by **MODIFY COMMAND**.

From the ASSIST Menu. **SET FORMAT TO** is found on the ■ *Set Up* ■ menu; **CREATE SCREEN** is found on the ■ *Create* ■ menu (as ■ *Create* ■ *Format* ■); and **MODIFY SCREEN** is found on the ■ *Modify* ■ menu (as ■ *Modify* ■ *Format* ■). As with other ASSIST menu commands that deal with files, you are asked for the drive designation and file name. Working with formats is the same whether you enter from the dot prompt or from the ASSIST menu.

Creating a Screen

We will illustrate the screen creation process by developing a screen that displays the description of a finished good and allows us to change the selling price of that item. See Figure 14-2 for an illustration of the finished screen. We begin the process with the **CREATE SCREEN** command (or, from the ASSIST menu, ■ *Create* ■ *Format* ■).

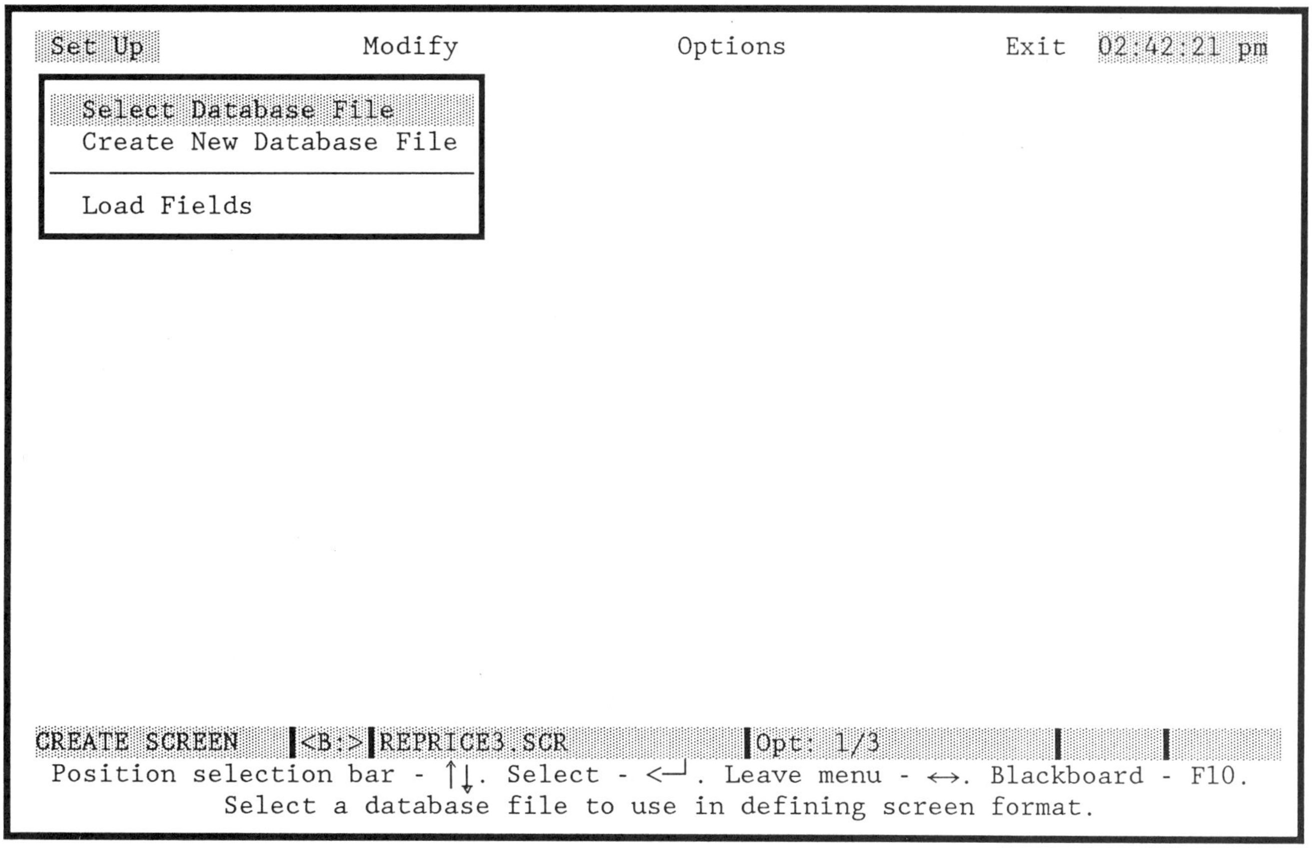

```
 Set Up              Modify              Options              Exit  02:42:21 pm
┌──────────────────────────┐
│ Select Database File      │
│ Create New Database File  │
│──────────────────────────│
│ Load Fields               │
└──────────────────────────┘





CREATE SCREEN    │<B:>│REPRICE3.SCR            │Opt: 1/3            │            │
  Position selection bar - ↑↓. Select - <┘. Leave menu - ↔. Blackboard - F10.
           Select a database file to use in defining screen format.
```

FIGURE 14-3 Creating a Screen: Selecting the Database File

For this illustration, I used the command **CREATE SCREEN REPRICE3**. Once the **CREATE SCREEN** command is given, from either the dot prompt or the **ASSIST** menu, you are presented with the menu illustrated in Figure 14-3.

The first action to take is to either ■ *Set Up* ■ *Select Database File* ■ or tell dBASE that you are going to create a new database file as you define the screen format. We will limit our discussion to the former case: using an existing file. The specific file is chosen by the usual process of moving the selection bar and pressing <CR>. If the file is already open, then you do not have to reopen it and you may move to the next step.

Next, choose ■ *Set Up* ■ *Load Fields* ■ to indicate which fields will be displayed on your custom screen. We use the selection bar and <CR> key to select both DESC and SELL_PRICE (see Figures 14-4 and 14-5). Note that the highlighted field is described at the bottom of the screen. The selected fields are placed on a *blackboard*, which is displayed by pressing the F10 key (Figure 14-6). If you decide later that more fields should be added to the blackboard, you may return to this option. Fields are loaded at the position of the cursor on the blackboard, and below.

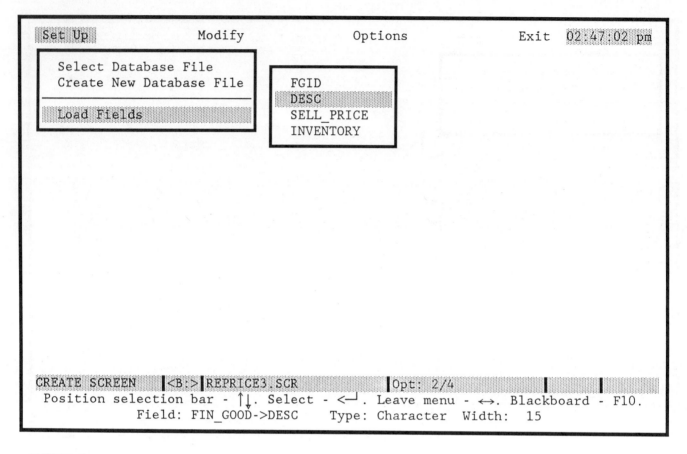

FIGURE 14-4 Creating a Screen: Loading Fields (I)

There are two ways to reposition the field names and input areas on the blackboard. First, you may press the Ins key and push text around by pressing <SPACE>, or using other standard editing keys, such as pressing <CR> to insert a line, moving everything below that point down one line. Second, you may *move* or *drag* a field input area (but not the associated field name), by placing the blackboard cursor in the highlighted area of the field and pressing <CR>. Use <UP>, <DOWN>, <LEFT>, and <RIGHT> to move the blackboard cursor to a new position for the field, then press <CR> to complete the move. If you decide to leave the field where it is, press Esc to exit the process. (See Figures 14-7 and 14-8.)

To add descriptive text, you position the blackboard cursor where you wish the text to appear, and type it. To remove text, use the Del or <BACKSPACE> keys to delete a character at a time, and ^T (Ctrl-T) to remove a word at a time.

Once the general appearance is set, you may press F10 for further options. For instance, to change the action for the DESC field from **GET** to **SAY**, I positioned the blackboard cursor in the field, then pressed F10 (the result is illustrated in Figure 14-9). At this point, I press <CR> to toggle between *Edit/GET* and *Display/SAY*. On the blackboard, **GET** areas are in reverse video and **SAY** areas are in normal video.

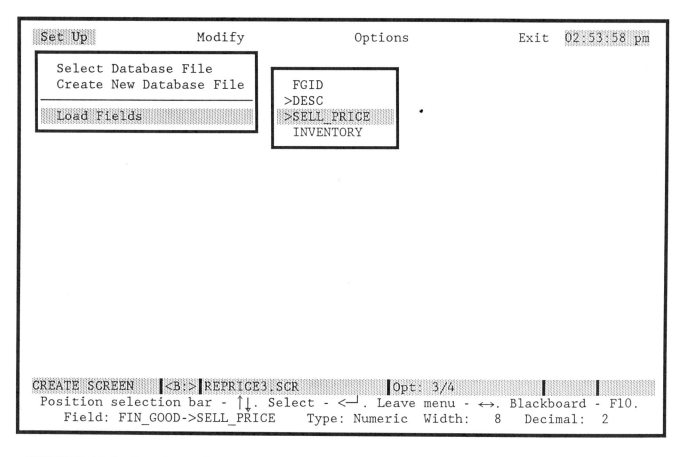

FIGURE 14-5 Creating a Screen: Loading Fields (II)

While in the ■ *Modify* ■ menu, I may change the field name, type, width, and picture function and template. If the field were numeric, I could also change the number of decimal places and specify the range of acceptable values. *Be very careful*: Some of the changes you make on this menu can affect the structure of the data file. I recommend that you do *not* change the name, type, or width here, but rather by using **MODIFY STRUCTURE** command. Make a backup copy of your database file before creating a screen.

The ■ *Options* ■ menu allows me to generate a text file image (the .FMT file), or to draw a window (box) or line. I must generate the text file (which will consist of a series of @ . . . **SAY** and @ . . . **GET** commands) before I can use the **SET FORMAT TO** command (or use the **ASSIST** menu sequence ■ *Set Up* ■ *Format for Screen* ■). If I intend to embed the screen into a command file, I must also generate the text file image for further editing with **MODIFY COMMAND**. The text file created by this screen consists of two lines:

```
@ 5, 5 SAY  FIN_GOOD->DESC
@ 7, 5 GET  FIN_GOOD->SELL_PRICE
```

and is stored in the file REPRICE3.FMT. The text file image is also generated when the process is exited by choosing ■ *Exit* ■ *Save* ■.

```
   Set Up              Modify              Options              Exit   03:29:42 pm
 DESC           XXXXXXXXXXXXXXXX
 SELL_PRICE     99999.99



















 CREATE SCREEN     |<B:>|REPRICE3.SCR              |Pg 01 Row 00 Col 00|          |
       Enter text.  Drag field or box under cursor with <┘.   F10 for menu.
                       Screen field definition blackboard
```

FIGURE 14-6 Creating a Screen: The Initial Blackboard

I have two methods to invoke this format:

set format to reprice3
do reprice3.fmt

In the first case, the commands **EDIT**, **APPEND**, and **CHANGE** will use my newly defined format instead of the default format data-entry (fields vertically aligned). A **READ** command will display the current record for input (effectively: **EDIT** for current record only). We will use this capability in the Guided Activity for this unit.

The second method for invoking the format is to use the **DO** command, with the name of the format file (*including the* .FMT *extension*). This has the effect of issuing the series of @ . . . **SAY** and @ . . . **GET** commands contained in the .FMT file. To enable data input, a **READ** command must follow the **DO** command.

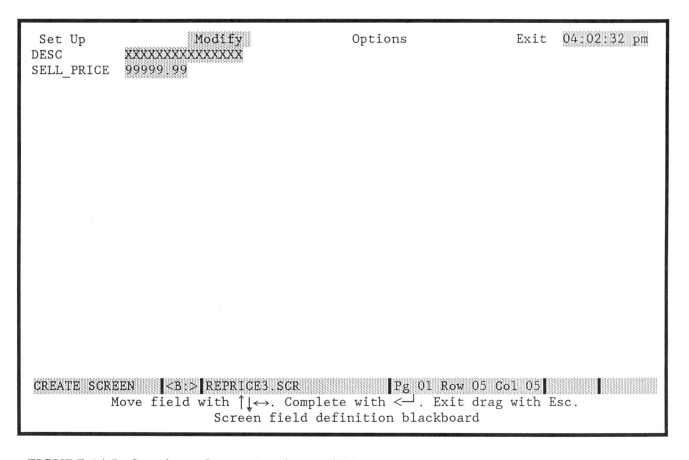

FIGURE 14-7 Creating a Screen: Moving a Field

GUIDED ACTIVITY

This activity requires you to use the full-screen input and output commands.

1. Follow the startup procedure for your version of dBASE as outlined in Unit 2.

2. Write a command file, using **MODIFY COMMAND REPRICE2,** that will allow you to process each record in FIN_GOOD. As each record is read, the description and selling price should be displayed on the screen. Input a new price to replace the old prices in the file with the new prices shown in Table 14-2. This program should use the full-screen input and output commands.

   Before sitting down at the computer, outline the commands that will accomplish the following tasks.

✔ CHECKPOINT
Write the commands on the lines to the right of the tasks.

a. Clear dBASE and open the file FIN_GOOD.   _____

```
 Set Up              Modify              Options              Exit   04:23:00 pm




       XXXXXXXXXXXXXXXXX

       99999.99












 CREATE SCREEN    |<B:>|REPRICE3.SCR              |Pg 01 Row 05 Col 05|Ins    |
       Enter text.  Drag field or box under cursor with <--.  F10 for menu.
              Field: FIN_GOOD->DESC    Type: Character  Width:  15
```

FIGURE 14-8 Creating a Screen: The Final Placement of the Fields

b. Start a loop that will continue until end
   of file is reached.   _____

c. Clear the screen.   _____

d. Output the DESC field at row 5, column 5.   _____

e. Input the new price at row 7, column 5.   _____
   (two commands)

                                                          _____

f. Move forward one record.   _____

g. Terminate the loop.   _____

3. When you have finished the program, exit from **MODIFY COMMAND** by typing ^W. Try
   the program by typing **DO REPRICE2**. If the program has no errors, you will be able to
   input the new prices, as illustrated in Figure 14-2. (Some of the prices are changed from
   those that you input in Unit 13, some are the same.) If the program has errors, use
   MODIFY COMMAND REPRICE2 to edit, and try again.

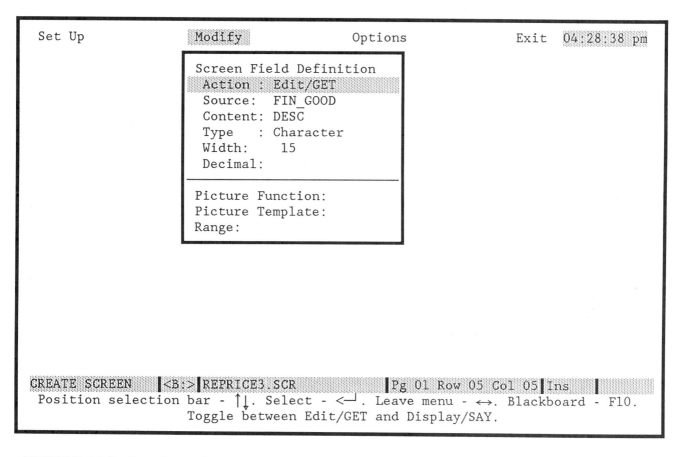

FIGURE 14-9 Creating a Screen: The Modify Menu

TABLE 14-2 New Prices for Finished Goods

Description	New Selling Price	Description	New Selling Price
Apple Tarte	0.84	Large Sprite	0.85
Big Jac	1.45	Jac Meal /Co/Ap	2.45
Cheese Burger	0.77	Jac Meal /Co/Ch	2.45
Cherry Tarte	0.83	Jac Meal /Sp/Ap	2.45
Giant Coke	0.99	Jac Meal /Sp/Ch	2.45
Giant Sprite	0.99	Regular Coke	0.59
Hamburger	0.65	Regular Fries	0.49
Large Coke	0.85	Regular Sprite	0.59
Large Fries	0.70		

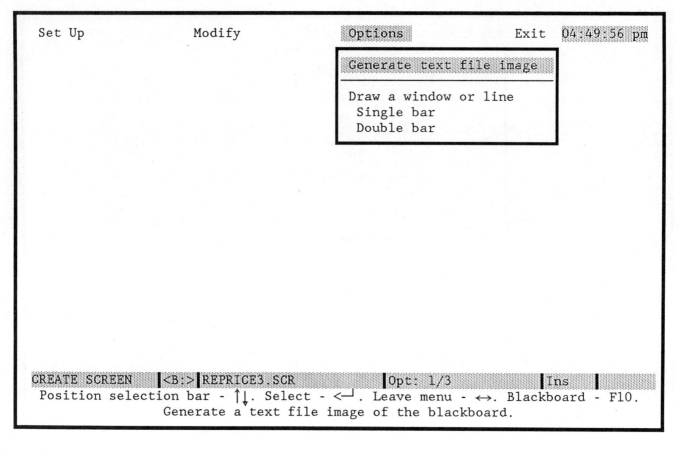

FIGURE 14-10 Creating a Screen: The Options Menu

4. After the program runs successfully, **LIST TO PRINT** to prove that you have made the changes. Then **TYPE REPRICE2.PRG TO PRINT** to make a copy of your command file.

5. (dBASE III Plus only.) Now, use the **CREATE SCREEN** process, as illustrated in Figures 14-3 through 14-10, to create an input screen named REPRICE3 that will accomplish these **@ . . . SAY** and **@ . . . GET** commands. Then, create a command file named REPRICE3.PRG that contains the following commands:

```
clear all
use fin_good
set talk off
set format to reprice3
do while .not. eof( )
    read
    skip
enddo
set talk on
```

Test your program with the command **DO REPRICE3**. (If you accomplished the input for REPRICE2, you will not have to change any prices.)

6. *For Additional Practice*: If you would like additional practice using the full-screen input and output commands, do the following.

   a. Create and test a command file which displays the contents of the MAILING database file on the screen. Follow the example in the section entitled "Functions for Full-Screen Input and Output" in this unit.

   b. Create a command file for the input of new prices to the COMSTOCK database file created in Unit 13. The general logic of the program follows; I leave it up to you to determine the precise commands (some of the tasks listed below may require more than one command). You may decide to create a screen format, use @ . . . commands, or use **INPUT** and **ACCEPT** commands.

   > *clear dBASE*
   > *open the COMSTOCK file*
   > *enter the date (which will be the same for all records)*
   > *start a loop*
   >   *replace the DATE field with the new date*
   >   *display NAME and DATE fields*
   >   *input and replace CLOSE field*
   >   *move to next record*
   > *end of loop*

   c. Test your command file by entering the following data:

NAME	DATE	CLOSE
Ashton-Tate	04/02/87	22.250
Compaq Computer	04/02/87	29.625
Digital Equipment	04/02/87	164.875
Hewlett-Packard	04/02/87	55.875
IBM	04/02/87	148.000
Lotus Development	04/02/87	25.500
Micropro	04/02/87	5.000

6. When you have completed this activity, give the command **QUIT** to exit dBASE. Remember to backup your work. If everything is proper, turn off the computer and return the dBASE software to the Lab Supervisor.

REVIEW QUESTIONS

1. What is meant by screen addressing?

*2. What is the address of the upper right corner of the screen?

*3. When will dBASE fail to stop to allow you to input data into an @ . . . **GET** statement?

DOCUMENTATION RESEARCH

Using the reference manual, determine the answers to the following questions which deal with the commands discussed in this unit. I recommend you also write the reference manual page number by the discussion of the command in this unit.

1. @ . . . SAY — what are functions in the **PICTURE** option?

2. @ . . . GET — if you are using this command to input dollars and cents, what must be in the **PICTURE** template?

3. READ — what is the relationship of this command to the **CLEAR** command?

4. SET DEVICE TO . . . — how does this command treat @ . . . **GET** statements?

5. SET STATUS ON/OFF — what is the relationship between this command and the "scoreboard"?

6. @ . . . TO — what @ . . . **GET** function works with this command to limit the input area of a wide field?

7. SET FORMAT TO . . . — how can you use multi-page formats?

8. CREATE SCREEN {screen filename} — what changes may you make to a database file structure while using this feature?

ED AND BRUCE SPECIALTIES (II)

This application exercise requires you to build a command file to revise the E&BS mailing list.

1. Follow the startup procedure for your version of dBASE as outlined in Unit 2.

2. As you may recall, E&BS has a file called MAILING.DBF that contains information concerning products ordered by its customers. (See Application D.) As customers order products, the file has been updated by editing the customer records. The edit process is dreadfully slow, however, and E&BS has been keeping lists of who has ordered which products (see Tables E-1, E-2, and E-3).

3. You have been asked to write a command file that will help automate the procedure. The command file should do the following:

   a. Reset dBASE, then ask the user which type of product is to be updated.

   b. Open the file MAILING.

   c. Start a loop that will continue until the end of file is reached.

   d. Clear the screen.

   e. Output the FIRST_NAME field at row 8, column 10 and the LAST_NAME field at row 8, column 21.

   f. Input the value of the appropriate field (CLOTHES, GADGETS, or SP_FOOD) at row 10, column 20.

   g. Move forward one record.

   h. Terminate the loop.

TABLE E-1 Persons Who Have Ordered Clothes

First Name	Last Name
Lillian	Forget
Tillie	Gillespie
Carla	Hasenzahl
David	Hoang
Robert	Kipp
Jessica	Lowe
Mary Kay	Moser*
Mary	Prucha
Khosrow	Sheikh
Laura	Streich
Sharon	Tackes
George	Wood
Michael	Ziebert

* This person is not in the Student Version of MAILING.DBF.

4. Most of the above should be easy by now, but steps a and f are a bit tricky. We want to make this program general enough to update each of the three logical fields, one at a time. Therefore, we must know which field is to be updated, and write the command in step f to accept any of the field names. In step a, you will need a menu that allows the user to indicate which of the three types of purchase is to be updated. You may create the menu with the following set of commands:

```
clear all
m_choice='0'
do while .not. m_choice$'123'
    clear
    text
    Which type of purchase are you updating:

    1   Clothes

    2   Tools and Gadgets

    3   Specialty Foods

    endtext
    wait '    Enter 1, 2, or 3 .. ' to m_choice
enddo
```

These commands will capture the user's choice in a memory variable called M_CHOICE. The first statement is used to create and initialize M_CHOICE. A variable must be created before it may be used in a {condition} or @ . . . GET statement. The remainder of the statements are designed to allow only a valid entry. You should ponder the rationale behind the DO WHILE loop, which is called an *error trapping routine*.

TABLE E-2 Persons Who Have Ordered Tools and Gadgets

First Name	Last Name
Karrie	Asselin
Ralph	Blumenthal
Audie	Brueckman
Vilis	Cahill
Fred	Davis
Lois	Farley
Joyce	Fromstein
Mary Pat	Gritzmacher
Grace	Huckstep
Donna	Ladish
Kenneth	Melsheimer
Kenneth	O'Malley
Jack	Oswald
Stephanie	Weber
Linda	Wild

Once the choice is captured, and still a part of step a, you must assign the proper field name to a memory variable, which will be referenced in step f. The following **DO CASE** logic should follow the commands above:

```
do case
    case m_choice='1'
        m_field='CLOTHES'
    case m_choice='2'
        m_field='GADGETS'
    case m_choice='3'
        m_field='SP_FOOD'
endcase
```

Finally, in step f, you may use the variable M_FIELD in the @ . . . **GET** command:

```
@ 10,20 get &m_field
read
```

This command uses the & (macro function) to substitute the contents of a character-type memory variable (M_FIELD) into a command.

5. The remainder of the program is up to you. Create the program under the name REVISE and test it until it works. When it does work properly, use the program to enter the data from the three tables (which will require you to execute the program three times). When you execute the program, you will be presented with the names and the current value of the field (see Figure E-1). If the current value is False and the name appears in the table, then change the name to True by pressing the letter T. If the current value is already True, or if the current value is False and the name does not appear in the table, then press <CR> to move to the next record.

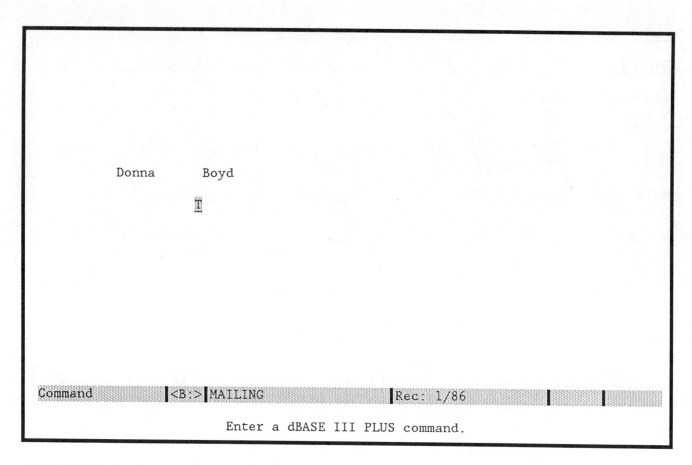

Donna   Boyd

| Command | <B:> MAILING | Rec: 1/86 | | |

Enter a dBASE III PLUS command.

FIGURE E-1 The REVISE Program in Operation

6. As you work with this program, think of ways to make it more efficient from the user's point of view. Is there any way to eliminate the need to go through all records in the file each time you update records? Is there a way to skip records that already have a True for the field in question? What other improvements would you suggest?

7. When you are finished with this exercise, **QUIT** to exit dBASE. Remember to backup your work, then turn off the computer and return the dBASE software to the Lab Supervisor.

TABLE E-3 Persons Who Have Ordered Specialty Foods

First Name	Last Name
Richard	Caulker
Lillian	Forget
Deborah	Helbert
Eileen	Kotnik
Marcia	Pate
Laura	Streich

UNIT
15
MULTIPLE FILES

This unit is devoted to a discussion of the use of multiple files in dBASE. With dBASE III, you may have ten files open at once, and there are fairly simple methods for juggling the open files to gain needed information.

LEARNING OBJECTIVES

1. At the completion of this unit, you should know

   a. what a work area is,

   b. what an alias is,

   c. the difference between the selected work area and other open work areas.

2. At the completion of this unit, you should be able to

   a. open multiple files,

   b. read field contents of any open file,

   c. write data to any field in any open file.

IMPORTANT COMMANDS

SELECT
USE
FIND
SEEK

OPENING MULTIPLE FILES

dBASE allows the use of multiple files by assigning each to a different *work area*. A work area is a logical concept; we need not be concerned with exactly how dBASE manages work areas. Consider a work area to be like a hotel room: there is only one occupant (data file) per room, the occupant may change, we can reach the present occupant by calling the room number, we can visit only one room at a time, and a given occupant can be in only one room at a time.

dBASE III allows you to have data files open in up to ten different work areas: 1 through 10 (or A through J). The **SELECT** command is used to indicate which work area is to be used in subsequent operations. It is possible to use fields in any file, regardless of which work area is selected. The general form of the command is

> **select** *n*   *Where* n = 1 *to* 10, *or* **A**, **B**, **C**, . . . **J**, *or a file alias.*

which selects one of the work areas for future operations. Records and fields in all areas are available for input. Output (i.e., **REPLACE**) is to the file in the selected work area only. Positioning (e.g., **GOTO**, **SKIP**, etc.) affects only the selected file, unless **SET RELATION** is activated (see Unit 16).

Files are specified as follows. When dBASE is loaded, or after a **CLEAR ALL**, the primary (A) area is active. Any file used at this time will be the primary file. Start a command file with the following sample commands if you want both first and second work areas active:

> **clear all**
> **use primfile**
> **select b**
> **use secofile**
> *Any statements here will affect secondary file.*
> **select a**
> *Any statements here will affect primary file.*
> **select b**
> **use difffile**
> *A different secondary file is used and the previous secondary file is closed. Any statements here will affect the new secondary file.*

ALIASES AND PREFIXES

To refer to fields in files (work areas) other than the currently selected area, it is necessary to use aliases or prefixes. The alias may be specified in the **USE** command:

> **use difffile alias df**

If no alias is specified, then the file name and the work area are interchangeable as the alias. Examples:

> **select b**
> **use raw__matl**   *No alias is specified, so the file name (RAW__MATL) and work area (B) are default aliases.*

use mailing alias ebs   *The alias for this file is EBS.*

use fin_good index fin_good alias fg   *Both index and alias are specified.*

As mentioned earlier, fields from any work area data file may be used in expressions. Fields in files other than the currently selected file must be referred to by aliases. Aliases may be upper- or lowercase, and do not count as part of the ten-character limit for field names. The alias is combined with the field name as follows:

alias->field_name

where the *arrow* is a combination of the hyphen and the greater-than sign. The following are legitimate field references:

raw_matl->desc   *The field* DESC *in a data file used with alias* RAW_MATL.

b->cost   *The field* COST *in a data file used in the second work area.*

ebs->clothes   *The field* CLOTHES *in a data file used with the alias* EBS.

I recommend that you get in the habit of using the file name as the alias; then you do not need to remember which file was opened in which work area. The examples in the remainder of this book use that method.

The alias may also be used with the **SELECT** command after the file is open:

select raw_matl   *Selects* RAW_MATL, *regardless of which work area it is in.*
select ebs   *Selects the file with the name or alias* EBS.

MULTIPLE FILE OPERATIONS

There are many possible multiple file operations, several of which are discussed in this and the following units.

One of the first uses that people make of multiple files is to look up data in a second file based on information in the first file. This is usually accomplished by indexing the second file on some key expression that also appears in the primary file. As data are entered into the primary file, the secondary file is checked for relevant information.

For instance, assume that a store has a list of all customers and their credit limits in a file that is indexed on customer account number. As orders are entered into an orders file, the credit file is checked to ensure that the order total does not exceed the credit limit.

As another example, a file of two-letter state abbreviations, minimum and maximum zip code values, and full state names may exist to assist in an address-entry application. This file would be indexed on state abbreviation. As an address is entered, the abbreviation is checked against the abbreviations list, the zip code is checked against the minimum and maximum allowable for that state, and the full state name is displayed as a check for the operator.

In each of these cases, either the **FIND** or **SEEK** command is used to link the two files. When the key expression is entered, dBASE attempts to find the match in the other file. For instance, if the state abbreviation is entered into a memory variable called M__ABBR and the check file is in the second work area, then the following would be used:

```
select 2
seek m_abbr     or     find &m_abbr
select 1
```

Note that the second work area must be selected before the search, and that the primary area is reselected after the search.

If there is a find (e.g., the customer number is found in the credit file), then the checking proceeds. If there is no find, then the operator is informed that some error has been made. Also, if the other items are not as specified (e.g., credit limit exceeded), then another type of error message is presented to the operator. A program to accomplish credit checking would look like the following:

clear all	
set talk off	
use orders	*This file contains the customer orders for the day.*
select b	
use accounts index accounts	*This file contains information about the customers, including credit limit and prior balance, and is indexed on customer account number.*
select orders	
do while .not. eof( )	*Loop through all records in ORDERS.*
select accounts	
seek orders->acct__no	*Searches ACCOUNTS file for a match to the account number of the current record in the ORDERS file.*
do case	
case .not. found( )	*Determines when a match is not found.*
? "Account number not found:"	*Prints error message.*
case (accounts->prior__bal + orders->amount) > accounts->limit	
	Determines when credit limit is exceeded.
? "New purchase plus prior balance exceeds credit limit:"	
display off accounts->prior__bal, accounts->limit, ;	
accounts->limit-accounts->prior__bal	
otherwise	
? "Acceptable transaction:"	
endcase	
select orders	
display off	*Displays the current order.*
wait	
?	*Prints blank line between orders.*
skip	
enddo	
set talk on	

GUIDED ACTIVITY

This activity requires you to use two data files.

1. Follow the startup procedure for your version of dBASE as outlined in Unit 2.

2. Write a command file called LOOKUP that will compute the cost of raw materials in a given Chez Jacques menu item. The program should accept an FGID as input, and read through the MIX file for all records that match that FGID. For each match, the program should locate the corresponding RMID in the RAW_MATL file, multiply the RM_QTY in MIX by the COST in RAW_MATL, and keep a running sum. When no more matches with the FGID are found, the sum should be printed and the program should terminate.

Before sitting down at the computer, outline the commands that will accomplish the following tasks.

✔ **CHECKPOINT**

Write the commands on the lines to the right of the tasks.

a. Reset dBASE and open the file MIX (two commands). _____

_____

b. Index MIX on FGID. _____

c. Select the second work area. _____

d. Open the file RAW_MATL. _____

e. Index RAW_MATL on RMID. _____

f. Select the MIX file. _____

g. Set a memory variable called TOTCOST to 0 (zero). _____

h. Input the FGID. _____

i. Find the first match in MIX. _____

j. Start a loop that will continue until the FGID in the MIX file does not match the input FGID. _____

k. Select the RAW_MATL file. _____

l. Find the record in RAW_MATL that matches the RMID in the MIX file record. _____

m. Select the MIX file. _____

n. Multiply RM_QTY in MIX file by COST in RAW_MATL file and add to TOTCOST. _____

```
. do lookup
mix.ndx already exists, overwrite it? (Y/N) Yes
   100% indexed          82 Records indexed
raw_matl.ndx already exists, overwrite it? (Y/N) Yes
   100% indexed          19 Records indexed
0
Enter FGID 1007
          0.10
Record No.      61
          0.16
Record No.      62
          0.26
Record No.      63
          0.30
Record No.      64
          0.32
Record No.      65
      0.32
.
```

Command Line |<B:>|MIX |Rec: 65/82 | |

Enter a dBASE III PLUS command.

FIGURE 15-1 The LOOKUP Program in Operation
Note: Items entered by the user are in **boldface**.

o. Move to the next record in MIX.   _____

p. Terminate the loop.   _____

q. Print the result.   _____

3. When you have finished the program, exit from modify command and test the program by typing **DO LOOKUP** and entering various valid FGID numbers. If you are using the Student Version, use FGID numbers of 1006 and above. (See example in Figure 15-1.) If the program does not operate properly, revise and test again.

   If you get tired of telling dBASE that it is OK to reindex the files, you can give the command **SET SAFETY OFF**, which tells dBASE to ignore the fact that it is about to write over an existing file. You should **SET SAFETY ON** when you are finished testing the program. These commands may be included in the command file, before and after the indexing operations.

4. **TYPE LOOKUP.PRG TO PRINT** to make a copy of the program.

5. *For Additional Practice*: If you would like additional practice using two files, do the following.

    a. **QUIT** to exit dBASE. Obtain the Exercises Disk and copy the files ORDERS.DBF and ACCOUNTS.DBF to your data disk. Reenter dBASE.

    b. USE ACCOUNTS. Display the structure. This file is the same as the Ed & Bruce MAILING.DBF, except that it has three extra fields:

Field	Field name	Type	Width	Dec
10	ACCT_NO	Character	4	
11	PRIOR_BAL	Numeric	7	2
12	LIMIT	Numeric	7	2

    c. Index the file on the ACCT_NO field, creating an ACCOUNTS.NDX.

    d. Create a command file named CREDCHK.PRG. Enter the sample program contained on page 248 into CREDCHK.

    e. Test the program. You should find some acceptable transactions, and some which are not.

5. When you have completed this activity, give the command **QUIT** to exit dBASE. Remember to backup your work. If everything is proper, turn off the computer and return the dBASE software to the Lab Supervisor.

REVIEW QUESTIONS

1. What is a work area?

2. What is an alias?

3. What is the difference between the selected work area and other open work areas?

4. Assume that a file named SOX is open in the second work area, that the file INDIANS is open in the primary (first) work area, and that the primary work area is currently selected. How would you compute and display the following?

    *a. The sum of the fields RED in the SOX file and CLEVELAND in the INDIANS file,

    *b. The difference between RED in the SOX file and WHITE in the SOX file.

*5. Continuing the situation in question 4, how would you place the number *200* in the field RED in the SOX file? (Two commands are needed.)

DOCUMENTATION RESEARCH

Using the reference manual, determine the answers to the following questions which deal with the commands discussed in this unit. I recommend you also write the reference manual page number by the discussion of the command in this unit.

1. SELECT — under what condition would the command **SELECT P** work in dBASE III?

2. USE — what will be the alias if none is specified?

UNIT 16

RELATIONAL DATA BASE OPERATIONS AND VIEWS

In this unit we provide an introduction to relational data base operations using dBASE. In relational data base operations, one data file is linked, through a key value, to another data file. A movement in one of the data files will cause a corresponding movement in the other data file. Relational operations are very useful in creating sophisticated applications involving diverse kinds of data. We also introduce the concept of a view: a set of fields and files related to solve specific problems.

LEARNING OBJECTIVES

1. At the completion of this unit, you should know

    a. what a relation is,

    b. what a view is.

2. At the completion of this unit, you should be able to

    a. establish a relation between two files,

    b. establish a view of two or more files.

IMPORTANT COMMANDS

    SET RELATION TO {key expression} INTO {alias}
    SET RELATION TO {numeric expression} INTO {alias}
    CREATE VIEW {view filename}
    SET VIEW TO {view filename}

CONCEPTS OF RELATIONAL OPERATIONS

A *relational data base* is one in which various *tables* are linked together through *key* expressions. Although there is some debate in the professional community as to whether or not dBASE is a true relational *data base management system*, its capabilities are very similar to a relational DBMS.

dBASE uses the term *data file* instead of the more common terms *table* or *relation*. Either term refers to a row by column matrix of data, such as the data files we have used throughout this manual.

Relation Defined

A *relation* is a link between two data files (such as dBASE .DBF files). As the record pointer is moved in one file, the record pointer in the other file is moved to a corresponding record. In dBASE, relations are established through *key expressions* and *indexes*. dBASE also allows us to link by record numbers. The method for linking will be discussed later in this unit.

Types of Relations

Several types of relations may be established. The type of relation affects the method of linking the files together. These types parallel the traditional family structure, which is used as an example.

One to One (1:1) Relation. A husband and wife are in a 1:1 relationship: a husband has (no more than) one wife, and a wife has (no more than) one husband. In a 1:1 relation, there may be no match for a given case (e.g., a wife without a husband — divorced or widowed), but there may not be more than one match for a given case (e.g., a wife with many husbands).

Another example of a 1:1 relation is states and capital cities.

Where a 1:1 relation exists, the files may be directly linked such that a (record pointer) movement in one results in a movement to the corresponding record in the other.

One to Many (1:M) and Many to One (M:1) Relations. A mother and her children are in a 1:M relation: each mother may have many children, but each child may have only one mother. The *one* (mother) file may have zero, one, or several matches with the *many* (child) file, but the *many* file may have only zero or one match with the *one* file.

Another example of a 1:M relation is the state abbreviation verification example discussed in Unit 15. A given state may appear in many different addresses, but a given address is in only one state.

The starting point determines whether the relation is many to one or one to many. Starting with the mother or the state, the relation is one to many. Starting with the child or the city, the relation is many to one. The distinction is important when we need to locate corresponding data.

Where an M:1 relation exists, the *many* file may be directly linked to the *one* file such that a movement in the former (child) results in a movement to the corresponding record in the latter (mother). The reverse is not true, however. In a 1:M relation, the *one* file may be linked to the *many* file such that a movement in the *one* file leads to a movement to one of the matching records in the *many* file (you will find *one* of the children); the remainder of the matches in the *many* file must be found by some other method. Typically, the *many* file is indexed on the key used to match the two, and the second and succeeding matches will be the following (logical) records.

Many to Many (N:M) Relation. Parents and children are in an N:M relation: each parent may have many children, and each child may have many (i.e., two) parents. Either file may have zero, one, or many matches with the other file.

Another example of an N:M relation is the Chez Jacques menu and raw materials application in this manual.

Where an N:M relation exists, the files are linked through an intermediate file called a *link file*, such as the MIX.DBF file. This file contains keys to both of the files (i.e., FGID, RMID) as well as information unique to the intersection (e.g., the RM_QTY, which is the amount of the specific raw material in the specific menu item).

ESTABLISHING RELATIONS

Relations are established with the **SET RELATION** command. The general forms of the command are

> **set relation to {key expression} into {alias}**
> **set relation to {numeric expression} into {alias}**

which will cause all sequential commands to perform positioning on both selected and alias data files. That is, whenever a record pointer movement is made in the selected (*from*) file, the record pointer in the alias (*to*) file is moved to the corresponding record. You may then make other movements in the *to* file, and these do not affect the *from* file. Up to nine relations may exist at one time, but no more than one relation may be established from any given file.[1]

To establish a relation, both files must have been opened (in two different work areas). The work area of the *from* file must be selected when the **SET RELATION** command is given.

If **{numeric expression}** is used, the **{alias}** file will be positioned to the record number matching the expression. The **{alias}** file must not be indexed (or, opened with an index).

The **{key expression}** alternative is more often used because no assumptions need be made about the physical order of the **{alias}** file. If **{key expression}** is used, the **{alias}** file must be indexed on that key. For instance, two files might have ACCT_NO (account number) fields. The following would establish a relation such that any movement in ORDERS would cause the record pointer to move to the corresponding ACCT_NO in ACCOUNTS.

---

[1] In Application G, we will achieve the *effect* of setting two relations from one file, but we must outwit dBASE to do so.

```
clear all
select a
use orders
select b
use accounts index accounts
select orders
set relation to acct_no into accounts
```

This method is much easier than the **SELECT . . . SEEK . . . SELECT** syntax described in Unit 15. Whenever the record pointer is moved in ORDERS, dBASE performs the equivalent of **SELECT ACCOUNTS, SEEK ORDERS->ACCT_NO, SELECT ORDERS** to move the record pointer in ACCOUNTS to the appropriate record, without any programming to that effect.

USING RELATIONS

This section contains three examples of how relations may be used. For these examples, assume that you have two files, WIVES and HUSBANDS; that each is indexed as noted (with no duplicates, i.e., there are not two husbands with the name 'John Smith'); and that each has the same structure.

Field	Field name	Type	Width	Dec
1	LAST_NAME	Character	15	
2	FIRST_NAME	Character	10	
3	SPOUSE_LN	Character	15	
4	SPOUSE_FN	Character	10	
5	AGE	Numeric	2	
6	INCOME	Numeric	6	

You have already given the following commands:

```
clear all
set safety off
use husbands
index on upper(last_name+first_name) to husbands
select b
use wives
index on upper(last_name+first_name) to wives
set safety on
set relation to upper(spouse_ln+spouse_fn) into husbands
```

As you read the examples that follow, remember that the relation is established from the WIVES file to the HUSBANDS file.

Note that the {key expression}, UPPER(SPOUSE_LN+SPOUSE_FN), does not have to use the same field names as the {index key}, UPPER(LAST_NAME+FIRST_NAME), but the contents of the expressions must be the same. For instance, the record for me in the HUSBANDS file would have 'Ross   ' as LAST_NAME and 'Steven   ' as FIRST_NAME. The record for my wife in WIVES should have 'Ross   ' as SPOUSE_LN and 'Steven   ' as SPOUSE_FN. If so, then the relation will point to my record in HUSBANDS whenever the pointer is moved to her record in WIVES. All expressions have been converted to uppercase to remove any inconsistencies in capitalization in the two files.

Because the relation is established from WIVES to HUSBANDS, the WIVES file must be selected and used for movements. Moving to a particular wife in the WIVES file will cause movement in the HUSBANDS file to her husband, but moving to a husband in the HUSBANDS file will not cause movement in the WIVES file to his wife.

Computing

To compute total family income of a given family, move the record pointer to the wife's record (which will move the pointer to the corresponding husband's record) and give the command

? husbands->income+wives->income

which adds the INCOME field from both HUSBANDS and WIVES files and displays the result.

Reporting

Reports may also refer to related files. Before defining the report (**MODIFY REPORT** command), establish the relation as above. If you exit dBASE or change the relations, you will also have to establish the relation before executing the report (**REPORT FORM** command).

Report columns may contain fields from the alias file (e.g., **HUSBANDS->AGE** in a column entitled "Husband Age") and also computations (e.g., **HUSBANDS->INCOME+ WIVES->INCOME** as in the example above).

Listing

The **LIST** and **DISPLAY** commands may also refer to fields in the related file. For instance, you might give the command

list off last_name,spouse_ln,age,husbands->age for (last_name)<>(spouse_ln)

to obtain a list of the ages of all couples who do not share the same last name.

VIEWS

A *view* is a particular way of looking at the data in a database, usually customized for a particular application.[2] The view determines which files are open, how they are related, which fields are available from those files, and filter condition and screen format if desired. View files have the extension .VUE, and may be created, modified, and invoked from either the dot prompt or the **ASSIST** menu. The relevant dot prompt commands are

---

[2] View file capabilities are not available in the original version of dBASE III.

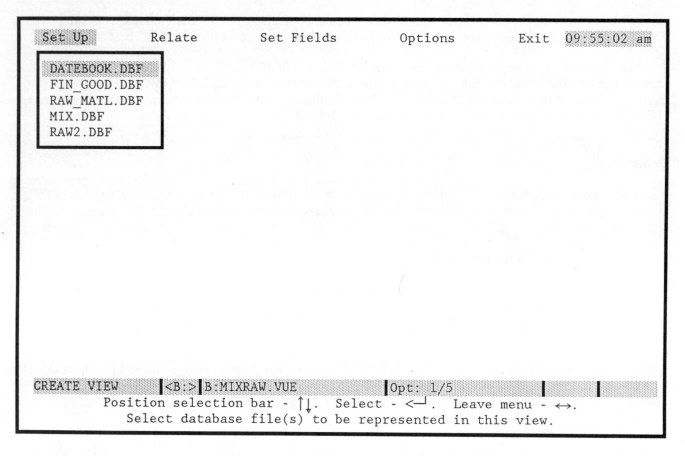

FIGURE 16-1 Creating a View: Selecting the Files to be Included

create view {view filename}
modify view {view filename}
set view to {view filename}

If you have already opened the files and set the relations you want included in your view, you may create the view from the existing status with the command

create view {view filename} from environment

The view thus created may be subsequently modified.

From the ASSIST Menu. SET VIEW TO is found on the ■ *Set Up* ■ menu (as ■ *Set Up* ■ *View* ■); **CREATE VIEW** is found on the ■ *Create* ■ menu (as ■ *Create* ■ *View* ■); and **MODIFY VIEW** is found on the ■ *Modify* ■ menu (as ■ *Modify* ■ *View* ■). As with other **ASSIST** menu commands that deal with files, you are asked for the drive designation and file name. Working with views is the same whether you enter from the dot prompt or from the **ASSIST** menu.

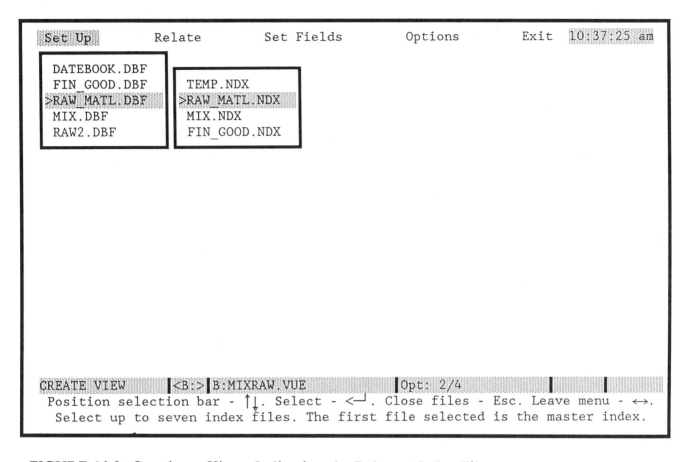

FIGURE 16-2 Creating a View: Indicating the Relevant Index File

Creating a View

We will illustrate the view creation process by creating a view of the mix and raw material data files. The view should include the RMID field (which serves as the link between the two), FGID and RM_QTY fields from MIX.DBF, and DESC and COST fields from RAW_MATL.DBF. The process is started with the **CREATE VIEW** command (or, from the **ASSIST** menu, ■ *Create* ■ *View* ■). I name the file MIXRAW (dBASE adds a .VUE extension automatically). The first screen is used to specify which files are to be included in the view. (See Figure 16-1.)

As usual, files are selected by highlighting and then pressing <CR>. Once a file is selected, you will be asked to specify the relevant indexes (Figure 16-2). If your view includes a relation, the first index of the target file (the one that the relation is set *into*) must be the index that matches the {key expression} of the relation. Normally, you will select all files and relevant indexes before proceeding beyond the ■ *Set Up* ■ menu. In this case, I indicated that RAW_MATL.DBF should be used with RAW_MATL.NDX, and MIX.DBF should be used with MIX.NDX. Recall that RAW_MATL is indexed on the RMID field, while MIX is indexed on the FGID field.

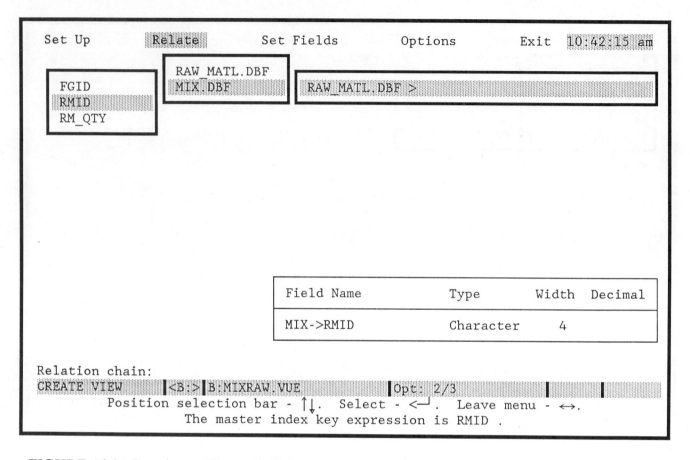

FIGURE 16-3 Creating a View: Defining a Relation

The next step is to define the relations. On the ■ *Relate* ■ menu, choose the file that the relation is to be set *from*, then the file that the relation is to be set *into*. If your relation chain includes three or more files, you must start with the primary file — the one that will not have any relation set into it. Once you choose the primary file, all others (in this case, there is only one other) will be displayed as potential targets. Press <CR> to enter the {key expression} for the relation. To get help, you may press the F10 key, and dBASE will display a list of fields in the primary data file. The index key of the target data file is displayed at the bottom of the screen (see Figure 16-3). If you have more than one relation to set, you may repeat the process to set a relation from the second file into a third file.

The next step in defining a relation is to indicate which fields should be displayed. In this case, I choose all fields in MIX (FGID, RMID, and RM_QTY), but only two fields in RAW_MATL (DESC and COST). Note that dBASE will assume that you want *all* fields included, and you must tell it which to exclude (see Figure 16-4). I excluded RMID because it is already included from the MIX file, and I excluded INVENTORY and LAST_ORDER because my application does not need them.

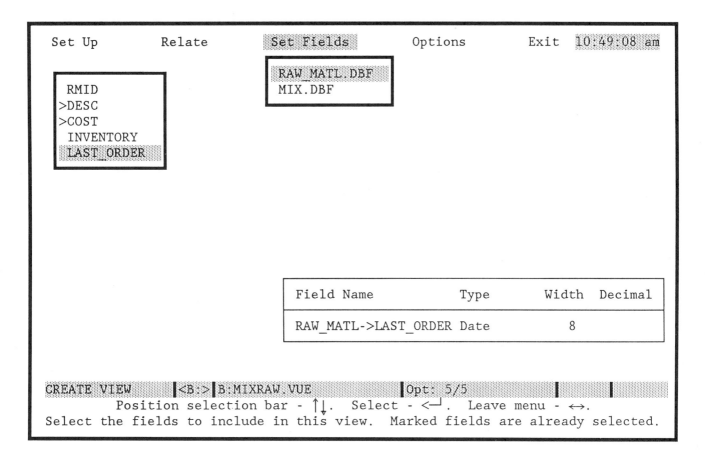

FIGURE 16-4 Creating a View: Setting the Fields to Be Included

dBASE offers two options for the view file: setting a filter condition through a query file (see Unit 5); and setting a custom screen format through a format file (see Unit 14). The query and format files must exist before you selecting them in this option. The ■ *Options* ■ menu is illustrated in Figure 16-5. For this example, I did not choose either option. In general, the sequence for creating a sophisticated view will be as follows:

1. Define the files, relations, and fields.

2. Exit (save) from the view creation process.

3. Create the screen and query files.

4. Modify the view file to include the screen and query files.

Once the view creation or modification process is exited, the view is in effect for the remainder of the dBASE session, or until you set another view (**SET VIEW TO . . .**). To disconnect a view without establishing another, use **SET VIEW TO** without specifying a {**view filename**}.

```
 Set Up          Relate          Set Fields       Options        Exit    10:56:44 am
                                                  ┌─────────────────────────────────────┐
                                                  │ Filter:                             │
                                                  │ Format:                     .       │
                                                  └─────────────────────────────────────┘

















 CREATE VIEW       │<B:>│B:MIXRAW.VUE                │Opt: 2/2        │           │
           Position selection bar - ↑↓.   Select - ◁┘.   Leave menu - ↔.
         Select a screen format to use with full-screen commands for this view.
```

FIGURE 16-5 Creating a View: The Options Menu

The view affects many database operations. For instance, I used the **ASSIST** menu sequence

■ *Retrieve* ■ *Display* ■ *Specify Scope* ■ *All* ■ *Execute the command*■

to display all records in the view, a screenful at a time (see Figure 16-6). The records are displayed in the order of the primary data file (here, MIX in the logical order defined by MIX.NDX). Note that appropriate data from RAW_MATL is also displayed.

You may also use **EDIT, BROWSE, REPLACE, SUM, AVERAGE, COUNT, REPORT,** and **LABEL** based on the view you have established. If you **EDIT**, the changes you make will go to the appropriate fields in the appropriate records of the proper file. For instance, changing the DESC field in our example will affect the RAW_MATL file. If you were to locate the FGID/RMID combination of *1001/0001* (*Big Jac/all-beef patty*), and change the DESC field to *ground round*, then all finished goods that have that raw material will now display *ground round* instead of *all-beef patty*. In effect, you have selected RAW_MATL and edited record 1, without having to give the specific commands.

```
 Set Up  Create  Update  Position  Retrieve  Organize Modify Tools    11:13:36 am


Record#  FGID RMID RM_QTY DESC                COST
      1  1001 0001      2 all-beef patty      0.10
      2  1001 0002      2 sp. sauce (oz.)     0.01
      3  1001 0003      1 lettuce leaf        0.01
      4  1001 0004      2 cheese slice        0.02
      5  1001 0005      4 pickle slice        0.03
      6  1001 0006      1 ch. onion (oz.)     0.06
      7  1001 0007      1 sesame seed bun     0.12
      8  1002 0001      2 all-beef patty      0.10
      9  1002 0002      2 sp. sauce (oz.)     0.01
     10  1002 0003      1 lettuce leaf        0.01
     11  1002 0004      2 cheese slice        0.02
     12  1002 0005      4 pickle slice        0.03
     13  1002 0006      1 ch. onion (oz.)     0.06
     14  1002 0007      1 sesame seed bun     0.12
     15  1002 0011     11 Coca Cola (oz.)     0.05
     16  1002 0014      1 12 oz. cup          0.03
     17  1002 0010      4 fren. fry (oz.)     0.01
Press any key to continue...
ASSIST            <B:> MIX                    Rec: 1/82
```

FIGURE 16-6 Display as a Result of the View

Some commands, such as **APPEND, DELETE, FIND, SEEK, LOCATE,** and **CONTINUE,** cause movement or changes to the primary file, although {search conditions} may include any of the fields in the view.

This section has provided a brief introduction to the view file capabilities available in dBASE III Plus. These capabilities are very powerful and move dBASE toward a true relational database management system.

GUIDED ACTIVITY

This activity requires you to establish and use a relationship between two files. You may use either the **SET RELATION** or the **SET VIEW** capabilities of dBASE.

1. Follow the startup procedure for your version of dBASE as outlined in Unit 2.

2. Write a command file called RELATE that will compute the cost of raw materials in a given Chez Jacques menu item. The program should accept an FGID as input, and read through the MIX file for all records that match that FGID. For each match, the program should locate the corresponding RMID in the RAW_MATL file, multiply the RM_QTY in

MIX by the COST in RAW_MATL, and keep a running sum. When no more matches with the FGID are found, the sum should be printed and the program should terminate.

This is virtually the same program as the one you created in Unit 15, except that you should set a relation between MIX and RAW_MATL instead of using the **SEEK** command. (You may also create and invoke a view file instead of including the relation-setting commands in your command file.)

Before sitting down at the computer, outline the commands that will accomplish the following tasks.

✔ **CHECKPOINT**

Write the commands on the lines to the right of the tasks.

a. Reset dBASE and open the file MIX. _____

_____

b. Index MIX on FGID. _____

c. Select the second work area. _____

d. Open the file RAW_MATL. _____

e. Index RAW_MATL on RMID. _____

f. Select the MIX file. _____

g. Set a relation to RAW_MATL based on RMID. _____

h. Set a memory variable called TOTCOST to 0 (zero). _____

i. Input the FGID. _____

j. Find the first match in MIX. _____

k. Start a loop that will continue until the FGID
   in the MIX file does not match the input FGID. _____

l. Multiply RM_QTY in the MIX file by COST in the
   RAW_MATL file and add to TOTCOST. _____

m. Move to the next record in MIX. _____

n. Terminate the loop, _____

o. Print the result. _____

```
. do relate
mix.ndx already exists, overwrite it? (Y/N) Yes
  100% indexed            82 Records indexed
raw_matl.ndx already exists, overwrite it? (Y/N) Yes
  100% indexed            19 Records indexed
0
Enter FGID 1006
          0.10
Record No.      57
          0.16
Record No.      58
          0.26
Record No.      59
          0.30
Record No.      60
          0.30
.
Command Line     |<B:>|MIX                        |Rec: 60/82           |Ins    |
                   Enter a dBASE III Plus command.
```

FIGURE 16-7 The RELATE Program in Operation
Note: Items typed by the user are in **boldface**.

3. When you have finished the program, exit from modify command and test the program by typing **DO RELATE** and entering various valid FGID numbers. If you are using the Student Version, use FGID numbers of 1006 and above. (See illustration in Figure 16-7.) If the program does not operate properly, revise and test again. You may eliminate the "OK to overwrite" questions by **SET SAFETY OFF**, and you may eliminate the reporting of record numbers and intermediate mathematic results by **SET TALK OFF**.

4. **TYPE RELATE.PRG TO PRINT** to make a copy of the program.

5. *For Additional Practice*: If you would like more practice using relations, modify the CREDCHK program you created in Unit 15 to take advantage of relations.

6. When you have completed this activity, give the command **QUIT** to exit dBASE. Remember to backup your work. If everything is proper, turn off the computer and return the dBASE software to the Lab Supervisor.

REVIEW QUESTIONS

*1. What is a relation?

2. List the types of relations, and give an example of each.

3. What is a view? How is a view different from a relation?

DOCUMENTATION RESEARCH

Using the reference manual, determine the answers to the following questions which deal with the commands discussed in this unit. I recommend you also write the reference manual page number by the discussion of the command in this unit.

1. SET RELATION TO . . . — how is the relation disconnected?

2. CREATE VIEW {view filename} — what do all .VUE files contain? What else *may* they contain?

3. CREATE VIEW {view filename} FROM ENVIRONMENT — although this command was not discussed in detail in the unit, it can be very useful. What does it accomplish?

4. SET VIEW TO {view filename} — how is a .VUE file closed?

UNIT

17

OTHER MULTIPLE FILE OPERATIONS

In this final unit, we discuss additional multiple file commands. One of the commands is used to update one file based on information contained in another file. Another command is used to create a new file based on the associations between the information contained in two source files. This unit also contains a discussion of a command that is used to create a data file of summary information.

LEARNING OBJECTIVES

1. At the completion of this unit, you should know

   a. what an update operation is,

   b. what a join operation is.

2. At the completion of this unit, you should be able to

   a. update one data file based on information contained in another,

   b. join two files to create a third based on some logical relationship between the two files,

   c. create a file containing subtotals of the data in another file.

IMPORTANT COMMANDS

UPDATE ON {key} FROM {alias} REPLACE {field} WITH {expression} RANDOM
JOIN WITH {alias} TO {file} FOR {condition}
TOTAL ON {key} TO {data file}

UPDATING A DATA FILE

Updating is the process of changing the information in one file based on the information contained in another. You performed updates manually in Units 13 and 14, when you entered new prices in the menu file. This section tells you how to perform the same operation automatically.

The general forms of the **UPDATE** command are

update on {key} from {alias} replace {field} with {expression}
update on {key} from {alias} replace {field} with {expression} random

These commands change the information in the selected file based on the information in the {alias} file, which is a dBASE data file.

Both files must be sorted or indexed on {key}, unless the **RANDOM** qualifier is used. **RANDOM** allows the **FROM** file to be in any order, but the selected file must be indexed on {key}. The {key} field must be the same (name, type, width) in both data files.

If the **WITH {expression}** involves fields from the {alias} file (which is usually the case), those fields must be referred to by their alias.

For example, assume that you have two files, INVENTOR.DBF and CHANGES.DBF, with new prices in CHANGES. Both files have PART_NO and PRICE fields, and you want to update the INVENTOR file with information from CHANGES. INVENTOR is indexed on PART_NO.

clear all
use inventor
index on part_no to inventor
select b
use changes
select inventor
update on part_no from changes replace price with changes->price random

Note that the file to be updated is selected before the update operation. Study this example carefully, for you will be expected to perform a similar operation in the Guided Activity for this unit.

CREATION OF A FILE OF RELATIONS

Joining is the process of merging fields from two files to create a third file. The command used is the **JOIN** command.

join with {alias} to {file} for {condition} fields {field list}

which uses two databases to create a third whenever some condition is met.

JOIN goes to the first (logical) record in the selected data file and evaluates each record in the alias data file against that record. Whenever the {condition} is true, a record is output to the **TO** file. After each record in the alias file has been evaluated, the selected file is advanced one record and the process repeats, until all selected file records have been evaluated. **JOIN** takes a long time to complete. If there are 1000 records in each file, then 1,000,000 comparisons must be made.

Note that the potential output of this procedure is the product of the number of records in the selected file times the number of records in the alias file. Thus, if each file had 1000 records, and {condition} was always true, then 1000 records would be output for each record in the selected file (1000 times 1000 = 1,000,000).

The output file will consist of the **FIELDS** specified, or, if the **FIELDS** specification is not present, will consist of all selected file fields and as many of the alias file fields as will fit. Alias file fields must be referred to with the **ALIAS->FIELD_NAME** syntax.

For example,

```
clear all
select a
use first
select b
use second
select first
join with second to new for id=second->id
```

will create a file called NEW.DBF with fields from both FIRST and SECOND. A record will be output for every match of ID numbers. If an ID number exists in one file but not the other, no record will be output.

Alternative Methods for Joining Two or More Files

The **JOIN** command is slow, and often does more than is needed. In many cases, establishing a relation or a view of the files will be sufficient. For example, remember the view of MIX and RAW_MATL we established in Unit 16. To see the data in both files, based on a match between the RMID field in each, we could do any of the following.

alternative 1:
```
clear all
use mix
select 2
use raw_matl
select mix
join with raw_matl to mixraw for rmid=raw_matl->rmid
```

alternative 2:
    clear all
    use mix
    select 2
    use raw_matl index raw_matl
    select mix
    set relation to rmid into raw_matl

alternative 3:
    clear all
    set view to mixraw

No new file is created in alternatives 2 and 3. In most cases, the relation or view is sufficient for database queries. If we *must* have a file with the related data, then add the command

copy to mixraw fields fgid, rmid, rm_qty, raw_matl->desc, raw_matl->cost

to alternative 2, or the command

copy to mixraw fields fgid, rmid, rm_qty, desc, cost

to alternative 3. These commands would create the same file as the **JOIN** command in the first alternative would have created, but much more quickly because the comparisons (82 times 19 = 1558) do not need to be made.

CREATION OF A FILE OF SUBTOTALS

The **TOTAL** command is used to compute subtotals of numeric fields and place those subtotals in a separate data file. The subtotals are computed for distinct groups of data, based on a key field. The general forms of the command are

total on {key} to {data file}
total on {key} to {data file} fields {list} for {condition}

The **{key}** *field must be a character-type field for the command to function properly.* The open database must be either sorted or indexed on the **{key}** field before the **TOTAL** command is given. All records with the same **{key}** value become a single record in the **TO {data file}**. Numeric-type fields named in the **FIELDS {list}** (which is optional) will contain totals. If no **FIELDS {list}** is present, all numeric-type fields are totaled. Other type fields will contain the contents of the first record in that set.

The **TO {data file}** will have the same structure as the data file from which the totals are drawn. If numeric-type fields are not wide enough to contain the totals, then data will be lost and the fields will be filled with *******s. Before using the **TOTAL** command, you should check the structure of the file, and modify it if necessary, to ensure that all numeric fields are wide enough. If the **TO {data file}** existed before, it will be replaced.

This command is useful for creating summary information for input into spreadsheet programs. For instance, if you had a data file ACCOUNTS.DBF of customers with fields for city and prior account balance (among others), you could easily create a summary file with total account balances by city:

> **use accounts**
> **index on city to temp**
> **total on city to citytot**
> **use citytot**
> **display all city, prior_bal**

If your data file contained records with information on people in thirty-seven different cities, CITYTOT.DBF would contain thirty-seven records, each with the total account balance in a specific city. The field CITY would contain the name of the city to which the totals pertained. Other character-, date-, and logical-type fields will contain the contents of those fields in the first record for a given city (and may be irrelevant for the task at hand).

GUIDED ACTIVITY

This activity requires you to use the **UPDATE** command.

1. Follow the startup procedure for your version of dBASE as outlined in Unit 2.

2. Create a file named PRICECH with the following structure:

Field	Field name	Type	Width	Dec
1	FGID	Character	4	
2	NEW_PRICE	Numeric	6	2

3. Enter the following data into PRICECH.DBF

FGID	NEW_PRICE
1005	2.50
1002	2.50
1004	2.50
1003	2.50
1007	0.89
1009	0.51

4. Update FIN_GOOD.DBF based on the information in PRICECH.DBF, as illustrated in Figure 17-1.

✔ CHECKPOINT
What command do you use for the update?

_____

5. Do a screen print to show the commands used, and **LIST TO PRINT** to demonstrate that the command worked.

```
. clear all
. use fin_good
. index on fgid to fin_good
fin_good.ndx already exists, overwrite it? (Y/N) Yes
   100% indexed            17 Records indexed
. select b
. use pricech
. select fin_good
. update on fgid from pricech replace sell_price with pricech->new_price random
      6 records updated
.
```

```
Command Line        <B:> FIN_GOOD               Rec: 16/17          Ins
```

Enter a dBASE III PLUS command.

FIGURE 17-1 Illustration of the **UPDATE** Command
Note: Items entered by the user are in **boldface**.

6. *For Additional Practice*: If you would like to try another of the multiple file commands, duplicate the example for the **TOTAL** command. (If you did not complete the *Additional Practice* section of Unit 16, follow the instructions in that section to copy ACCOUNTS.DBF to your data disk.)

7. When you have completed this activity, give the command **QUIT** to exit dBASE. Remember to backup your work. If everything is proper, turn off the computer and return the dBASE software to the Lab Supervisor.

REVIEW QUESTIONS

1. What is an update operation?

2. What is a join operation?

*3. If you were to use the **TOTAL** command on the RAW_MATL file, indexed by RMID, how many records would be in the file created by **TOTAL**? Why?

DOCUMENTATION RESEARCH

Using the reference manual, determine the answers to the following questions which deal with the commands discussed in this unit. I recommend you also write the reference manual page number by the discussion of the command in this unit.

1. UPDATE ON {key} FROM {alias} REPLACE {field} WITH {expression} RANDOM — what will happen if the {key} field is not unique in the target database?

2. JOIN WITH {alias} TO {file} FOR {condition} — what is the minimum number of records in the target {file}? the maximum number of records?

3. TOTAL ON {key} TO {data file} — what will appear in character-, date-, and logical-type fields of the target data file?

APPLICATION

F

CHEZ JACQUES (III)

This application exercise requires you to use multiple file capabilities of dBASE. There are many possible methods for accomplishing this exercise.

1. Follow the startup procedure for your version of dBASE as outlined in Unit 2.

2. Write a command file named BOM.PRG that will compute a Bill of Materials for all items in the finished goods file. (A sample Bill of Materials appears in Figure F-1.) The Bill of Materials that you compute may have different numbers as a result of changes you have made in the finished goods and raw materials files, and if you are using the Student Version, FGID numbers of 1005 and below have no raw materials.

The Bill of Materials should

a. print the finished item description and selling price;

b. list all raw materials with description, quantity (in the finished product), and cost;

c. compute and print the total cost of the raw materials in the item and the margin (price minus cost).

You have done much of the necessary work for items b and c in the Guided Activities for Units 15 and 16. Your program will need another loop to circulate through the finished goods file, with the loop through the mix file included within the finished goods loop. The basic structure of the program will therefore be

```
      reset dBASE
      set talk off
      open all files, index and set relations as necessary
      start loop through finished goods file
          start loop through mix file
              list and sum for raw material
              next record in mix file
          end of mix file loop
          next record in finished goods file
      end of finished goods file loop
      set talk on
```

I leave it to you to fill in the details.

3. Print a copy of your bill of materials. Do this by giving the command **SET PRINT ON** before you give the command **DO BOM**.

4. Print a copy of your command file.

5. When you have completed this exercise, exit dBASE. Remember to backup your work. If everything is proper, turn off the computer and return the dBASE software to the Lab Supervisor.

```
Hamburger
-------------------------------------------------
all-beef patty   1       0.10
pickle slice     2       0.03
regular bun      1       0.10
catsup (oz.)     1       0.04
Selling Price        0.62
Total Cost               0.30
Margin                            0.32

Cheese Burger
-------------------------------------------------
all-beef patty   1       0.10
pickle slice     2       0.03
regular bun      1       0.10
catsup (oz.)     1       0.04
cheese slice     1       0.02
Selling Price        0.89
Total Cost               0.32
Margin                            0.57
```

FIGURE F-1 Portion of a Bill of Materials

APPLICATION

G CHEZ JACQUES (IV)

This application makes additional use of the Chez Jacques database. You are asked to accomplish several tasks that reflect the types of operations performed in "real-life" database management. This application consists of four parts.

PART 1 AN ON-SCREEN BILL OF MATERIALS

In Part 1, we will explore further the use of multiple files with a sample program that accomplishes a variation of the Bill of Materials requested in Application F. This part is unlike previous applications, where you are given a task and asked to develop the commands to accomplish the task. Here, you are given the commands, in two program files, and must determine *how* they accomplish the task. Then, you are challenged to add to the program.

Start by copying the files OSBOM.PRG, OSBOM2.PRG, and MIX2.DBF from the Exercises Disk to your data disk. You should already have the files FIN_GOOD.DBF and RAW_MATL.DBF on the same data disk. Once the files are copied, give the DOS commands

    type b:osbom.prg>prn
    type b:osbom2.prg>prn

to make copies of the two program files (if you are using a hard-disk system, change **b:** to **a:** or **c:** — whichever has your data-file disk).

Now, enter dBASE and **DO OSBOM**. You should see a bill of materials for the first item in FGID-order (the Big Jac). Pressing the following keys will cause the program to react as indicated.

Press:	Result:
<DOWN ARROW>	Next item in FGID-order is displayed.
<UP>	Previous item in FGID-order is displayed.
<LEFT>	User is prompted to enter FGID of item to be displayed.

Press:	Result:
PgDn	Item after next item in FGID-order is displayed (program skips an item).
PgUp	Item prior to previous item in FGID-order is displayed (program skips an item in reverse order).
Home	First item in FGID-order is displayed.
End	Last item in FGID-order is displayed.
<CR>	Program terminates.

Try all of these keys, making note of the screen display and comparing the results to the bill of materials you created in Application F. Notice the message line at the bottom of the screen. Look at the listing of the programs you obtained earlier and try to determine which commands are responsible for which effects. (A listing of each program also appears at the end of this Application.) Five of the effects are especially notable and are discussed further.

The Leap-Frog Relation. In Unit 16, I said that dBASE will allow you to set only one relation from a given file. That is technically true, but there are times when we can achieve the effect of two relations set from one file, either using the **SET RELATION TO . . .** command, or while establishing a .VUE file. Notice that, early in the program, we set a relation from MIX2 into RAW_MATL, based on the RMID field (of MIX2). Then we set a relation from RAW_MATL into FIN_GOOD, *based on the FGID field of MIX2*. We have effectively set two relations from MIX2: one into RAW_MATL and the other into FIN_GOOD. Whenever we move in MIX2, we cause a movement in RAW_MATL based on the key for that relation (RMID field in MIX2). Whenever we move in RAW_MATL, we cause a movement in FIN_GOOD based on the key for that relation (FGID field in MIX2).

The Customized Message. The **SET MESSAGE TO . . .** command is used to alter the informational message which is displayed at the bottom of the screen. In this case, I created a message which included normal text as well as three special graphics characters using the **CHR( )** function. The codes for the <ARROW> graphics characters are

    24 <UP ARROW>
    25 <DOWN ARROW>
    26 <RIGHT ARROW>
    27 <LEFT ARROW>

I found these and other graphics codes in Appendix G of the *IBM PC BASIC Manual*.

Capturing a Keypress. The **INKEY( )** function is used to capture any key pressed by the user and store the numeric equivalent of that key in the memory variable KEY. The value of KEY is then used to determine which of the options to follow. The values returned by **INKEY( )** for the most common control keys are presented in Table G-1. (These are *not* the same as the values returned by **READKEY( )**.)

Calling a Subprogram. The command **DO OSBOM2** appears repeatedly through OSBOM, in each case executing the subprogram/command file named OSBOM2.PRG. Since the same series of commands is executed after each choice (except <CR>) made by the user, I was able to put those commands in a separate file and use that file as a subroutine.

TABLE G-1 INKEY( ) Values

Key Pressed by User	Value of INKEY( )
\<LEFT ARROW>	19
\<RIGHT>	4
\<UP>	5
\<DOWN>	24
Home	1
End	6
PgUp	18
PgDn	3

If no key has been pressed the value of INKEY( ) is 0 (zero).

Using Limited Scopes. Within OSBOM2.PRG, we capitalize on the fact that the logic of the main program has moved us to the first record in MIX2 which has the FGID of interest, and that the value of that FGID is stored in a memory variable named GOOD. We use **SUM . . . WHILE** to compute the total raw materials cost without having to go through the entire file, and **DISPLAY . . . WHILE** to quickly display the relevant raw materials.

You may be wondering why this application uses a file named MIX2, and all other Chez Jacques exercises have used MIX. The reason is because of a curious trait (in other words, a *bug*) of dBASE. When I tried to get the SUM command to work in OSBOM2, it would work fine for all items *except* the last finished good in the MIX file. I even changed the last item, and still had the problem. There was no way I could get the command to sum the costs for the last item in the list, so I changed the list by adding a dummy item (FGID = '9999', RMID = '9999', RM_QTY = 0) to MIX2. Except for this last record, MIX and MIX2 are identical. To make the program display the last *real* item, the logic is written to analyze the next-to-last item.

Positioning. The sixth special effect of OSBOM is how it determines which FGID to analyze. I leave it to you to analyze the logic of each **CASE** within the **DO WHILE .T.** loop.

The Endless Loop. Finally, notice how an endless loop and **DO CASE** logic are used to cycle the program until the user presses \<CR>.

My Challenge to You

Modify OSBOM to add the following features:

» If the user enters an invalid FGID after pressing \<RIGHT>, the program should inform him or her of that fact and ask again.

» Add an option for the \<LEFT ARROW>, which will display all finished goods, one at a time, pausing for the user to press a key before continuing from one to the next.

PART 2 A REVERSE BILL OF MATERIALS

Jacques has just been informed that his last shipment of cheese was tainted. Since he prides himself on using the finest ingredients, he will pull all items from his menu which use cheese. Which items must be (temporarily) eliminated?

In anticipation of further crises, Chez Jacques would like you to prepare a *reverse bill of materials* — a list of each raw material and the menu items in which it is used. Do so by creating a command file with the name RBOM.PRG. You might wish to use the logic of LOOKUP (Unit 15), RELATE (Unit 16), BOM (Application F), or OSBOM (Part 1 of this application) as a starting point.

PART 3 SALES

Assume that the following items were sold earlier today. Change the raw materials inventory to reflect these sales. Write a command file named SALES.PRG to accomplish this task.

Apple Tartes	25
Jac Meal /Co/Ch	30
Giant Coke	10
Large Fries	35

PART 4 MARGINS

For this exercise, you may wish to modify the file structure to add additional fields. On which menu item does Chez Jacques make the largest margin? The largest margin as a percent of sales price?

OSBOM.PRG

```
************************************
* OPEN FILES, ESTABLISH RELATIONS *
************************************
CLEAR ALL
SET TALK OFF
SET HEADING OFF
SET SAFETY OFF
USE FIN_GOOD
INDEX ON FGID TO FIN_GOOD
SELECT B
USE RAW_MATL
INDEX ON RMID TO RAW_MATL
SELECT C
USE MIX2
INDEX ON FGID TO MIX2
SET RELATION TO RMID INTO RAW_MATL
SELECT RAW_MATL
SET RELATION TO MIX2->FGID INTO FIN_GOOD
SELECT MIX2
SET SAFETY ON
SET MESSAGE TO CHR(25)+' next  '+CHR(24)+' prev.  PgDn 2d next  '+;
   'PgUp 2d prev.  Home first  End last  '+CHR(26)+' enter'
GOOD=FGID
DO OSBOM2                              && Displays information
************************
* START AN INFINITE LOOP *
************************
DO WHILE .T.
   KEY=INKEY()                         && Determines last key pressed
   DO CASE
      CASE KEY=0                       && No key has been pressed
         LOOP
      CASE KEY=4                       && User enters number
         CLEAR
         ACCEPT 'FGID: ' TO GOOD
         SEEK GOOD
         DO OSBOM2                     && Displays information
      CASE KEY=5 .AND. .NOT.BOF()      && <UP> one item
         SKIP -1        && moves to last record of most recent list
         GOOD=FGID
         SEEK GOOD      && moves to first record of most recent list
         SKIP -1        && moves to last record of desired list
         GOOD=FGID
         SEEK GOOD      && moves to first record of desired list
         DO OSBOM2      && Displays information
      CASE KEY=24 .AND. .NOT.EOF()     && <DOWN> one item
```

Program listing continues on following page.

```
                  GOOD=FGID       && will already be at first record of desired list
                  DO OSBOM2       && Displays information
            CASE KEY=3 .AND. .NOT.EOF()       && PgDn -- skip one item down
                  GOOD=FGID
                  LOCATE REST FOR FGID<>GOOD  && moves to next unique FGID
                  GOOD=FGID
                  DO OSBOM2                    && Displays information
            CASE KEY=18 .AND. .NOT.BOF()       && PgUp -- skip one item up
                  SKIP -1       && moves to last record of most recent list
                  GOOD=FGID
                  SEEK GOOD     && moves to first record of most recent list
                  SKIP -1       && moves to last record of list to skip
                  GOOD=FGID
                  SEEK GOOD     && moves to first record of list to skip
                  SKIP -1       && moves to last record of desired list
                  GOOD=FGID
                  SEEK GOOD     && moves to first record of desired list
                  DO OSBOM2     && Displays information
            CASE KEY=1                          && First Item (Home)
                  GO TOP
                  GOOD=FGID
                  DO OSBOM2                      && Displays information
            CASE KEY=6                          && Last Item (End)
                  GO BOTTOM
                  SKIP -1
                  GOOD=FGID
                  SEEK GOOD     && moves to first record of desired list
                  DO OSBOM2     && Displays information
            CASE KEY=13                         && Return (<CR>)
                  SET MESSAGE TO
                  SET TALK ON
                  SET HEADING ON
                  RETURN
      ENDCASE
ENDDO
```

OSBOM2.PRG

```
CLEAR
TOTALCOST=0
PRICE=FIN_GOOD->SELL_PRICE
SUM RM_QTY*RAW_MATL->COST WHILE GOOD=FGID TO TOTALCOST
SEEK GOOD
? "FGID  Description    Sell Price"
DISPLAY OFF FGID, FIN_GOOD->DESC, FIN_GOOD->SELL_PRICE
? "RMID Qty Description          Cost        Ext."
DISPLAY OFF RMID, RM_QTY, RAW_MATL->DESC, RAW_MATL->COST,;
   RM_QTY*RAW_MATL->COST WHILE FGID=GOOD
? "    Total Cost         Margin"
DISPLAY OFF TOTALCOST, PRICE-TOTALCOST
```

APPENDIX

A GETTING STARTED ON YOUR MICROCOMPUTER

This appendix covers the knowledge necessary to use applications software and the Disk Operating System (DOS) with the IBM PC or compatible microcomputers. It is not intended to make you an expert in DOS, but to provide some level of competence by setting forth the necessary operations external to the software discussed in this manual.

PART 1 THE KEYBOARD

The IBM and other personal computers have over 80 keys, about 40 more than most type-writers. An illustration of the keyboard appears inside the back cover of this manual. Many of the "extra" keys have symbols or mnemonics rather than characters. To minimize confusion, the following conventions are used in THE MICROCOMPUTING SERIES.

Keys with multiple character names have those names spelled out in Small Type, usually followed by the word *key*. Examples include the F1 key, the Ins key, the Home key, and the Del key. Keys with symbols only have the key name enclosed in < > signs:

<TAB>   Gray key just below the Esc key, marked with two arrows.

<SHIFT>   Gray keys: one between the Ctrl and Alt keys, the other just above the Caps Lock key, marked with hollow upward arrows.

<BACKSPACE>   Gray key in top row of keyboard with arrow pointing to the left.

<CR>   Gray key between the <BACKSPACE> and PrtSc keys, marked with bent arrow.

<ARROW KEYS>   White keys on the right of the keyboard, each marked with an arrow; also called <UP>, <LEFT>, <DOWN>, and <RIGHT>. Note that <LEFT> and <BACKSPACE> are different keys and perform different functions in most software packages.

A-1

We assume that you know how to use the <SHIFT> key to obtain an uppercase letter or a symbol character, and we do not explicitly mention the <SHIFT> in most cases.

FUNCTION KEYS

These ten keys are located in two columns along the left edge of the keyboard. Most application software packages make special use of these keys. Although these keys also have special meanings when used by DOS, we ignore those uses here to avoid confusion with the application program that is the subject of this manual.

MULTIPLE KEY COMBINATIONS

On a typewriter, <SHIFT> is used in conjunction with a letter key to produce a capital letter. The same is true on a computer. On a computer, the Ctrl and Alt keys also act as modifying keys; if either of these is used in conjunction with another key, the original meaning of the letter key is modified. These keys are manipulated in the same manner as <SHIFT>. For example, to enter Alt M (sometimes written Alt-M or Alt + M), hold down the Alt key then press M.

TOGGLE KEY FUNCTIONS

Toggle keys act as on-off switches. Press a toggle key once and the function is activated, press it a second time and the function is deactivated. The toggle keys are the Num Lock key (which activates the numeric keypad), the Scroll Lock key (used in only a few software packages), the Ctrl-PrtSc combination (which directs screen display to the printer as well), and the Caps Lock key.

CAPS LOCK KEY

The Caps Lock key shifts all alphabetic (A . . . Z) characters to upper case, but has no effect on any other key. (This is unlike a typewriter, where the Shift Lock key changes numeric character keys to symbols.) The Caps Lock key is a toggle key. If you are typing in capital letters and need one or two lower case letters (such as in the word *McCLELLAN*), then pressing <SHIFT> plus the letter you wish in lower case will yield the desired effect.

NUMERIC KEYPAD KEYS

These are the keys on the right side of the keyboard arranged as a 10-key pad. The keys with arrows on them are referred to as <ARROW KEYS>, or as <UP>, <LEFT>, <RIGHT>, and <DOWN>. The other keys in this group are referred to by the text that appears on them: Home, PgUp, PgDn, End, Del, and Ins. The numeric function of the keys can be activated by using the Num Lock key (a toggle). Most of these keys have no effect when in DOS, but are used by many application programs to control movement on the screen.

PART 2 STARTUP AND SHUTDOWN PROCEDURES

LOADING DOS

Loading DOS means transferring some of the programs in the Disk Operating System from a *System Disk* into the computer's memory. You must load DOS before you can use any application software or any of the system's utilities.

Some application software requires you to use the DOS disk to load the system before using the application program disk. Other application software gives you instructions on how to install DOS onto the software program disk in order to make the software self-loading and provide some system functions without having to switch disks.

THE DOS PROMPT

The DOS or system prompt (A>__ with most floppy disk systems and C>__ with most hard disk systems) tells you that it is your turn to type information; that is, you must tell DOS what to do next by entering a command. The DOS prompt will appear on the screen after you have successfully loaded DOS. *Many of the command examples in this appendix show the DOS prompt, but you should not type the A> or C>, it has already been supplied by DOS.*

STARTUP PROCEDURES IF THE MICROCOMPUTER SYSTEM IS TURNED OFF

Floppy Disk Systems

1. Insert the DOS disk or a program disk on which DOS has been installed into Disk Drive A. (This is the left-hand drive on IBM PCs. Your instructor or lab supervisor will tell you if otherwise on the equipment you are using.)

2. When the disk is fully inserted, close the drive door. You should not have to force the door closed; if the door is not closing easily, remove and reinsert the disk.

3. With a dual-disk system, insert the disk you will use for your data files into Disk Drive B.

4. When the disk is fully inserted, close the drive door.

5. If a printer is attached to your computer, make sure that it is turned on and that the POWER, READY, and ON LINE lights (or their equivalent) are on.

6. Turn on the power switch. On IBM PCs, this is at the rear of the right side of the computer. On some other PCs, the power switch is on the rear of the computer. On some systems, you must also turn on the monitor (display screen) power switch.

7. When the red disk-in-use light goes off, DOS should be loaded. You may need to adjust the contrast and brightness controls on the monitor. In most cases, you will be asked to enter the date and time.

8. The next step is dependent upon specific software. For the DOS commands discussed in this appendix, leave the DOS disk in Drive A. For the software discussed in this manual, appropriate instructions are presented in Part 1.

Hard Disk Systems

1. If a printer is attached to your computer, make sure that it is turned on and that the POWER, READY, and ON LINE lights (or their equivalent) are on.

2. Turn on the power switch. On IBM PC/XTs, this is at the rear of the right side of the computer. On some other PCs, the power switch is on the rear of the computer. On some systems, you must also turn on the monitor (display screen) power switch.

3. When the red disk-in-use light goes off, DOS should be loaded. You may need to adjust the contrast and brightness controls on the monitor. In most cases, you will be asked to enter the date and time.

4. The next step is dependent upon specific software. For the DOS commands discussed in this appendix, you may place the disk you will use for your data files in the disk drive. For the software discussed in this manual, appropriate instructions are presented in Part 1.

STARTUP PROCEDURES IF THE MICROCOMPUTER SYSTEM IS TURNED ON

Floppy Disk Systems

1. Insert the DOS disk or a program disk on which DOS has been installed into Disk Drive A. (This is the left-hand drive on IBM PCs, your instructor or lab supervisor will tell you if otherwise on the equipment you are using.) You may need to adjust the contrast and brightness controls on the monitor.

2. When the disk is fully inserted, close the drive door. You should not have to force the door closed; if the door is not closing easily, remove and reinsert the disk.

3. With a dual-disk system, insert the disk you will use for your data files into Disk Drive B.

4. When the disk is fully inserted, close the drive door.

5. If a printer is attached to your computer, make sure that it is turned on and that the POWER, READY, and ON LINE lights (or their equivalent) are on.

6. Load (or reload) DOS by pressing and holding, in order, the Ctrl, the Alt, and the Del keys. After pressing Del, *release all three keys.*

7. When the red disk-in-use light goes off, DOS should be loaded. In most cases, you will be asked to enter the date and time.

8. The next step is dependent upon specific software. For the DOS commands discussed in this appendix, leave the DOS disk in Drive A. For the software discussed in this manual, appropriate instructions are presented in Part 1.

Hard Disk Systems

1. If a printer is attached to your computer, make sure that it is turned on and that the POWER, READY, and ON LINE lights (or their equivalent) are on. You may need to adjust the contrast and brightness controls on the monitor.

2. Load (or reload) DOS by pressing and holding, in order, the Ctrl, the Alt, and the Del keys. After pressing Del, *release all three keys.*

3. When the red disk-in-use light goes off, DOS should be loaded. In most cases, you will be asked to enter the date and time.

4. The next step is dependent upon specific software. For the DOS commands discussed in this appendix, you may place the disk you will use for your data files in the disk drive. For the software discussed in this manual, appropriate instructions are presented in Part 1.

SETTING THE DATE AND TIME

We strongly recommend that you set the date and time in the computer each time you begin a work session. This will allow the computer to *time stamp* your files so you will know when you last edited a file and, if you have the same file on many disks, which version of the file is most current. (Some microcomputers have a clock built in which will automatically set the time. If your system has this feature, the operating system disk will normally bypass the date and time queries and you may skip these procedures.)

When Loading DOS

The setting of the date and time at startup is illustrated in Figure App-1.

1. When DOS asks for the current date, type today's date using the following format: mm/dd/yy *or* mm-dd-yy, replacing mm with the number of the month (e.g., 03 for March), and so on. Press <CR> after entering the year number. *Do not type the name of the day, even though DOS will show you the name of the day.* If you make an entry that DOS does not recognize, an *invalid date* message will be displayed and you will be asked to reenter.

2. When DOS asks for the time, type the current time using the format hh:mm:ss.hs. (In most cases, hours and minutes -- hh:mm -- are sufficient; any number not entered is set to 0 [zero].) You must use the 24-hour clock, i.e., 10 A.M. is entered as **10**, while 1:25 P.M. is **13:25**. If you make an entry that DOS does not recognize, an *invalid time* message will be displayed and you will be asked to reenter.

```
Current date is Tue  1-01-1980
Enter new date: 3-22-86
Current time is  0:00:51.41
Enter new time: 12:40


The IBM Personal Computer DOS
Version 2.10 (C)Copyright IBM Corp 1981, 1982, 1983

A>_
```

FIGURE App-1 Setting the Date and Time at Startup
Note: Items entered by user are in **boldface.**

Resetting the Date

If you entered the wrong date or forgot to set the date when you started the system, you may reset the date with the **DATE** command:

1. Type **date** followed by <CR>.

2. Enter the appropriate date as discussed above.

Resetting the Time

If you entered the wrong time or forgot to set the time when you started the system, you may reset the time with the **TIME** command:

1. Type **time** followed by <CR>.

2. Enter the appropriate time as discussed above.

SHUTDOWN PROCEDURES

1. Make sure you have followed the proper escape or exit procedures for the software program you are using. Failure to follow such precautions may result in lost data.

2. When you have successfully exited the applications software or completed the last DOS command, you should have the command (A>__ or C>__) prompt.

3. Remove the disk(s) from the disk drive(s). Place the disk(s) in their protective jackets or other holders. *Do not shut the disk drive doors.*

4. Follow your organization's policy concerning turning the power off or leaving the system on. In general, it is advisable to leave the system on if someone else will be using it within a short amount of time; otherwise turn everything off. If you leave the system on, turn down the contrast control or type the DOS command **CLS** to protect the display screen.

PART 3 DOS COMMANDS

TO ISSUE COMMANDS

1. The command must be typed exactly as described in this appendix, including any spaces within the command.

2. Commands may be entered in uppercase or lowercase. DOS will convert them to uppercase.

3. Terminate all commands with <CR>.

4. If the command contains a typographical error, a missing space, or an extra space, the message *Bad command or file name* will appear after you press <CR>. If this happens, simply retype the command correctly. Many commands are disk files, and require that the DOS disk be present. If you get this message when you have not made a typographical error, check to see if the command is on the disk (using the **DIR** command discussed below).

TO CORRECT A TYPING MISTAKE BEFORE YOU PRESS <CR>

1. The <BACKSPACE> key may be used to correct errors made while in DOS. Characters will be erased as you backspace. The <LEFT ARROW> key has the same effect (in DOS). Once the mistaken character has been erased, type the proper character. If the remainder of the line (to the right of the error) was correct, press the <RIGHT ARROW> key to reinstate the characters. Otherwise, retype from the point of the correction.

2. If a line has many errors, you may prefer to press the Esc key, which will eliminate the line. A backslash (\ ) will appear and the cursor will move down one line. The line with errors may still appear on the screen, but it will not affect the command. You may now enter the corrected command.

TO STOP A COMMAND IN PROGRESS

1. Press the Ctrl key, then the Scroll Lock/Break key.

2. Release both keys; execution of the command will halt.

3. The system prompt (A>__ or C>__) will appear and the next command may be entered.

COMMAND AND FILE NAME PARAMETERS

Command and file names must be carefully entered into the system. Since most commands are special types of files, we can discuss parameters which apply to both *command names* and *file names*. Some parameters are required, and others are optional. If a parameter is omitted, the system will supply a default value. Upper- and lowercase letters are equivalent. The parameters you will see in this manual and some applications software manuals are explained in detail in Table App-1.

TABLE App-1 File Specification Parameters

[*filespec*]

The *file specification* is the complete description of the file, and may appear as [*filespec*] or as [*d:*][*filename*][.*ext*]

Examples: b:myfile.doc
           a:yourfile
           anyfile.bas
           thisfile

An explanation of each part of the [*filespec*] follows.

[*d:*]

This parameter is the drive indicator. Enter the drive letter followed by a colon to indicate the intended drive.

For example, to obtain a directory of the disk in Drive B (when B is not the default drive), type **dir b:** followed by <CR>. The system displays the directory of the disk in Drive B.

If you do not specify a drive in the command, the system assumes that the default drive is intended. For example, if the default drive is Drive A and you type **dir** followed by <CR>, the system displays the directory of the disk in the A drive.

[*filename*]

You may assign any name to a file as long as it meets the following criteria: The name assigned to the file can be from one to eight characters long; the only valid characters are A to Z 0 to 9 $ & @ % / \ __ - ( ) ' ' { } # !

Some versions of DOS and some applications software programs will not accept all of these characters. We recommend the use of the letters, numbers, and the __ (underscore) character for greatest compatibility.

[.*ext*]

The extension is optional for many situations, and pre-assigned by the applications software in other instances. The extension is from one to three characters long, preceded by a period, and follows immediately (no space) after the filename.

The characters listed above are the only valid characters. If an extension is assigned to the file (by you or by the software), it must be included as part of the [*filespec*] whenever you wish the system to locate the file.

THE DEFAULT DRIVE

The letter in the DOS prompt indicates the default drive. The default drive is the disk drive to which DOS will go automatically if you do not type a drive specification as part of a command or file name. On floppy disk systems, the default drive is usually A; on hard disk systems the default drive is usually C. Entering another drive letter will override the default. If you intend to perform a number of operations (Copy, Erase, Rename, etc.) on the files in the drive that is not the default, you may wish to change the default disk drive.

Changing the Default Drive

To change the default drive to B, type

A>**b:**<CR>   *The colon is required!*

To change the default drive to A, type

B>**a:**<CR>

To change the default drive to C, type

A>**c:**<CR>

The last command will not work unless you have a hard disk drive or a specially configured PC. Remember that the A> illustrated in the commands is supplied by the system, not typed by you.

PREPARING A DISK FOR USE

The **FORMAT** command is used to prepare a blank disk for use (a disk cannot be used to store programs or data until it is formatted) or to erase an entire disk which contains data you no longer need. The disk can then be reused. Unless you wish to use the **FORMAT** command to erase a disk, you need format each disk only once.

CAUTION: The **FORMAT** *command will effectively erase the entire contents of the disk.* If you have any doubts about the contents of the disk you are going to format, obtain a directory of the disk to insure that it does not contain any files you wish to keep (see the **DIR** command discussion in this appendix).

To Format a Disk

1. DOS should be loaded and the DOS disk should be in the default drive.

2. Type either

     A>**format b:**<CR>   *Floppy disk system; DOS disk in Drive A.*

     C>**format a:**<CR>   *Hard disk system; DOS on hard disk which is Drive C.*

```
A>format b:/v
Insert new diskette for drive B:
and strike any key when ready

Formatting...Format complete

Volume label (11 characters, ENTER for none)? steve ross


   362496 bytes total disk space
   362496 bytes available on disk

Format another (Y/N)?n
A>_
```

FIGURE App-2 Formatting a Disk with Volume Label
Note: Items entered by user are in **boldface.**

3. When the system prompts you to insert a new disk in the designated drive, make sure that the disk you wish to format is in the drive.

4. Press any key to begin the formatting process.

5. When the formatting process is complete, you will be asked if you wish to format another disk. If so, press the letter **Y** and follow the screen prompts to insert another disk. If you are finished formatting, press the letter **N**. Your data disk is now ready for use with the system.

Format with Volume Label

By using the /v option, you put an electronic label on your disk. When the **DIR** or **CHKDSK** commands are used, this electronic volume label will be displayed. The operation of the **FORMAT/V** command is illustrated in Figure App-2.

1. DOS should be loaded and the DOS disk should be in the default drive.

2. Type either

    A>**format b:/v**<CR>   *Floppy disk system; DOS disk in Drive A.*

    C>**format a:/v**<CR>   *Hard disk system; DOS on hard disk which is Drive C.*

3. When the system prompts you to insert a new disk in the designated drive, make sure that the disk you wish to format is in the drive.

4. Press any key to begin the formatting process.

5. When the system asks for the Volume label, enter any meaningful label, such as your name, identification number, or the contents of the disk. Use only legal file name characters. Press <CR> when the label is complete.

6. After the label is entered, you will be asked if you wish to format another disk. If so, press the letter **Y** and follow the screen prompts to insert another disk. If you are finished formatting, press the letter **N**. Your data disk is now ready for use with the system.

Bad Sectors

On occasion, the format process will report a number of bytes in *bad sectors* which means that the system was unable to format a portion of the disk. Often the problem is a speck of dirt, which will be dislodged if you try the format process once or twice more. If you receive a *bytes in bad sectors* message, answer **Y** to the *format another* prompt and leave the same disk in the drive. If the bad sectors persist after several tries, you should return the disk to where it was purchased and ask for a replacement.

THE DISK DIRECTORY

The directory, obtained by entering the **DIR** command, is a listing of the files on a specific disk. It is possible to display the directory of any disk on the system, and there are many variations of the command.

The Complete Directory

The **DIR** command, by itself, will display all files on the disk in the default disk drive. The [d:] parameter will yield the directory of the disk in a different drive. Examples:

    A>dir   *The directory of disk in Drive A (the default).*

    A>dir b: *The directory of disk in Drive B.*

    C>dir a: *The directory of disk in Drive A (hard disk system).*

An illustration of the use and result of the **DIR** command appears in Figure App-3. This command will tell you the disk volume label, how many files are on the disk, the size and date and time last modified of each, and the amount of space remaining on the disk.

Paused Directory

Once you have more than 20 files on a disk, you will not be able to see the entire directory on the screen at once. Use the **/p** option as illustrated in the following examples to cause the directory listing to pause after each screenful of information:

    A>dir/p
    A>dir b:/p
    C>dir a:/p

```
A>dir b:

 Volume in drive B is STEVE ROSS
 Directory of  B:\

KEYDOC11 DOC     3072   9-12-85    8:32a
KEYDOC2  DOC     2048   9-12-85    9:46a
FORMAT0  WKS     1536  10-20-85    9:27p
FORMAT1  WKS     1536  10-20-85    9:29p
EX1A     FW      1360   7-08-85    1:34p
EX1B     FW      7168   1-01-80   12:10a
SAMPLE_F FW     21952   9-16-85    1:21p
         7 File(s)    321536 bytes free

A>_
```

FIGURE App-3 Illustration of the **DIR** Command
Note: Command entered by user is in **boldface**.

Wide Directory

This form of the command produces a wide display of the directory, which lists only the file names and extensions, five across. Examples:

    A>**dir/w**
    A>**dir b:/w**
    C>**dir a:/w**

Printed Directory

The directory listing may be sent directly to the printer instead of to the screen by adding **>prn** after the command. Examples:

    A>**dir>prn**
    A>**dir b:>prn**
    C>**dir a:>prn**

DISK AND MEMORY STATUS REPORT

The **CHKDSK** command produces a disk and memory status report. The report will tell you how much space your files are using on the disk, how much space is available on the disk, and whether the disk has any bad sectors. This command will also indicate how much memory is installed and available in the computer system that you are using.

```
A>chkdsk b:
Volume STEVE ROSS   created Mar 22, 1986 12:43p


   362496 bytes total disk space
        0 bytes in 1 hidden files
    40960 bytes in 7 user files
   321536 bytes available on disk

   655360 bytes total memory
   453744 bytes free


A>_
```

FIGURE App-4   Illustration of the **CHKDSK** Command
Note: Command entered by user is in **boldface.**

1. The DOS disk should be in the default disk drive (normally Drive A on a floppy disk system, and normally Drive C on a hard disk system). If you want to check a disk *other* than the DOS disk, that disk must be in the other drive.

2. Type either

   A>**chkdsk**<CR>   *To check the DOS disk.*

   A>**chkdsk b:**<CR>   *To check the disk in the other disk drive.*

The result of the **CHKDSK** command is illustrated in Figure App-4. The *hidden file* is the volume label. The *bytes available on disk* refers to disk capacity. The *bytes free* refers to computer system capacity.

COPYING FILES

The **COPY** command allows you to transfer a copy of one or more files from one disk to another without erasing any of the data located on the disk to which you are copying, *except that a file from the source disk will overwrite a file with the same name on the target disk.* This is one method that may be used to backup data disks.

The disk that contains the files you wish to copy is called the *source disk*. The disk to which you are copying the files is called the *target* or *destination disk*.

In order to use this command, the target disk must be formatted and have sufficient bytes free (available) to hold the files being copied. The name of the file to be copied must be spelled correctly and include the complete *filespec* (drive designation if not the default drive, filename, and extension if present).

1. Place the source disk in one drive and the target disk in the other drive.

2. Type **copy**, a <SPACE>, enter the source drive, filename and extension next, another <SPACE>, then the target drive. Terminate the command with a <CR>. Consider the following examples.

   a. If the file you wish to copy is in Drive A and the target disk is in Drive B, you would type the command as follows:

      A>**copy a:filename.ext b:**<CR>

      Since a filename is not specified for the target (B), the file on the target disk will have the same name and extension on both disks.

   b. If the file you wish to copy is in Drive B and the target disk is in A, the command would be

      A>**copy b:filename.ext a:newname.ext**<CR>

      In this case, the file on the disk in A will have a different name and extension.

   c. To copy from the hard disk (C) on a PC/XT or other hard disk computer, the command would be

      C>**copy c:filename.ext a:**<CR>

      As in case a., the filename does not change.

   With each of these forms of the command, you are specifying that you want to copy the named file from the disk in the first drive designated to the disk located in the second drive. Although you do not need to name the default drive, we recommend that you always name *both* drives to insure that the copy goes in the proper direction.

3. If the system cannot find the file, it will indicate *File not found* and *0 file(s) copied*. Check the spelling of the filename. Be sure you have included an extension if the source file contained an extension. If you have made a mistake, you may reenter the command.

Copy Using the Global Match Character

When you wish to copy several files which have file name or extension in common, use the global match character (*****) to expedite the process.

1. Place the source disk in one drive and the target disk in the other drive.

2. Type **copy**, a <SPACE>, enter the source drive and filename next, another <SPACE>, then the target drive. Terminate the command with a <CR>. Consider the following examples.

a. If the file you wish to copy is in Drive A and the target disk is in Drive B, and the files to be copied have the same extension, you would type the command as follows:

A>**copy a:*.ext b:**<CR>

All files on the disk in the A drive with the extension *.ext* will be copied to the disk in the B drive. Neither filenames nor extensions will be changed.

b. If the file you wish to copy is in Drive B and the target disk is in A, and the files all have the same file name, the command would be

A>**copy b:filename.* a:**<CR>

All files on the disk in the B drive with the name *filename* will be copied to the disk in A. Neither filenames nor extensions will be changed.

c. To copy to the hard disk (C) on a PC/XT or other hard disk computer, the command would be

C>**copy a:filename.* c:**<CR>

All files on the disk in the A drive with the name *filename* will be copied to the hard disk (C). Neither filenames nor extensions will be changed.

With each of these forms of the command, you are specifying that you want to copy the named file from the disk in the first drive designated to the disk located in the second drive. Although you do not need to name the default drive, we recommend that you always name *both* drives to insure that the copy goes in the proper direction. There are many additional uses of the global replacement character which are not illustrated here.

3. If the system cannot find any files which match, it will indicate *File not found* and *0 file(s) copied*. Check the spelling of the filename or extension. If you have made a mistake, you may reenter the command.

Copy All Files

With this version of the **COPY** command, you can copy all files from the source disk to the target disk. The target disk must be formatted and must have sufficient room for all the files. Files already on the target disk will not be erased, *except that a file from the source disk will overwrite a file with the same name on the target disk.*

1. Place the source disk in one drive and the target disk in the other drive.

2. Type **copy**, a <SPACE>, enter the source drive and ***.*** next, another <SPACE>, then the target drive. Terminate the command with a <CR>. Consider the following examples.

a. If the files you wish to copy are in Drive A and the target disk is in Drive B, you would type the command as follows:

    A>copy a:*.* b:\<CR>

The files will have the same name and extension on both disks.

b. If the files you wish to copy are in Drive B and the target disk is in A, the command would be

    A>copy b:*.* a:\<CR>

c. To copy to the hard disk (C) on a PC/XT or other hard disk computer, the command would be

    C>copy a:*.* c:\<CR>

With each of these forms of the command, you are specifying that you want to copy all the files from the disk in the first drive designated to the disk located in the second drive. Although you do not need to name the default drive, we recommend that you always name *both* drives to insure that the copy goes in the proper direction.

3. If the system cannot find any files, it will indicate *File not found* and *0 file(s) copied*. If you have made a mistake, you may reenter the command.

COPYING AN ENTIRE DISK

The **DISKCOPY** command is used to copy the entire contents of one disk to another. The target disk will be formatted if necessary. Be careful when you use this command, because anything on the target disk will be erased and unrecoverable.

1. The DOS disk or another disk with the DISKCOPY.COM program file must be in the default drive.

2. Enter one of the following commands

    A>diskcopy a: b:\<CR>   *To copy from A to B*

    A>diskcopy b: a:\<CR>   *To copy from B to A*

depending on which drive will hold the source diskette and which will hold the target diskette. Note: This command cannot be used to copy to or from a hard disk, but can be used on a hard disk system to copy from one floppy disk to another.

3. When the program has been loaded from the DOS diskette, you will be told to insert the source and target diskettes, and press any key when ready. Make sure you put the proper disk in each drive, then press any key to commence the disk copy process. You may make multiple disk copies if you wish.

DELETING OR ERASING FILES

Two commands, **DEL** and **ERASE**, are used to delete a specified file or files from the disk. The two commands are equivalent.

1. The disk with the file to be deleted must be in one of the drives (and you must know which drive).

2. Use the appropriate form of the command. Examples:

    A>del a:filename.ext<CR>   A>erase a:filename.ext<CR>
    A>del b:filename.ext<CR>   A>erase b:filename.ext<CR>
    C>del a:filename.ext<CR>   C>erase a:filename.ext<CR>

3. If the file is found and erased, there is no message. You can use the global character with these commands, just as with the **COPY** command, but be careful. Multiple file erasures are somewhat risky: it is easy to erase more than you intended.

4. If the system cannot find the file, an error message appears. Check the spelling of the file name and extension, and retype the command if you have made an error.

PAUSE DISPLAY

If information is moving on the screen or scrolling "off the top" of the screen too fast for you to read it, you may cause the display to pause until you are ready to continue.

1. Press the Ctrl key, then the Num Lock key, then release both. Output to the screen is suspended until you press any other character key.

2. Press any character key (including <CR> and <SPACE>) to resume display. You may use the Ctrl-Num Lock combination as often as you wish.

PRINT SCREEN FUNCTION

The print screen function is available through DOS and remains active in most applications programs. This capability is especially useful when you are having problems and no one is available to help you. Use the following procedure to make a screen print and take that print to your instructor or a friend for help.

1. Make sure the printer is turned on (usually there is a light indicating POWER) and on-line (look for an ON LINE indicator).

2. Press and hold <SHIFT>, press the PrtSc key, then release both keys.

3. The cursor traces the entire screen as the text is sent to the printer, then returns to its previous position when the system is ready for the next operation.

PRINTER ECHO FUNCTION

The print screen function is a snapshot: a view of the entire screen at a point in time. The printer echo function is more like a movie: once activated, everything typed or sent to the screen also appears on the printer until the echo is deactivated. Printer echo *does not* work with most applications software, and is generally used in DOS operations.

To Activate Printer Echo

1. Make sure the printer is turned on (usually there is a light indicating POWER) and on-line (look for an ON LINE indicator).

2. Press and hold the Ctrl key, press the PrtSc key, then release both keys.

3. Nothing will seem to have happened. Test the echo status by pressing <CR> once or twice. You should hear (and see) activity on the printer: the command prompt (A> or C>) is printed and the paper advances each time you press <CR>.

4. If you get no response in Step 3, repeat Step 2. You may have held the PrtSc key down too long, effectively activating and immediately deactivating the printer echo function.

To Deactivate Printer Echo

1. Press <CR> once to clear any text which has been sent to the printer.

2. Press and hold the Ctrl key, press the PrtSc key, then release both keys.

3. Nothing will seem to have happened. Test the echo status by pressing <CR> once or twice. You should not hear (nor see) activity on the printer.

4. If you get a response in Step 3, repeat Step 2. You may have held the PrtSc key down too long, effectively deactivating and immediately reactivating the printer echo function.

APPENDIX

B ANSWERS

ANSWERS TO ✓CHECKPOINTS

page 50
3-12a. Remove the dBASE disk from Drive A.
3-12b. copy b:*.* a:

pages 73-74
4-3.   list to print for cost<0.10
4-4.   list to print for cost*inventory>10
4-5.   list to print for '(oz.)'$desc
4-6.   set heading off   *followed by*   list off for cost*inventory>50

pages 88-89
5-2a. use fin_good
5-2c. use raw_matl

page 109
6-5.   The 8 oz. cup record (number 5) is found first because it has the lowest RMID.

page 126
7-3.   replace all cost with cost*1.2
7-4.   change for 'cup'$desc
7-5a. delete for inventory>=100
7-5b. set deleted off   *followed by*   recall all

page 143
8-5.   set function 10 to 'DIR *.*;'
8-8.   copy to raw2
8-9.   copy to merge.txt fields desc, cost delimited
8-10. copy to inventry fields desc, cost, inventory type wks for inventory>100

pages   163-65
9-7.   index on rmid to temp *followed by* report form raw__matl to print
9-8.   report form raw__matl to print for cost*inventory > 10

page   174
10-7.   index on rmid to temp *followed by* label form raw__matl to print, 174
10-8.   label form raw__matl to print for last__order>=ctod('10/02/87')

pages   189-90
11-3.   sum cost*inventory to value
11-4.   sum inventory to k
11-5.   ? value/k

pages   217-18
13-2a. clear all   *followed by*   use fin__good
13-2b. do while .not. eof( )
13-2c. display desc,sell__price
13-2d. input 'New Price ' to new__price
13-2e. replace sell__price with new__price
13-2f. skip
13-2g. enddo

pages   235-36
14-2a. clear all   *followed by*   use fin__good
14-2b. do while .not. eof( )
14-2c. clear
14-2d. @ 5,5 say desc
14-2e. @ 7,5 get sell__price   *followed by*   read
14-2f. skip
14-2g. enddo

pages   249-50
15-2a. clear all
15-2a. use mix
15-2b. index on fgid to mix
15-2c. select b
15-2d. use raw__matl
15-2e. index on rmid to raw__matl
15-2f. select mix *or* select a *or* select 1
15-2g. totcost=0 *or* store 0 to totcost
15-2h. accept 'Enter FGID ' to m__fgid
15-2i. seek m__fgid *or* find &m__fgid
15-2j. do while fgid=m__fgid
15-2k. select raw__matl
15-2l. seek mix->rmid
15-2m. select mix
15-2n. totcost=totcost+mix->rm__qty*raw__matl->cost
15-2o. skip
15-2p. enddo
15-2q. ? totcost

page 264
16-2a.   clear all
16-2a.   use mix
16-2b.   index on fgid to mix
16-2c.   select 2
16-2d.   use raw__matl
16-2e.   index on rmid to raw__matl
16-2f.   select mix *or* select 1 *or* select a
16-2g.   set relation to rmid into raw__matl
16-2h.   totcost=0
16-2i.   accept 'Enter FGID ' to m__fgid
16-2j.   seek m__fgid *or* find &m__fgid
16-2k.   do while fgid=m__fgid
16-2l.   totcost=totcost+mix->rm__qty*raw__matl->cost
16-2m. skip
16-2n.   enddo
16-2o.   ? totcost

page 271
17-4.   update on fgid from pricech replace sell__price with pricech->new__price random

ANSWERS TO SELECTED REVIEW QUESTIONS

pages 8-9
1-4.   Maximum number of fields in dBASE III: 128.
1-5a.   4 bytes
1-5c.   4 bytes
1-5d.   3 bytes minimum, 4 bytes recommended so quantity can exceed 999.

pages 27-28
2-2a.   The F1 key invokes help menus.
2-2e.   The PgUp key moves to the previous record or screen display.
2-2f.   The Del key deletes the character at the cursor.
2-2g.   The ^End combination is used to exit and save from most editing situations.

page 50
3-2a.   TICKER,Character,4 (other names are possible, and greater width)
3-2b.   PRICE,Numeric,7,3
3-2c.   PHONE,Character,13
3-2d.   SMOKER,Logical (width of 1 is automatic)
3-2e.   DATE,Date (width of 8 is automatic)

pages 76-78
4-2.   the order in which the operations in conditions and expressions are performed.
4-4a.   False (capitalization is different)
4-4b.   False
4-4c.   True
4-4d.   True
4-4f.   True (age>size is False and .not. False is True)

4-4g. False (first condition is False; both must be True with .and.)
4-4h. True (one of the conditions is True)
4-4j. False (age = 25)
4-5.   list to print for (cost*inventory > 50)
4-6.   The $ must be used when the comparison does not start with the first character.

page 91
5-1.   use fin_good *followed by* count for (sell_price<1)
5-3.   use raw_matl *followed by* sum cost*inventory
5-5.   sum cost*inventory for (.not.('(oz.)'$desc))

page 110
6-3.   use raw_matl *followed by* index on rmid to raw_matl
6-4b. the order in which the data reside on the disk
6-4c. the order in which the data appear to be based on the index key
6-5a. find 0010
6-6a. The dot prompt without any "No Find" message.
6-6b. dBASE will display the message "No Find."
6-6c. dBASE displays the message "Record = n" where n is a record number.
6-6d. dBASE displays the message "End of LOCATE Scope."
6-7.   use fin_good *followed by* index on sell_price to temp *followed by* list
6-9.   Use LOCATE when you wish to process the records, LIST when viewing is sufficient.

page 127
7-2a. replace all age with age+1
7-2b. change fields name,phone for 'Marketing'$department
7-2c. locate for ('Smith'$last_name) *followed by* edit

page 144
8-3.   display status
8-6.   use raw_matl *followed by* copy to textfile fields desc,cost delimited

page 165
9-2.   use raw_matl index raw_matl *followed by* report form raw_matl

pages 190-91
11-1. a field is part of a data base, a variable is in memory
11-3a. store 'Genghis Khan' to name *or* name = 'Genghis Khan'
11-3b. store 16 to age *or* age = 16
11-4a. store name+'the Magnificent' to name *or* name=name+'the Magnificent'
11-4b. store age*2 to older *or* older = age*2
11-6. save to memory
11-7. restore from memory additive

page 205
12-2. another name for command file
12-3. a series of repeated instructions
12-4. modify command {filename}
12-6. do {filename}

pages 219-20
13-2a.   go 15
13-2b.   skip
13-2c.   find New York
13-3a.   accept 'Name: ' to m_name
13-3b.   input 'Age: ' to m_age
13-4.   ? m_name *followed by* ? m_age
13-5.   append blank
13-6.   replace

page 239
14-2.   0,79
14-3.   When you neglect to put a READ statement into the command file.

page 251
15-4a.   ? sox->red+indians->cleveland
15-4b.   ? sox->red - sox->white
15-5.   select b *followed by* replace red with 200

page 266
16-1.   a link between two data files

page 272
17-3.   19 records because each RMID is different

INDEX

SYMBOLS INDEX

#
#, 63

$
$, 62, 63, 150

&
&, 188, 211, 243
&&, 200

'
' . . . ', 62

"
" . . . ", 62

(
( ), 61

*
*, 61, 137, 200
**, 61

+
+, 61, 62, 170

-
-, 61, 62
->, 183, 247

/
/, 61

[
[. . .], 62

^
^, 61

{
{ }, 34

<
<, 63
<=, 63
<>, 63

=
=, 63, 184

>
>, 63
>=, 63

?
?, 137, 214
??, 214

@
@, 224, 226
@ . . . GET, 226
@ . . . SAY, 224
@ . . . TO, 227

ALPHABETIC INDEX

Notes

Notes

Notes

Notes

Notes

Notes

Notes

Notes

Notes

Notes

Notes

Notes

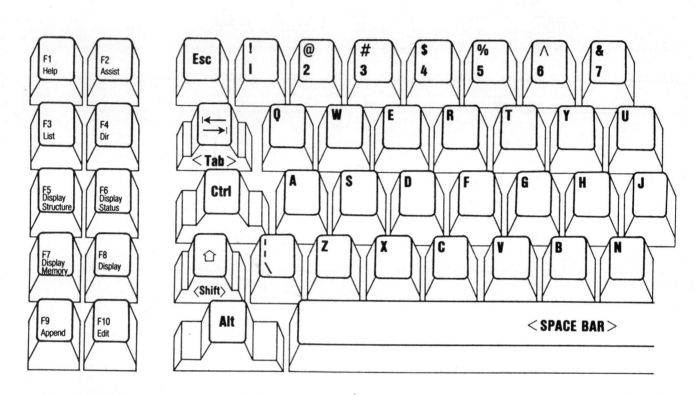

dBASE III KEYBOARD

F1   Help;
F2   Assist;
F3   List;
F4   Dir;
F5   Display Structure;
F6   Display Status;
F7   Display Memory;
F8   Display;
F9   Append;
F10   Edit;
The commands assigned to the function keys may be
changed—see Unit 8.

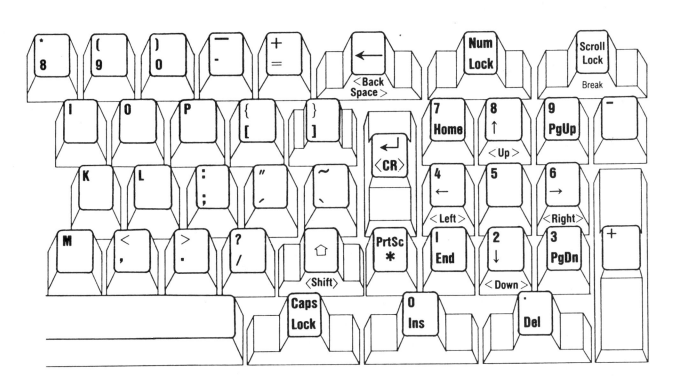

IBM PC™ Abbreviations

Esc—Escape Key	PrtSc—Print Screen Key
Ctrl—Control Key	Pg Dn—Page Down Key
Alt—Alternate Key	Ins— Insert Character Key
Num Lock—Number Lock Key	Del— Delete Character Key
Pg Up—Page Up Key	

Common dBASE Error Messages and Remedies

Command and Error Message	Cause and Remedy
. craete datebook ***** Unrecognized command verb** . create datebook	The command is misspelled, retype with proper spelling.
. modify form gizmo **Unrecognized phrase/keyword in command** **?** **modify form gizmo** **Do you want some help? (Y/N) No** . modify report gizmo	The word *form* is not correct, the proper keyword is *report*. The ? indicates the general location of the problem. Retype with proper keyword.
. list for age #= 35 **Syntax error** **?** **list for age #= 35** **Do you want some help? (Y/N) No** . list for age <> 35	The comparison operator is not correct. Retype with proper operator.
. list last__name,age **Variable not found** **?** **list last__name,age** **Do you want some help? (Y/N) No** . list name, age	There is no field in the data base with the name LAST__NAME. Retype with proper field name (DISPLAY STRUCTURE if you do not remember the field names.)
. list for age='35' **Data type mismatch** **?** **list for age='35'** **Do you want some help? (Y/N) No** . list for age=35	AGE is (probably) a numeric field, and '35' is character/text data because of the quote marks. Retype without quotes, or use the STR( ) function to convert AGE.
. use mailing index mailnig **File does not exist** **?** **use mailing index mailnig** **Do you want some help? (Y/N) No** . use mailing index mailing	There is no file MAILNIG.NDX on the default disk drive. This may be a spelling error, or the file may not exist. Use DIR *.NDX to see what is on the disk. (This problem can also occur with data files, use the DIR command to check.)
. use datebook . index on name to datebook **Too many files are open** **?** **index on name to datebook** **Do you want some help? (Y/N) No** . quit	The DOS disk used to start the PC did not contain the proper CONFIG.SYS file. You must exit dBASE and reset the computer with the proper DOS disk.